BURY MY HEART AT
COOPERSTOWN

BURY MY HEART AT
COOPERSTOWN

Salacious, Sad, and Surreal Deaths
in the History of Baseball

Frank Russo and Gene Racz

TRIUMPH
B O O K S
CHICAGO

Library of Congress Cataloging-in-Publication Data

Russo, Frank, 1959–
    Bury my heart at Cooperstown : salacious, sad, and surreal deaths in
    the history of baseball / by Frank Russo and Gene Racz.
        p. cm.
    ISBN-13: 978-1-57243-822-4
    ISBN-10: 1-57243-822-3
    1. Baseball players—United States—Death   I. Racz, Gene, 1964–
    II. Title.

GV865.A1R86 2006
796.357092'2—dc22

                                                            2005037778

This book is available in quantity at special discounts for your group or organization. For further information, contact:

Triumph Books
542 South Dearborn Street
Suite 750
Chicago, Illinois 60605
(312) 939-3330
Fax (312) 663-3557

Printed in U.S.A.
ISBN-13: 978-1-57243-822-4
ISBN-10: 1-57243-822-3

Design by Patricia Frey
Cover photographs courtesy of Frank Russo's private collection and Getty Images.
All other photographs courtesy of National Baseball Hall of Fame Library unless otherwise indicated.

Dedication

To my wife and partner, Joanne, who believed in me from practically the first moment we met and told me to never quit. To my mother, Rose, who has always been there for me! Guess what, we did it! To all my nieces and nephews, thanks from Uncle Frank! To all my in-laws, especially Rick DiCanio and Kurt Nellis, both of whom helped out with info and fascinating tidbits! Thank you to my mother-in-law, Vita DiGiovanni.

This book is also dedicated to the memory of my father, Frank, brother Joseph and sister Elaine, who are always with me in spirit. Also to the memories of my little ones, Podey, Pinky, and Babe, who crossed over while this work was being created. Also a special thanks to Dr. Neal Beeber of the Rutherford Animal Hospital, one of the great Yankees fans that I know. Yeah, I know, I am always fashionably late!

Thanks to Timmy and Barbara South. Hey Tim, will we ever live down the famous Fabian Kowalik incident at the HOF library?

This book is also dedicated to Kenny "Gunny" Dawson, USMC retired, and all the men and women of the United States Armed Forces fighting the real struggle of good versus evil.

To "the Coach," Robin Gunn and Trish Hackler, my two dear friends in Florida who always remind me how warm it is down there when it's 12 degrees in the middle of December.

—Frank Russo

To my loving parents, Zoltan and Eleanor, who always gave me the home-field advantage; my beautiful wife, Angie, who continues to keep me in the lineup despite my occasional slumps; and my sons, Alden and Garrett—they come ready to play every day.

—Gene Racz

Contents

George "Snuffy" Stirnweiss • Gus Sandberg's Blowout Loss
• Witness Tampering • Snakebitten • Badly Rattled • Ralph
"Socks" Seybold • Mike Donovan • Emil "Hillbilly" Bildilli
• Johnny Scalzi • Harold B. "Rowdy" Elliott • Harry
Wolverton • Howard Freigau • John "Rube" Benton • Karl
Drews • Mike Dorgan • Chet "Red" Hoff • Ken Hubbs •
Worst Seat in the House • Passing the Buck • Last Lap •
Kill the Umpire! • Killed by the Umpire! • Killed because of
the Umpire! • Billy Martin • Burt Keeley • Mike Fornieles •
Dick Radatz • Eddie Grant • Frank Eustace • Fred Holmes
• Al Kellett • Harry Blake • Joe O'Brien • Mike Kelley •
Ruppert Mills • Sandy Piez • Lewis "Snake" Wiltse • Bert
Myers • Jim McKee • Roberto Clemente • Thurman
Munson • John Kane

Newnam • Thomas "Parson" Nicholson • Willie Garoni •
Newt Halliday • John "Egyptian" Healy • Ed Hughes •
Kid McLaughlin • Tricky Nichols • Hank O'Day • John
Puhl • Yank Robinson • John Skopec • Fred Warner •
Marsh Williams • Rube Waddell • Lew Richie • Virgil
"Ned" Garvin

Pat Kilhullen • Pembroke Finlayson • Sherry Magee • Gene Krapp and Tony Suck • Matty McIntyre

Foreword

Here's the thing about baseball fans: it isn't just that we care. It isn't just that we care *deeply*. It isn't just that the daily marathon of a baseball season consumes a larger portion of our brains, our souls, and our nervous systems than anything else in our lives (and, yes, you can take *anything* as literally as you please). It isn't just that we can spew statistical numbers—755; 511; 56; 73; 4,256; .366— more easily than we can our own phone numbers (and if you needed to look up those numbers to know that they are Hank Aaron's career home-run total; Cy Young's career victory total; Joe DiMaggio's seminal hitting-streak number; Barry Bonds' single-season home-run mark; Pete Rose's all-time hit mark; and Ty Cobb's all-time batting average record, then perhaps you aren't as big a baseball fan as you thought).

Heck, it isn't just that we can spend hour upon hour upon hour in saloons, salons, and sacristies peacefully arguing about the game (unless the discussion revolves around the Red Sox–Yankees rivalry, in which case bloodshed is inevitable).

No. Baseball means *even more* to us than that.

Frank Russo gets that. He understands that. Since 1999, he has stewarded an amazing website called thedeadballera.com. At the time, I was a sports columnist for the Newark *Star-Ledger*, and when someone turned me onto that site, two things became immediately apparent:

1. I would need to be physically removed from my computer, so arresting was the content contained on that site.
2. I would need to write about this guy at once.

Which is what I did. And I have to tell you: at first, I was a little cautious. Let's face it, there was at least a 5 percent chance that a guy who spends so much time devoted to tracking and charting the demises—both unfortunate and inevitable— of baseball players might be a little odd. A little offbeat. A little different. A little...well, *out there*.

Of course, it took about 30 seconds of conversation to understand that Frank was simply that most wonderful brand of baseball fan. He's so devoted to the sport, so completely loyal to its history and to its legacies, and so steadfast in the baseball fan's belief that there is *never* a fact that is too trivial that he's created an astonishing encyclopedia of information, and he's managed to strike the absolute right balance between reverence and humor—not easy when you consider the fact that the primary subject matter is, you know, *dying*.

Devotees of thedeadballera.com already know this.

Readers of this book, which Frank has authored alongside the gifted journalist Gene Racz, you will soon discover the same thing, as soon as you make it past this testimonial. You will be informed, you will be entertained, you will be treated to hundreds of facts and tidbits of trivia that will make you the scourge of your next fantasy baseball draft. Mostly, you will be struck by the same thing I was the first time I found myself glued in front of the computer screen: if you really care about baseball, and if you truly care about the men who have comprised this wonderful game for a century and a half—and there are more and more of us every day who do care—then you will care deeply about each of the players profiled in *Bury My Heart at Cooperstown.*

I'm reminded of that first day I met Frank, back in January 1999, when we'd driven through the bitter New Jersey cold and walked to a grassy finger in the middle of Fernwood Cemetery in Jamesburg. He'd pointed to a simple slab of gray slate.

"There it is," he said.

And there it was, indeed: the final resting place of Franklin W. Hayes, revealing the kind of information (1914–1955) that wasn't on any of his baseball cards while he was playing for the Philadelphia A's, St. Louis Browns, Cleveland Indians, Boston Red Sox, and Chicago White Sox from 1933 until 1947, making six All-Star appearances as a catcher.

I have to confess that until our visit I had never even heard of Frankie Hayes, who had a lifetime batting average of .259 and hit 119 Major League home runs, and I consider myself the kind of rabid baseball fan whom people at cocktail parties either flock to or run away from, depending on their own levels of affinity for the game. Yet in learning about his death, I was moved to find out more about his life, meaning that by the end of the day, I'd become one more person touched by the life of a complete stranger who was—in the words of Casey Stengel—dead at the present time, and had been such for well over 44 years. I'd like to think that if he could have, Frankie Hayes would have bought Frankie Russo a beer and shook his hand in thanks for allowing him to be remembered.

When I was a kid, when baseball truly did have an all-encompassing grip on my soul and my daily existence, there were certain days that struck me deeply, so deeply that I still recall them today: the days when I would hear on the radio or read in the newspaper that a baseball player had died. I vividly recall where I was when I learned that Thurman Munson had been killed in a plane crash, that Lyman Bostock had been felled by a gunshot wound, that Danny Frisella had died in a dune-buggy accident, that Bob Moose was killed in a car crash on the way to a birthday party, that Danny Thompson had succumbed after a battle with leukemia.

Why?

I suspect part of it is the inevitable twinge of tragedy that accompanies the death of a young athlete, something that has fascinated people at least as far back as the British poet A. E. Housman, who famously penned these haunting words about athletes who were taken before their time:

> Now you will not swell the rout
> Of lads that wore their honours out
> Runners whom renown outran
> And the name died before the man.

Of course, in our minds, in our culture, athletes inevitably die two deaths: the physical and the athletic. The ones I mentioned earlier are, thankfully, the exception rather than the rule. But on some level, it's just as sad when old ballplayers die long after their on-field exploits so that hardly anyone remembers who they were, what they did, and how free they ran when they were young, unburdened by the troubles that inevitably occur away from a baseball diamond. Thanks to Frank's website, that hasn't been the case for quite sometime. Every player is accorded the same respect, whether it is Babe Ruth, the most famous player of all, who died of throat cancer in 1948, or Len Koenecke, an out-fielder for the Brooklyn Dodgers who hit 22 lifetime home runs before being killed at age 31 on September 17, 1935, after being "battered with a fire extinguisher in a plane by a member of the crew."

And thanks to this book by Frank and Gene, we have a volume that officially provides the same kind of insight on a variety of fresh topics. And you know the best part? Baseball devotees will love this book for their own reasons, but so will nonacolytes, too. Maybe in different sets of hands that would have been impossible to pull off. But in Frank Russo's and Gene Racz' hands, what you're about to read will soon become one of those books where the corners of the pages quickly wear away from overuse.

Enjoy.

—Mike Vaccaro
November 2005

Preface

When I launched my website—thedeadballera.com—in 1999, I never intended it to be macabre or depressing. I named it after a time in major league baseball before 1920—before the advent of the lively ball—and it was the only site at the time dedicated to the memory of deceased big leaguers.

Collecting close to 200,000 hits, the site took on a life of its own, and so did my baseball research. I found myself straying far from my original intent of simply documenting and compiling a comprehensive baseball necrology. I began chronicling the most interesting lives of ballplayers along with some very interesting deaths.

After all the time spent sifting through material in libraries and archives, I always find myself heading out to the actual grave sites of the deceased. Some may call it morbid, and maybe there's some truth to it, but tracking down the headstones and markers is always like standing before a little piece of history.

And like history itself, these ballplayers are much more than simply names and numbers in a book to me.

In order to bring the material to life, I entered into a collaboration with longtime sportswriter Gene Racz, who wrote essays to accompany the player profiles, which he also edited, reworked, and helped organize into a coherent volume.

Our curiosity about these players remains as strong as ever, and we hope you will find them interesting and entertaining as well.

—Frank Russo

Acknowledgments

Unknowingly, I actually first started collecting data for this book back in the summer of 1968 while away at military school. Many people have helped me over the years with my baseball research, and of those people many have become my good friends.

The majority of the player information used in this book was obtained from player files at the A. Bartlett Giamatti Research Center at the Baseball Hall of Fame in Cooperstown, New York. Over a five-year period, I made over 35 trips to Cooperstown, scouring more than eight thousand files.

So right off the bat, (bad pun, sorry!) I must thank the staff at the HOF library, especially my buddy, Freddy "the Real Stewie Griffin" Borowski. Also a special thank you to the woman I drove crazy on several occasions, the lovely Claudette Burke. And a special thanks must go out to the man with the craziest sense of humor I have ever known, Timmy "Wile E. Coyote" Wiles.

Additional information was obtained using ProQuest Historical Newspaper search and the archives of *The Sporting*

News. The majority of the transaction information used in this book was provided by retrosheet.org.

Over the years I have interviewed many relatives of deceased players. They provided many interesting facts and tidbits that helped to make this book what it is. Thank you to all!

Also, I have to thank my grave-hunting buddies. Grave hunters are the people who get their butts in the grass and do the hard work of finding and photographing the final resting places of the ballplayers.

To Russ "the Mad Monk" Dodge, whom I have been friends with for well over seven years now, and who also originally wrote several of the bios for the book, showing that he is one of the best and most knowledgeable baseball bio writers out there.

Connie Nisinger, "Conan the Librarian," my source in St. Louis, who, like me, proves that you have to be a little nutty to go out on a lousy day in November to snap a grave photo just for the hell of it!

Joyce Ellsworth, the "Queen of Cleveland." You are one of the best people I know, simply put.

Dave Lotz, my buddy in Texas who helped me with research when others flat-out refused.

I also want to thank the following SABR members who helped me out over the years with my research requests:

Stew Thornley, the first SABR member I got to know and an expert grave hunter, who is one of the foremost authorities on the final resting places of members of the Baseball Hall of Fame.

Eric Sallee, cousin of Harry "Slim" Sallee, Jim "the Sandman" Sandoval, a great guy and a damn fine man! Ron Henry of the SABR Vets Committee, Dave Vincent of the SABR Bio Committee, whom I have worked with closely for more than three years now. (Can you believe it? A Yankees fan and Red Sox fan getting along—amazing!) Also Bill Carle, head of the SABR Bio Committee and Richard Malatzky. Thanks also go out to Wesley Fricks, curator of the Ty Cobb Museum and to Cecelia

Tan, a great writer and true Yankees fan living in the heart of Red Sox Nation. Also the great Bill Deane!

Also special thanks to my agent, Kathi Paton. To my two buddies at the *New York Post*, Mike Vaccaro and his "Post Compadre" Kevin Kernan. So when do we all go to dinner?

I am eternally grateful to the various physicians I have been in contact with over the past 20 years, with extra special thanks going out to Dr. Jeremy Rothfleisch, MD; Dr. Lewis Levine, MD; and Richard DiCanio, RN, for their help with medical terminology and diagnosis. Their vast knowledge and experience was of the utmost help to me in clearing up several medical mysteries.

Also special thanks goes out to my buddy, Brian Van Horn, who helped out with his huge collection of vintage baseball cards. Also the staffs of the East Brunswick Public Library and the New Brunswick Public Library.

Also thanks to the caretakers, office workers, and security people of the cemeteries that I've visited over the past 25 years. Lastly, thanks to my neighbor Bob and his uncle, who helped send some wonderful information my way regarding Snuffy Stirnweiss.

Thank you to the Bear Paw Winery and the 7th Inning Stretch of Cooperstown, New York, for making my final research trip in October 2005 a most pleasant experience!

—Frank Russo

I'd like to thank Nicholas DiGiovanni, talented author and colleague, whose sage advice was instrumental in getting this book published. I would also like to thank my wife, Angie, whose professional editing skills and sound judgement helped keep the content sharp and the tone consistent.

—Gene Racz

Introduction

There's a hard bite in the chill wind gusting across the open expanse of St. Peter's Cemetery in New Brunswick, New Jersey. It's late February, and Frank Russo's black leather jacket is not getting the job done, but he's too absorbed in his search to notice. Head down, off in a familiar corner, he's foraging through the fallen leaves for the modest headstone of John "Pa" Harkins—city native who once pitched for the old Brooklyn Trolley Dodgers. He died of a heart attack in 1940.

"It's right here somewhere," said Russo, never more sure of himself on a grave hunt in his life. The former disc jockey and member of the Society for American Baseball Research (SABR) has cataloged hundreds and hundreds of deceased ballplayers in various categories and stories and put them on his website, thedeadballera.com.

Harkins was Russo's first because his final resting place is a short infield's throw from the Russo family plots. Tending them as a young boy with his father, he remembers being asked to salute an adjacent grave of a soldier who fell during World War I.

"We didn't know him, it's just that my father was a veteran and it was a basic sign of respect," said Russo. A seminal experience perhaps, recognizing and honoring the dead. It's something he would later turn into a hobby bordering on the obsessive—not with veterans, but with big leaguers.

Russo has a hard time himself explaining his passion for something that some would consider macabre. It has more to do with research than fetish. To him it's all about history—about getting a record or setting one straight.

As a member of SABR, he has a categorical mind that's also very much interested in the Civil War. His scholarly streak and burning curiosity drive him to dig deeper than simply names and dates.

Forgive the metaphor.

"You look at an obit, or a grave site, and your life gets summed up in one line—born here and died there. There's got to be more," said Russo. "The hardest thing about dying, I think, is not knowing that you will die but knowing that 100 years after you die no one will know that you even existed.

"A lot of people don't understand what I do. But it's simply saying, 'I remember.'"

—Gene Racz

BURY MY HEART AT
COOPERSTOWN

What a Way to Go

Flat-out bad luck or god-awful poor judgment. Those are the two major reasons most of the folks in this chapter met their demise.

Take, for example, minor leaguer James Phelps, who made a running catch during a game in Louisiana in 1909 and was bitten by a poisonous snake in the outfield. He finished the game and then died.

Then there's veteran Los Angeles Angels' catcher Gus Sandberg, who made his last earthly decision in 1930 when he decided to light a match to see how much gas was left in the tank of a car.

And how about retired New York Yankee George "Snuffy" Stirnweiss, father of six, who drowned in the Raritan Bay when his New York–bound train plunged into the water after the train's motorman suffered a heart attack?

Car accidents, blood poisoning, falling out of a window— there are plenty of ways to go. Interestingly, there's been only one fatality on the field in the history of major league baseball. That's when Yankees pitcher Carl Mays beaned Ray Chapman at the Polo Grounds in August of 1920.

The amateurs and minor leagues are a different story, with numerous accounts through the years of players and spectators alike getting killed by thrown balls and swung bats. At five ounces of wrapped rubber, string, and horsehide, the baseball makes a lethal projectile either leaving the hand at close to 100 miles per hour or flying out of a huge ballpark in a matter of seconds.

There's no shortage of fatalities occurring on the sandlots and in the stands. Maybe none is so strange as the incident which befell Bernard Lawrence Doyle, who was hit and killed by a stray bullet in the Polo Grounds bleachers. Police think it was fired during a belated Fourth of July celebration.

You couldn't make this stuff up if you tried.

George "Snuffy" Stirnweiss

When George "Snuffy" Stirnweiss boarded a New York–bound train on September 18, 1958, little did he know he was on the fast track to an unimaginable death.

An outstanding player for the Yankees during the war years, he led the American League in hits, doubles, and runs scored in 1944 and 1945 and was the AL batting champ in 1945.

Having retired from pro ball at age 33, Stirnweiss' Jersey Central train was headed to New York, where he worked as a businessman. But this would be anything but another day at the office. As fate would have it, the motorman suffered a heart attack, and the train ran through two signals before plunging off an open-lift bridge that connected the port of Elizabeth and Bayonne in New Jersey.

Stirnweiss, father of six, drowned in the Raritan Bay.

Yankees manager Joe McCarthy called the always-hustling Stirnweiss "one of the toughest competitors" he ever saw. Considered a marvelous teammate and friend to those who knew

him, Stirnweiss edged out Tony Cuccinello of the Chicago White Sox on the last day of the season for the AL batting crown. He was also an All-Star–caliber second baseman.

There are differing versions as to how he got the nickname "Snuffy." The first one has the moniker originating from his nasal condition brought on by hay fever. The other has it that he was named after the comic book character Snuffy Smith due to his colorful personality. Former major leaguer Hank Majeski supposedly hung the name on him, and it stuck.

3

The son of a New York City police officer, he played halfback at North Carolina, becoming a star football player during his tenure there. He joined the Yankees from the Newark Bears in 1943, taking over the second base duties from Joe Gordon the next year when Gordon left for military service. Stirnweiss had 4F status because of chronic ulcers.

Traded in June 1950 as part of a multiplayer deal with the St. Louis Browns, he spent 1951 and 1952 with Cleveland before retiring. He managed in the minor leagues before entering the business world.

Stirnweiss was only 40 years old at the time of the tragedy. When his body was found inside the train, he was clutching a rosary. His funeral was a sad affair, attended by former team-mates Phil Rizzuto and Jerry Coleman. who both remembered him as a great teammate and good man. He left his wife, Jane, and six children ranging in ages from 17 months to 15 years.

He was buried at the Mount Olivet Cemetery in Middletown, New Jersey (Section 29 of the Old Division, Lot 157, Grave 10). Hall of Fame football coach Vince Lombardi is buried just a scant few yards away.

Bizarre postscript: the number of the train Stirnweiss was riding when he died, 932, was played by literally hundreds of people the next day in the illegal pick-3 numbers games that were being run at the time. (The New Jersey lottery was not instituted until 1970). When they all hit the number, a report at the time said the only bookie with enough cash in reserve to pay it all out was a gent by the name of Newsboy Moriarty.

The other bettors got taken for a bad ride, so to speak.

Gus Sandberg's Blowout Loss

Considered one of the smartest catchers in the Pacific Coast League, Sandberg made a mental error in February 1930 that cost him his life. His tools of ignorance that day were a gas tank and a lighted match.

4

Sandberg's former manager Marty Krug was visiting him and noticed his car's needle was on empty. Sandberg volunteered to drain the gas from the tank of his car and put it in Krug's car so he could drive home. After draining the gasoline, Gus lit a match to see if it was empty.

Krug was standing by Sandberg's side and watched in horror as Sandberg took a blast of flame square in the face. Krug suffered burns on his hands trying to put the fire out. Sandberg suffered first-, second-, and third-degree burns on his face, neck, back, and shoulders. He died in the hospital that evening, leaving a widow and two young sons.

Sandberg was a veteran catcher at the time who had been traded from the Cincinnati Reds in 1925 to the Los Angeles Angels. He was well-liked and respected by teammates and rivals alike and was said to not have an enemy in the game.

Witness Tampering

Who needs a hung jury when you have a beaned witness?

How miffed must the prosecutor have been when his star witness was killed by a stray baseball while on break at a local park in Dallas on April 12, 1903?

Aaron Sokolowski, a witness in a murder case that was being tried in Orange, Texas, was waiting his turn on the witness stand when the judge permitted witnesses who were not needed for a considerable time to go watch a baseball game.

Sokolowski's testimony was considered important to the prosecution, which wound up without it when Sokolowski died that afternoon. He was fatally struck by a ball as he leaned back against a low fence behind home plate. The wild pitch caught him in the right temple, and he passed away two hours later.

Snakebitten

Playing outfield for the Ralleyville nine in Monroe, Louisiana, on July 24, 1909, James Phelps made a running catch on a long fly ball. He backed into a bog after hauling it in and felt a sharp pain in his leg. He had been bitten by a water snake.

Incredibly, he opted to finish the game, playing through the last inning as his leg began to balloon from the venom. Twenty-four hours later, he was dead.

The newspaper account reported that another player was bitten on the same grounds a few years before and also died soon afterward.

Badly Rattled

Country merchant Benjamin Nolan was taking in a ballgame on June 5, 1895, in Eckerty, Indiana, when a full-grown rattlesnake took his life. Nolan was bitten several times before the serpent locked its fangs onto him. It had to be pried off of him and killed—all three feet of it, including eight rattles and a baton.

Ralph "Socks" Seybold

It was an ordinary car accident in 1921 that took the life of one of the most extraordinary players of his day—Ralph "Socks" Seybold.

When the American League began play in 1901, legendary manager Connie Mack formed the Philadelphia Athletics and brought Seybold with him from the Western Association. In Mack's eyes, Seybold was "the steadiest and most serviceable of players."

And serve steadily he did. Seybold hit .300 three times, topping 90 RBIs three times. He was consistently among the American League leaders in homers and was second in RBIs in 1907 and fourth in 1902. He also led the league in doubles in 1903 with 45. Not an especially good fielder, he nonetheless had two unassisted double plays from the outfield in 1907.

Seybold strung together a 27-game hitting streak in 1901, bested only by teammate Nap Lajoie, who hit safely in 28 straight.

His best season was 1902, when he batted .316 with 97 RBIs and an American League–leading 16 home runs. The A's won the pennant that year, and his 16 dingers stood as a league record until a young upstart by the name of Babe Ruth shattered it with 29 in 1919.

An injury in 1908 ended his major league career. The accident in 1921, three days before Christmas, ended his life when he lost control of his car and drove over an embankment, breaking his neck. He was 51 years old and was buried at the Brush Creek Cemetery in Irwin, Pennsylvania.

Mike Donovan

Michael Berchman Donovan was blown away on payday.

It was actually a freak accident that cost the ex-ballplayer his life. He went to pick up a check as an employee for Consolidated Edison on February 3, 1938. He wound up taking a bullet in the neck from a coworker whose gun accidentally discharged.

Shortly after noon that fateful day, Donovan and a fellow security guard and friend, Joseph Courtney, entered the paymaster's office on the ninth floor of the Con Ed building, which was located on 14th Street and Irving Place in New York City. Both men were preparing to draw their pay as they entered a small anteroom when Courtney attempted to pull a handkerchief from his back pocket. Somehow, the handkerchief had become entangled with his semi-automatic pistol, which discharged when Courtney jerked at it.

The bullet struck Donovan in the neck, and he died within a few minutes. When police arrived, they immediately charged Courtney with unlawful possession of a weapon. Even though Courtney had a valid pistol permit, he did not have a permit for the semiautomatic that killed his friend.

Police were suspicious of the far-fetched scenario given by Courtney, who was held on a technical charge of homicide. He posted bail totaling $2,500—$500 for the gun possession and $2,000 for the homicide charge.

Eventually, the prosecutor's office ruled the shooting purely accidental.

A native New Yorker, Donovan was born on October 18, 1883. Except for seven games at the big league level—two with Cleveland and five with the Highlanders—he was a career minor leaguer.

He debuted against the Chicago White Sox on May 29, 1904. In the 5–4 Naps victory, Donovan replaced Nap Lajoie at short-stop after the Naps' player/manager was tossed from the game for arguing with umpire Frank Dwyer. In his last major league game, Donovan went 2 for 4 and played third base in a 7–5 loss to Cleveland.

Donovan's minor league odyssey included stops at Shreveport, Louisiana; Toledo, Ohio; Troy, Michigan; Fall River, Massachusetts; Johnstown, Lancaster, Reading, Wilkes-Barre, and Williamsport, Pennsylvania; and Elmira, New York.

He was living at 180 Claremont Avenue in Manhattan at the time of his death, and he was survived by his wife, the former Mary Clarke, and two married daughters, Sally and Marjorie. He was buried at the Calvary Cemetery in Woodside Queens (Section 9, Range 181) in the Clarke family plot.

Emil "Hillbilly" Bildilli

Emil Bildilli's best appearance came when he hurled a two-hitter at Yankee Stadium, pitching for the St. Louis Browns on April 30, 1940. His last appearance came when the car he was driving ran off the road and side-swiped a tree just north of Hartford City, Indiana, on September 15, 1946.

Nicknamed "Hillbilly," Emil Bildilli never did quite live up to his reputation as a pitcher with star potential. The left-hander pitched the majority of his career (five seasons) with the Browns and had his best season in 1940, appearing in 28 games with 11 starts. He went 2–4 with a 4.60 ERA.

Bildilli's road to the majors was a slow and rocky one. He began his pro career when he signed with the Monessen, Pennsylvania, team of the Mid-Atlantic League in 1936. He moved on to Terre

Haute, Indiana, and Johnstown, Pennsylvania, before his contract was sold to St. Louis in 1937.

In his major league debut on August 24, 1937, he got shelled by the Washington Senators—lasting only four innings in the Browns' 9–6 loss, which included surrendering a home run to Buddy Lewis in the third inning. He made only four appearances that year, giving up 12 runs before the Browns' management sent him back to the minors. In 1938 he appeared in five games for St. Louis, going 1–2. In between, he made some minor league stops in Johnstown; San Antonio, Texas; and Springfield, Illinois. He pitched again for San Antonio in 1939 before being called back up to the Browns where he went 1–1 in two games.

After being sent down to the minors—in Toledo, Ohio— once again in 1941, Bildilli decided to quit baseball and take a job with the Muncie, Indiana, fire department. He continued to pitch semi-pro ball.

Bildilli was returning home from a game at Fort Wayne on the fateful night when he apparently fell asleep at the wheel. He suffered multiple injuries in the accident, including a skull fracture. He turned 34 the next day. He left a wife and daughter.

Johnny Scalzi

Johnny Scalzi's major league career with the Boston Braves lasted all of two games with only one at-bat. He struck out. He was then forced to retire when his old college football back injury flared up.

His career as a scout for the newly formed New York Mets had a similarly short life—stopped dead in its tracks soon after it began when he crashed into an oncoming car near Port Chester, New York, on September 27, 1962.

Considered one of the all-time best football players in Georgetown history, Scalzi might have turned to a career in the NFL if not for his injury. But he was also an outstanding infielder for the Hoyas and, as graduation neared, he mulled over offers for both football and baseball. With the advice of his family, he signed a contract with Boston.

Scalzi remained in baseball after hanging up the cleats and eventually became president of the Colonial League before landing his job with the Mets. He had just finished supervising a tryout camp at the Polo Grounds and was driving to his home in Stamford, Connecticut, when his car went out of control and crashed.

He died from his injuries a short time later. He was 55 years old and was buried at St. John Cemetery in Darien, Connecticut.

Harold B. "Rowdy" Elliott

Indiana native Harold B. "Rowdy" Elliott made his major league debut with the Braves on September 24, 1910. He came to bat only twice, with no hits in three games that season. He did not return to the majors until the 1916 season when called up by the Chicago Cubs. Elliott appeared in 23 games in 1916 and 85 in 1917. After just five games in 1918, he joined the service. After his return in 1919, he played in the Pacific Coast League with the Oakland Oaks. In 1920 he was called back to the majors, where he played one more season for the Brooklyn Robins, hitting .241 in 41 games.

He died on February 12, 1934, at the age of 33, when he fell out of an apartment window in San Francisco. No one knows why or how he fell. He was laid to rest at the San Francisco National Cemetery, in the Presidio (Plot C, Grave 768).

Harry Wolverton

Harry Wolverton was a solid third baseman with a .278 lifetime average. He batted over .300 for the Phillies in 1901 and 1903, and once rapped out three triples in a July 13, 1900, game.

But his real claim to fame, or infamy, was managing the Yankees to the worst record in team history, a 50–102 record in 1912. He had built a solid reputation in the minor leagues as manager, piloting teams in the Tri-State, Eastern, and Pacific Coast leagues before he came to New York to guide the Yankees in their last season at Hilltop Park. That season, the team was so beset by injuries that he frequently used himself as a pinch-hitter.

Known as a free spirit, he was noted for wearing a sombrero and was a cartoon-like figure as he puffed cigars in the dugout. After his career, he settled in Oakland, California, where he had managed in the Pacific Coast League. He died when he was run over by a hit-and-run driver there on February 4, 1937.

Wolverton is buried at the Cypress Lawn Memorial Park in Colma, California.

Howard Freigau

Going off the deep end is not always such a bad thing—especially when it comes to unlit swimming pools.

In July 1932 while playing for the Knoxville Smokies of the Southern Association, Freigau decided to go for a late-night swim to cool off from the severe summer heat. In the sweltering darkness, the talented utility player plunged headlong into the shallow end, breaking his neck and drowning. He was only 32 years old.

A gifted athlete, Freigau could have been a professional basketball player had there been a pro league at the time. He was an All-American hoop star at Ohio State University, where he also played baseball and went on to become a lifetime .272 hitter in the majors.

Adept at playing all four infield positions, he became a highly valued utility specialist. It was a role he found hard to shake. When he did get a chance to play every day, he never embarrassed himself. His career high for RBIs was 71 in 1925, most of which were accumulated after he was traded to the Cubs from St. Louis.

Freigau is buried in the Woodland Cemetery in Dayton, Ohio.

John "Rube" Benton

Ageless John "Rube" Benton was still going strong on his 50th birthday, hurling for the Erwin, North Carolina, club on June 27, 1937. He had no plans to officially give up pitching as the winter rolled around. But in December of that year, on a visit to his brother in Ozark, Alabama, he got caught in an eight-car pileup, killing both him and a passenger with whom he was riding.

During his major league career, the port-sider was a solid, often spectacular pitcher who had the misfortune of playing for some terrible teams—he once lost 20 games for Cincinnati. Eventually, he got the chance to show off his pitching prowess when he joined the New York Giants. The staff was being rebuilt after the departure of three of its mainstays: Christy Mathewson, Rube Marquard, and Jeff Tesreau.

Some considered Giants manager John McGraw crazy for bringing in a pitcher like Benton. But Rube did not disappoint. He had the best years of his career with New York and appeared in two games during the 1917 World Series, going 1–1. He won Game 3 against Eddie Cicotte, 2–0.

Steady and reliable, he averaged 13 wins and 230 innings pitched per year for his career. He continued pitching decent ball even after he rejoined his old team, the Reds, for the last three years of his career. After his major league career ended in 1925, Benton continued on in the minors for seven years. Benton is buried in the Baptist Church Cemetery in Salemburg, North Carolina.

Karl Drews

Karl Drews was run down by a drunk driver in plain view of his 17-year-old daughter on August 15, 1963.

Another promising pitcher who never did quite reach his potential, Drews was a Staten Island, New York, native whose high-water mark came in 1952 when he won 14 games for the Phillies, with five shutouts and an ERA of 2.72. The beginning of his career was auspicious as well, when he went 6–6 in 1947 for the Yankees, World Series champs that year.

In between, there were ups and downs. Purchased by the St. Louis Browns in 1948, he played two seasons before getting sent to the minors. After spending 1950 in the bushes, he caught on with the Phillies the following season and eventually called it quits in 1954.

His final earthly appearance came when the car he was driving in with his daughter stalled near a construction site in Dania, Florida. Drews tried to flag down motorist Earl Richard Johnson, who wound up running him down. Johnson was charged with DUI and causing an accident.

Drews was 43 years old and was buried at the Hollywood Memorial Gardens in Hollywood, Florida.

Mike Dorgan

The routine operation would be a success, but the patient would die.

Mike Dorgan may have thought he would suffer less pain after he underwent knee surgery to correct injuries from his rough-and-tumble playing days. The procedure, performed in April 1909, looked to have gone well before complications set in, eventually causing death due to blood poisoning.

Dorgan was as versatile a performer as you could find during the early years of professional baseball. He played every position on the diamond, even going 8–7 as a pitcher. He became one of manager Jim Mutrie's favorite players when he joined the Giants in 1883.

Whenever Dorgan filled in behind the plate, he wore no catcher's mitt or even a mask. Instead, he wore a rubber glove and a piece of rubber to cover his teeth and mouth. His no-holds-barred style of play led to several severe injuries, most notably knee damage that eventually ended his career.

Later in life, he suffered from severe arthritis and at times walked with a bad limp. As he lay on his death bed, he was asked several times if he would play with the same reckless abandon if he had to do it all over again.

His answer was always "yes," and he said he had no regrets. He was 55 years old and was laid to rest in St. Agnes Cemetery in Syracuse, New York.

Chet "Red" Hoff

Talk about going the distance. Chet Hoff lived to the amazing age of 107, making him the oldest living former major leaguer in history. Born a decade before the Yankees ever even existed as a franchise, the righty nicknamed "Red" pitched only a handful of games for the New York team known as the Highlanders. The highlight of his big-league stay was coming in to a game in relief and striking out the great Ty Cobb.

Hoff pitched in only a total of 23 major league games with a record of 2–4 and a 2.49 ERA.

After his 100th birthday, he enjoyed his status as one of baseball's oldest players. In September 1993 Hoff was asked to appear at a ceremony in the garden of the Columbia-Presbyterian Medical Center in New York City. The 102-year-old dedicated a bronze plaque on the site where home plate was believed to have been at Hilltop Park.

Hoff was still a fairly spry person who, all things considered, was in good health when he took a fall that caused complications that killed him on September 17, 1998. One of Hoff's teammates on the 1912 Highlanders, Paul Otis, lived to the age of 101. Hoff is buried between his two wives, both of whom he outlived, at the Dale Historical Cemetery in Ossining, New York (Section 3, Lot 30, Grave 3).

Ken Hubbs

"Hubbs of the Cubs" was a perfect poster boy for the hard-luck Chicago team, and his untimely and tragic death in a plane crash can be seen as another sad chapter in the franchise's enduring misfortune.

He burst upon the big-league scene in Chicago in 1962, not only winning the National League Rookie of the Year but becoming the first rookie to win a Gold Glove. He set a major league record with 78 errorless games—handling 418 chances at second base in that stretch.

He also set a National League record with 661 at-bats that season.

A member of the Colton, California, team that lost the championship game of the Little League World Series to Schenectady, New York, in 1954, Hubbs died in careless fashion after deciding to take off in a Cessna airplane as a blizzard set in on February 16, 1964. He and a friend were heading back to Hubbs' home in Colton after playing in a charity basketball game in Utah sponsored by the Mormon Church. Airport officials at Provo warned of hazardous conditions, but that failed to deter the overconfident Hubbs who had just received his pilot's license two weeks earlier.

The plane barely traveled five miles when it crashed, killing Hubbs and friend Dennis Doyle.

Hubbs, who should have been a fixture at Wrigley Field for years, was only 22 years old. He was buried at the Monticello Cemetery in Loma Linda, California (Space 5, Section 129 in the Garden Fairhaven).

Worst Seat in the House

Bernard Lawrence Doyle was settling into his seat in the upper tier grandstand of the Polo Grounds on July 5, 1950. He was with a friend who brought along his 13-year-old son. Little did Doyle know that Row 3, Section 42 held the worst seat in the house that day. Maybe of all time.

It was 12:20 PM, about an hour before the first pitch of a doubleheader between the Brooklyn Dodgers and the New York Giants. As the teams warmed up down on the field, a spectator seated in front of Doyle recalled hearing a loud, popping noise. When he turned around he saw Doyle slump forward, blood gushing from his head. He was rushed to Harlem Hospital where he died.

An autopsy revealed a gunshot wound to the temple, with the trajectory of the bullet pointing downward. Police believed that a shot had been fired from outside the ballpark by someone celebrating the Fourth of July, and that the stray bullet struck Doyle. A search of nearby Coogan's Bluff, which overlooked the Polo Grounds from behind home plate, turned up a spent .22 caliber cartridge.

Most of the spectators on hand were unaware of the tragedy that took place. Many thought Doyle had simply been taken ill and needed medical attention. Word of the shooting did filter down to the players after the end of the first game. Dodgers second baseman Jackie Robinson said when the shooting was confirmed, his teammates were talking more about it than the ballgame.

Doyle, of Fairview, New Jersey, was 56 years old. An unemployed freight sorter at the time of his death, he was known as Barney Doyle in boxing circles where he was at one time a fight manager in small local clubs in Jersey. He once managed James Braddock, former world heavyweight champion.

Passing the Buck

Who says keeping score isn't a contact sport?

On October 27, 1902, Thomas Walker was sitting on a fence with two other boys, one of whom was keeping score. As the ballgame unfolded before them in Bellefontaine, Ohio, Walker unfolded his buck knife. The boy keeping score asked if he could use it to sharpen his pencil which had grown dull. As Walker got ready to pass the knife over, a foul ball struck his hand and drove the blade into his chest, severing an artery and causing instant death.

Last Lap

Patrolman John Salo, who had gained national notoriety as a marathon runner, crossed the finish line for the last time in Newark, New Jersey, on October 5, 1931. While on duty at the Third Ward Ball Park, Salo was accidentally hit in the head by a ball thrown by a player. Unconscious, he was rushed to nearby St. Mary's Hospital, where he came to only to die later that evening. Ziggy Mayo, pitcher of the Bergen nine who threw the ball, was questioned and absolved of blame.

Salo, known as the "Flying Finn," was a native of Finland who won C. C. Pyle's transcontinental footrace in 1929 for a purse of $25,000. He took second in the previous race. Married with one child, he was 38 years old.

Kill the Umpire!

Samuel Powell ruled that a three-run homer in the seventh inning was foul on the night of May 1, 1899, in Birmingham, Alabama. Two local teams, the Reds and the Blues, were going at it, and Frank McCoy of the Blues took exception to having his longball called back. McCoy called Powell a "sneaking thief," and Powell got the first lick in, knocking McCoy down and stamping on him.

McCoy grabbed a bat, and instead of swinging for the seats, he took a cut at Powell's head and connected. No one could call that shot back, and Powell died instantly.

Killed by the Umpire!

Students at Methodist University in Chattanooga, Tennessee, were playing baseball on February 23, 1888, when base runner J. C. Johnson forgot to touch home as he crossed the plate. Umpire

Ben Magill called him on it, touching off a dispute that ended with Magill crushing Johnson's skull with the swing of the bat. Both men were 21 years old. Magill fled the scene and had not been captured at the time the story appeared in the newspaper.

Killed because of the Umpire!

One controversial call by an umpire equaled three dead and a fourth seriously injured south of the border on April 7, 1935. The deadly mêlée erupted between the two amateur teams in the state of Jalisco, Mexico, and quickly worsened when spectators charged the field. The three killed were hit with bats. The fourth person was hurt by a flying bottle before the cops came and restored order.

Billy Martin

Throughout his career, Billy Martin loved to go out carousing with his teammates and friends. It was a lifestyle that ultimately wound up getting him killed when the car he was riding in crashed on Christmas Day, 1989.

A tactical genius in spikes, he was one of the game's greatest managers. Yet many people remember Martin more for his rowdy, hard-drinking ways than for his on-field accomplishments.

As a player, he was a second baseman who logged 11 years in the majors, which included winning four World Series with the Yankees. He was the MVP in the 1953 fall classic.

As a manager, he gained a reputation as someone who could win anywhere. Wherever he went as a skipper—Minnesota, Detroit, Texas, Oakland, New York—he had success. He was fired by Yankees owner George Steinbrenner five times, but managed to lead the Bronx Bombers to two league titles and one World Series championship.

Born May 16, 1928, in Berkeley, California, his parents separated when he was young. His mother always referred to the

delinquent father as "the Jackass." Martin was raised by his mother in poverty, and grew up rough and tough on the streets. He brought that same attitude to the diamond, where he eventually excelled for the minor league Oakland Oaks, managed by Casey Stengel.

Stengel left Oakland in 1949 to manage the Yankees, but promised Martin that he would bring him to New York sooner than later. That promise was kept in 1950 when Stengel brought the brash, cocky Martin in for spring training. Martin made the team, bringing the same, hard-nosed style of play to the Yanks that worked so well in the PCL.

Not the most talented player, he made up for any lack of physical skills with sound fundamentals and a heart as big as the George Washington Bridge.

These are precisely the kind of players they say make great managers, and Martin was one of them. He got the most out of his players and was always a step ahead of the play. Nothing between the lines went unnoticed by him. (Recall the famous pine-tar incident when Martin noticed that the sticky substance went too far up the barrel of the bat of Kansas City Royals' George Brett, who had a home run nullified after Martin protested to the umpires.)

No doubt, Martin had his problems—drinking and brawling chief among them. Yankees general manager George Weiss traded Martin to Kansas City in 1957 because he believed Martin was a bad influence on Mickey Mantle and Whitey Ford. The last straw for Weiss was a brawl at the famed Copacabana nightclub on Martin's 29th birthday.

Ironically, Martin had little to do with the punch-up on that occasion.

On May 16, 1957, several members of the Yankees, including Mantle, Yogi Berra, and Hank Bauer, were out on the town in celebration of Martin's birthday. After dinner at Danny's Hideaway, the group, which included their wives, went to see a show at the Copacabana nightclub that featured Sammy Davis Jr. Also in the audience that night were two bowling teams that were celebrating winning their league championships. Several members of the bowling teams who had been drinking heavily began shouting racial slurs at Davis.

The Yankees took offense. Hank Bauer, a former Marine, told them in no uncertain terms to cut it out. The bowlers barked back at the Yankees. Both groups got up and met by the cloak room. The next thing anyone knew, one of the bowlers got laid out by one of the club's bouncers.

According to Mantle, "It looked like Roy Rogers rode through on Trigger, and Trigger kicked the guy in the face."

The fight, which was front-page news, gave Weiss the excuse he needed to dump Martin, whom he felt didn't have enough class to wear the pinstripes. Martin was traded on June 15, 1957, along with Woodie Held, Bob Martyn, and Ralph Terry to the Kansas City Athletics for Ryne Duren, Jim Pisoni, and Harry Simpson.

When Weiss died in 1972, it was said that Mantle half jokingly mentioned to Martin that the two of them should both go to Weiss' wake. Billy, asked his buddy why, and "the Mick" half-jokingly replied, "To make sure the son of a bitch is really dead."

After New York, Martin's career took a nomadic turn. He played for Kansas City, Detroit, Cleveland, Cincinnati, and Minnesota. While at Minnesota, he turned to coaching, and in 1969 guided the Twins to a first-place finish in the American League's West Division.

Next, he came on board as manager for Detroit in 1971 and led the Tigers to second, first, and third place in the American League East.

Martin's turbulent years as Yankees manager are well documented. But lost in the soap-opera-like series of fires and re-hires is his strong managerial performance that saw him win the pennant in 1976 and a World Series in 1977.

He also brought winning ball back to Oakland in the early 1980s.

Despite his volatile temper, Martin was beloved by his teammates and had scores of friends in the game, including Tony La Russa, Joe Torre, and Tommy Lasorda, to name a few. There was a side to Martin that would give the shirt off his back to those in need. When New York journalist and sports talk show host Art Rust Jr. became faint from the heat before a game at Yankee Stadium in the 1980s, it was Martin who took charge, making sure he was taken care of by medical staff.

But the media found it tall too easy to harp on Martin's negative side.

When he was killed in a pick-up truck crash on an icy road on that fateful Christmas night, the press had a field day. Early reports stated that Martin, who had been out drinking with a friend, was the driver of the pick-up truck that crashed in Johnson City, New York, a few scant yards from the entrance to Martin's residence. Throughout the nation, sports talk-radio hosts fanned the flames of criticism and lambasted Martin for his drinking, brawling ways. It was an easy time for Yankees haters to swarm out of the woodwork, and the on-air criticism of Martin continued even four months later when the Yankees placed a plaque in his honor in Monument Park, at their stadium, on Opening Day in 1990.

Martin was a passenger that night in the truck that his friend Bill Reedy was driving when it crashed. And when details of the tragic evening came to light, it was discovered that on the last night of his life, Martin bought Christmas dinner for two homeless men.

His funeral at St. Patrick's Cathedral in Manhattan was a solemn affair, attended by former President Richard Nixon, Mantle, Berra, Ford, and many other former and present Yankees, including Don Mattingly and Steinbrenner.

Martin, 62, was laid to rest at the Cemetery of the Gate of Heaven in Hawthorne, New York (Section 25, Plot 21, Grave 3). He is buried in the same section as Babe Ruth.

Burt Keeley

Born in Wilmington, Illinois, where he pitched for the hometown club, Burton Elwood Keeley was signed out of Notre Dame University in 1908 by Joe Cantillon, manager of the Washington Nationals.

He made his pro debut on April 18, 1908, with a 3–1 victory over the Red Sox. While with the Nationals, he roomed with the legendary Walter Johnson.

"Walter and I roomed together," he told a newspaper in a 1948 interview. "And he was a wonderful fellow. He said to me, 'You must have had something to get up here, and the way I see it, it's no harder than pitching back in the sticks where the batters swing at everything.'

"He used to make three times as much as I did and used to leave a roll of bills on the dresser and tell me if I need anything to help myself," Keeley once said. "Then he never let me pay him back. He was king, all right, in every way."

Unfortunately for Keeley, he wasn't able to master the major league hitters as well as he did in the bush leagues. He went 6–11 in 1908 and got sent to Omaha, Nebraska, after only two appearances in 1909.

He was forced out of baseball in 1911 due to injuries he received in a railroad mishap and returned to Chicago in 1912 to manage the Chicago entrant in the United States League. He then saddled up for a year in the Federal League.

After he retired, he worked many years for the Wilson Sporting Goods Company. His heart, though, was still in the game, and he took to managing girls' softball teams in the greater Chicago area. One of his biggest thrills managing was in 1942 when his Garden City team won both the state and regional titles before losing the national championship to the New Orleans Jax 4–1 in Detroit.

On April 27, 1952, Keeley, age 62, fell and fractured his neck at his home in Ely, Minnesota. Pneumonia eventually set in, and he passed away less than a week later, at just after midnight on May 3.

He was laid to rest at the Ely Cemetery on May 6, 1952, leaving his widow Mae and the many friends whom he had touched over the years.

Mike Fornieles

Mike Fornieles played parts of 12 seasons in the major leagues with five teams, but it wasn't until his trade to Boston in 1957 that he finally found his niche as an ace reliever in the Red Sox bullpen.

Born Jose Miguel Fornieles Torres in Havana, Cuba, on January 18, 1932, Fornieles threw a one-hitter in his big-league debut with the Washington Senators on Tuesday, September 2, 1952.

The performance was as spectacular as it was unexpected.

Fornieles was an emergency fill-in starter that night against the Philadelphia Athletics. Right-hander Paul Sanchez, who also played with Fornieles in Havana, was supposed to pitch but went down with a stomach ailment. On short notice, Senators' scout "Papa" Joe Cambria sent up Fornieles as a replacement and the 5'11" side-armer surrendered only a second-inning single to the Athletics catcher, Joe Astroth. Only one base runner got on after the third inning.

Fornieles continued to pitch well after his debut, including eight innings of scoreless relief against the Red Sox in a 5–3 Washington victory.

Despite a 1.37 ERA during his four-game trial, Washington management decided not to wait to develop the youngster. While Fornieles was pitching "lights out" in the Cuban Winter League, the Senators traded him to the Chicago White Sox on December 10, 1952, for veteran pitcher Chuck Stobbs.

The trade proved to be a good one initially for both clubs— Stobbs won 11 games for D.C. while Fornieles twirled to an 8–7 record with Chicago. Finding only nominal success as a starter and long reliever during his stay on the South Side, he was traded to the Baltimore Orioles on May 21, 1956, along with Connie Johnson, George Kell, and Bob Nieman for Jim Wilson and Dave Philley. The trade startled White Sox fans, who felt that their team gave up too much in the deal. At Baltimore, Fornieles pitched under .500 ball, and it appeared he would never fulfill his potential.

Fornieles blossomed when he was sent to the Red Sox for Billy Goodman in June of 1957, thanks in part to manager Pinky Higgins, who found that when he used Fornieles in relief, later in games, that his fastball and curve tended to be more effective. Fornieles would only start 10 more games in the majors as he headed to the pen, eventually taking over for Leo Kiely as the Red Sox closer in 1959.

He led Boston in relief appearances and saves for the next three years, and led the American League in saves (14) and appearances (70) in 1960. The next year he collected a career-high 15 saves.

By 1962, however, he was saddled into a long relief role and was replaced as closer by the fire-balling Dick Radatz.

Fornieles stayed with Boston until mid-June of 1963, when he was purchased by his old organization, the Twins (Washington moved to Minnesota after the 1960 season). The reunion did not prove to be fruitful. He went 1–1 with a 4.76 ERA in 11 games, the last of his major league career. Released by Minnesota that July, he signed a contract with the Reds before the 1964 season, but failed to make the roster in spring training.

During his career, Fornieles would return to Cuba each winter to pitch in the Cuban Winter League. This afforded him the luxury of seeing his wife and family. He was able to continue that practice until the regime of Fidel Castro informed him that he could not leave Cuba to play in the U.S. unless he promised that he would return. Fornieles already planned to stay in the United States, but told Communist officials that he would return after the 1960 season. Cuban authorities only allowed him to take $5 out of the country with him, enough to pay the cab fare at the airport. He was able to sneak $200 in the fingers of his baseball mitt and never looked back.

Sadly, he never was able to coax his wife to come to America with their daughter Marina. Fornieles stated publicly that he believed that his wife and her family were committed to the Marxist cause of the new regime.

Fornieles divorced his wife and married Olga Vasco de Gama Gomes.

After his career, he sold cars and gained a reputation for his good demeanor and willingness to talk of his glory days in the majors.

Fornieles died at the Bayfront Medical Center in St. Petersburg, Florida, on Wednesday, February 11, 1998, as the result of injuries from a fall at his home in Bay Harbor, Florida. He was 66 years old, and survived by his daughter and two brothers, both of whom lived in Havana. He was cremated and his ashes were retained by his family.

Dick Radatz

Interestingly, Detroit native Richard Raymond "Dick" Radatz died in virtually the same way as the man he replaced in the Boston bullpen—Mike Fornieles, who died in February of 1998 after suffering injuries from a fall at home.

Known as "the Monster" or "Moose" because of his size (6'5", 235 pounds), Radatz had an intimidating presence on the field backed up by a blazing fastball.

Off the field, he was known for his wonderful demeanor.

Radatz pitched for the Michigan State Spartans in the late 1950s. Signed by the Boston Red Sox as an amateur free agent before 1959 season, he replaced Mike Fornieles as the Boston closer in 1962, notching 24 saves. The big right-hander led the league with 62 appearances and nine relief wins and was chosen the American League Fireman of the Year.

Radatz was one of the top relievers of the 1960s, accruing 100 saves and 49 wins over a four-year span from 1962 to 1965. He typically pitched multiple innings per appearance, averaging 134.6 innings and 68 appearances per season.

Radatz said he always considered the 1964 All-Star Game, the one in which he gave up a three-run homer to Johnny Callison with two outs in the ninth to lose 7–4, the biggest disappointment of his career.

On the suggestion of former Red Sox great Ted Williams, Radatz started developing a sidearm sinkerball in spring training in 1965. But while the action of throwing sidearm gave him a very good sinker, it was not effective for throwing his fastball. Hence, he lost movement and speed with his blazer. What followed was a so-so season in 1965, and a scant 19 innings of work in 1966. He was traded to the Cleveland Indians on June 2 of that season for Don McMahon and Lee Stange.

Radatz had lost his pinpoint control. It was more mental than physical, but either way, he was never able to regain his dominating form of earlier years and bounced around several organizations his last few seasons.

All told, he pitched seven seasons in the majors for Boston, Cleveland, Detroit, the Chicago Cubs, and Montreal. He had lifetime record of 52 wins and 43 losses, with 122 saves and a 3.13 ERA. In 1963 and 1964 he made the All-Star team.

One of baseball's great urban legends was Radatz's record against Mickey Mantle. Radatz always maintained that he struck out his buddy Mantle 54 times in 67 attempts. No one ever doubted the record or even checked the real stats. It was SABR researcher Dave Smith who finally dug up the truth. Radatz actually only struck out Mantle 12 times in 16 at-bats. Still, not bad.

What is also factual is that Radatz holds the major league record for strikeouts in a season by a relief pitcher with 181 in 1964.

In 1997 Radatz was inducted into the Red Sox Hall of Fame. He was also a friend of the Jimmy Fund—an organization that helps children and adults with cancer.

On Wednesday afternoon, March 16, 2005, Radatz, who had been suffering problems with his legs for some time, lost his balance and fell down a flight of stairs. When police arrived at his home at 17 Hilltop Lane in Easton, Massachusetts, at 3:27 PM, they found him lying unconscious on the floor at the bottom of the stairs. Paramedics were unable to revive him. Radatz had struck his head on a carpet-covered concrete floor and suffered severe head trauma. He was 67 years old and was remembered at the Red Sox opening day ceremonies at Fenway Park that April.

Radatz's body was taken back to his home state of Michigan, where he was laid to rest at the Holy Sepulchre Cemetery in Southfield.

Eddie Grant

Eddie Grant was a Harvard graduate who became the first of three major league players killed in World War I.

All told, he played 10 years in the majors, making his big-league debut by belting out three hits with the Cleveland Naps of the American League.

After a stint in the minors, he resurfaced in the majors with the 1907 Phillies, taking over as leadoff batter in 1908. He led the NL in at-bats in 1908 and 1909.

Grant became a fine-fielding third baseman, fast on the bases and dependable in the clutch. In 1915, after two-and-a-half seasons with the Giants, where he was a favorite of John McGraw, he left baseball and became a practicing lawyer in New York City.

When war was declared on Germany in the "War to End All Wars," he joined the 307th Infantry Regiment, 77th Infantry Division, entering the service from New York. He was leading a mission in the Argonne Forest to rescue the "Lost Battalion" when he was killed by German fire.

Grant is buried at the Meuse-Argonne American Cemetery in Romagne, France (Plot A, Row 2, Grave 24).

A monument in his honor was placed in center field at the old Polo Grounds in New York. Each Memorial Day there was a wreath-laying ceremony at his plaque.

Frank Eustace

While playing for Reading, Pennsylvania, Frank Eustace was credited with being the second player ever to make an unassisted triple play in the Pennsylvania State League. He turned the trick in a contest against the Carbondale Stars on July 18, 1892.

Incredibly, he supposedly performed the same feat again while playing third base in a game between Pottsville, Pennsylvania, and Lebanon, Pennsylvania, on September 6, 1902. An article appearing in the July 20, 1909, edition of the *Chicago Daily Tribune* attests to the achievement.

Eustace debuted for the Louisville Colonels on April 16, 1896, against the Chicago Colts. At shortstop that day he had three hits and scored twice. Unfortunately, his first day in the pros was spoiled by a 10-run first-inning outburst by Chicago.

Eustace went on to play for Hartford; Indianapolis; Springfield, Massachusetts; and Utica before heading back to Pottsville in 1903 to open a business. The game pulled him back as a manager in 1904 with the York, Pennsylvania, club of the Tri-State League. The next year, as both manager and captain of the Concord, New Hampshire, club, he led the team to the New England League pennant.

This put Eustace's services in great demand. A bidding war for him ensued between the Haverhill and Manchester clubs of the New England League that was settled in Manchester's favor by the league secretary in 1906. Eustace stayed there until taking on duties in Roanoke, Virginia, for the 1908–1909 season.

He closed out his career with his hometown team of Pottsville in 1910 and later worked at a steel mill there. An avid hunter, Eustace was killed on October 20, 1932, when he accidentally fell off a railroad trestle at Connors Crossing, Pennsylvania, while training his hunting dogs. Eyewitnesses said he spun around and fell as if experiencing a dizzy spell.

He was buried at the Mount Laurel Cemetery in Pottsville, Pennsylvania.

Fred Holmes

You could say that Fred Holmes got killed for the best seat in the house. Actually, he took a pummeling that caused his death from a fellow patient at a mental hospital in an argument over a chair as they watched TV.

It was an ignominious death for a man who contributed to the game as a player and promoter.

In his all-too-brief big-league "career" (two games), he made his debut for the Highlanders in the second game of a doubleheader between Chicago and New York on Sunday, August 23, 1903. Holmes walked and had five putouts and a miscue at first base in his lone appearance of the year. New York split the twin bill with the White Sox.

On April 24, 1904, playing for the Chicago Colts, he smashed a double (his only major league hit) in a 4–3 loss to the Cardinals. In that game, Holmes had the privilege of catching the legendary Hall of Fame pitcher Mordecai "Three Finger" Brown before 11,000 fans at St. Louis.

Holmes became a player/owner of a popular semi-pro ball club in Chicago known as "Fred Holmes' Arions" that played in the highly competitive Park Owners Baseball Association. He was able to maintain a certain amount of fame and credibility as the Arions' leader, something he never was able to achieve in the majors.

He was admitted to the Chicago State Hospital in Norwood Park, Illinois, on January 24, 1956, for mental illness. His stay lasted just a little over three years before he took his fateful beating on Friday afternoon, February 10, 1956, at about 1:00 PM. Holmes had emphysema, and he suffered a traumatic rupture of his lungs and multiple fractured ribs. He lasted through the weekend, passing away on Monday the 13th, at the age of 76.

His death certificate read that he was still married at the time of his demise. He was laid to rest in Mount Olive Cemetery (Block 22, Grave 97) in Chicago two days later. Wire services completely omitted Holmes' baseball career from the obituaries that they briefly ran—a brief and incomplete final account for a very popular player who gave his all on the semi-pro fields of the Windy City.

Al Kellett

Al Kellett had a better career on the hardwood than the diamond—logging 117 games with three teams in the American Basketball League after a short stay in the majors.

It's unknown why he opted for a career on the mound right out of college since he was an All-American hoops star at Columbia University.

What's also unknown is the exact cause of the skull fracture that killed him at age 58—he passed away due to a brain laceration and hemorrhage.

Kellett's debut in the majors is also unresolved. Most record books have him down as debuting on July 1, 1923, yet, *The New York Times* of June 30, 1923, in a column called "Caught at the Plate," and box scores reported around the country, including in the *Atlanta Journal-Constitution*, have him making his debut against the Yankees two days earlier, on Friday, June 29, 1923. (*The New York Times* identified him as Francis Kellett.)

Kellett made his final major league appearance when he pitched on Saturday, August 30, 1924, for the Red Sox in the first game of a doubleheader against his old club, the Athletics. The A's swept both games by scores of 18–7 and 7–2.

After the season, Kellett signed to play barnstorming basketball for Eddie Holly's Majors. The team was comprised of current and former major leaguers and featured Al Schact and Nick Altrock. A fine all-around player, he eventually played in the ABL with Philadelphia, Trenton, Chicago, and Brooklyn—scoring a total of 756 points, averaging 6.5 points per game.

Kellett was living in New York City at 319 West 94ᵗʰ Street, when he died at Bellevue Hospital on July 14, 1960. He left his wife, Helen, and was buried at the Ferncliff Cemetery in Ardsley, New York.

Harry Blake

Before playing pro ball, Harry Blake was a circus acrobat, and his coordination and flexibility helped make him a versatile player. He became a fairly sure-handed fielder with a decent stick—churning out six seasons in the majors, where he batted .252 with eight homers and 253 RBIs.

Blake started his career with the Ironton club and later signed on with Charleston, West Virginia; Staunton, Virginia; and then Atlanta in 1894. In July of that year, he was purchased by the Cleveland Spiders, becoming a utility man who could play outfield, shortstop, second base, and first with equal adroitness. He even appeared in one game at catcher.

The Portsmouth, Ohio, native debuted for Cleveland on July 9, 1894, in a 16–15 win over the Washington Nationals. Blake's skills were always in great demand, and rumors always abounded that other clubs were willing to trade with Cleveland for his services. Blake stayed with Cleveland for three years, except for a brief stay with the Fort Wayne, Indiana, club.

Blake was having problems batting during the 1898 season with Milwaukee when his physician recommended that he quit cigarette smoking. He acquiesced. (He might have been willing to try anything, batting .245 at the time.) On March 29, 1899, he was assigned to the St. Louis Perfectos by the Cleveland Spiders, part of the movement of players that was going on during the duel-ownership days of syndicate baseball.

After his big-league career ended, he toiled in the minors for teams like Worcester, Massachusetts; Syracuse, New York; Brockton, Pennsylvania; Pueblo, Colorado; and Lincoln, Nebraska, retiring about 1910.

Blake was residing in a rooming house at 650 East 39th Street in Chicago when he died in a fire on October 19, 1919. His remains were taken back to his hometown of Portsmouth, Ohio, where he was buried at the Greenlawn Cemetery.

Joe O'Brien

There's an old schoolboy's rhyme urging safety in chemistry class that goes: Johnny was a chemist, but he's not one anymore, because what he thought was H_2O was H_2SO_4.

Joe O'Brien's needless death through accidental poisoning could have been avoided through accurate labeling by his careless wife, Jean, who inadvertently left the words "Rhubarb Soda" on a bottle of potassium cyanide.

Like water and hydrochloric acid, they are also two very different compounds with very different effects.

On Wednesday, May 29, 1929, O'Brien woke up with a headache and indigestion at his home at 551 West 157th Street in New York. O'Brien's wife advised him to take some rhubarb and soda that was in a bottle in the medicine cabinet. On his way through the kitchen, O'Brien saw another bottle with the same label, picked it up, and headed into the bathroom. After half an hour, his wife, worried that he had not yet come back out, entered the bathroom to find her husband sprawled on the floor, dead.

Apparently, about eight years before, Mrs. O'Brien had made the solution to use as an insecticide, and had kept it tucked away in the bottom of a closet. (She apparently put the deadly mixture into the first convenient bottle she saw lying around.) The night before the tragedy, she had taken the poison out and dabbed it on some pieces of bread in order to kill a mouse that had been making a pest of itself. She had simply forgotten to put the poison back, thus leading to her husband's tragic demise at the age of 54.

O'Brien, a native of Milwaukee, was an executive in minor and major league baseball for over 25 years, including a post as president of the American Association from 1905 to 1909.

His death was widely mourned, as he had become a fairly popular figure in baseball circles. He left his wife and two children. He was buried at St. Raymond's Cemetery in the Bronx.

The fate of the mouse remains unknown.

Mike Kelley

"Knock 'em down and pick 'em up!" was the personal credo for Michael Joseph Kelley who spent 52 years in baseball as a player/owner, manager, and entrepreneur.

33

The last minor league boss of Ted Williams, Kelley could be brash, bellicose, and overbearing at times. Yet, he never held a grudge and had literally hundreds of friends in the game. He was no less than a father-figure for many rookie pitchers and rookie umpires, and always maintained good working relationships within the majors and other minor league circuits like the PCL.

His strong persona continually served him well in terms of making connections and finding talent. In fact, Kelley always used to brag about how he never needed scouts to find talent. He maintained that by good ties with umpires, he would always be able to find out about the best talent.

"I got all the dope on players from umpires," he said. "I cultivated their friendship. Umpires make the best scouts and it doesn't cost as much."

Born December 2, 1875, in Templeton, Massachusetts. Kelley knew his father was disappointed that he wanted to become a professional ballplayer. The lack of approval only fueled his desire to excel.

And excel he did, embarking on a long career as both a player and a manager. A noteworthy moment in his career was being traded along with Honus Wagner and several other players to Pittsburgh from Louisville in 1899.

In 1902 he became the first baseman/manager of the St. Paul Saints of the American Association (AA), staying there until 1905. At St. Paul he was a teammate of Miller Huggins, a friendship that lasted until Huggins' untimely death in 1929.

Kelley rated his friend Miller Huggins as the greatest manager of all-time and, pound for pound, considered Ty Cobb and Wagner to be the best major leaguers. Babe Ruth and Lou Gehrig were also high on his list.

Of his American Association teams, he was most proud that he took Joe Houser off the scrap heap to become the AA's home-run hitting champion.

Kelley became a rich man wheeling and dealing players—sending hundreds of them to the majors. He once bought the contract of Bubbles Hargrave for $500, eventually turning around and selling him to the Reds for $25,000. Righteous bucks in those days.

Kelley's clubs were always competitive, and he was the last of the independent owners in the American Association when he sold out in 1946.

He kept a keen interest in the game right up to the time of his death. He lived with his wife, the former Margaret Morrison, at 2820 Brookwood Terrace in Minneapolis.

On May 25, 1955, Kelley fell several times outside his home, sustaining a comminuted fracture—a broken, splintered, or crushed bone—of his right femur. Despite his advanced age of 80, doctors at the Mt. Sinai Hospital had no choice but to operate and install a prosthetic device. Unfortunately, Kelley was also suffering from several other medical problems, including cirrhosis of the liver, which caused fatal complications.

Kelley died at 5:10 AM on June 6, 1955. The official cause of his death was cerebral anemia involving the vital center due to congestive heart failure.

He was buried on June 9, 1955, at the Lakewood Cemetery in Minneapolis.

Ruppert Mills

A teammate of Knute Rockne at the University of Notre Dame, where he competed at the end position, Ruppert Mills played in 41 games for the 1915 Newark Peppers of the Federal League. The 6'2" first baseman batted .201 with 16 RBIs.

Mills had left the game and was practicing law when he drowned in a boating excursion on Lake Hopatcong in New Jersey on July 20, 1929.

A good track and field man in high school, Mills got entangled in contractual red tape at the outset of his career after the Federal League went belly-up. In a bizarre episode, Mills was forced to work out by himself in an empty stadium for a club that no longer existed to fulfill contractual obligations with the Newark Peppers. Eventually, a settlement was reached and he gained his release.

After getting signed by Detroit, he entered the service in 1917 when America entered World War I. He then quit the game to embark on a successful career as an attorney. He was one of the negotiators who represented the Meadowbrook Club, the owners of Meadowbrook Field, when that venue was chosen as the new home for the Newark team of the International League. He was a counsel-at-large for the Veterans of Foreign Wars and also had a successful political career with the Essex County Republican Party.

On July 20, 1929, Mills, who lived on Roseville Avenue in Newark, was on holiday and in the midst of a canoeing excursion with a friend at Lake Hopatcong when disaster struck. The canoe capsized, and Mills drowned while attempting to help his partner.

Mills, who at the time was an under-sheriff and had recently won the Republican nomination for Essex County sheriff, was only 36. A captain with Troop A of the 102nd Cavalry, he was buried with full military honors at St. Mary's Cemetery in East Orange, New Jersey.

Sandy Piez

The son of German immigrants Anton and Huldah Hornick Piez, Charles William "Sandy" Piez was considered to be a fast and heady base runner.

He met a chilling demise in an icy brook in Absecon, New Jersey.

Normally a left fielder, he started his pro career in Greenville, South Carolina, and then Richmond of the Virginia League before being purchased by the New York Giants in June 1913.

Giants manager John McGraw inserted him into the lineup for his debut on April 17, 1914. He was used mostly as a pinch-hitter/runner, but the season was a bust for "McGraw's Minions" who looked like a bunch of tired old men.

Piez made his final big league appearance in a twin bill with the Giants on October 6. In game one, a 5–1 victory over the Phillies, Piez was the offensive star. He had two hits, one of them a bases-loaded triple, and also scored a run while making two putouts as the center fielder. The three RBIs were the only ones he would ever produce in a major league uniform.

Before he entered pro ball, Piez attended Rutgers University, where he starred on the baseball team. After his playing career, he returned to his alma mater to coach the Scarlet Knights. He was known for his preparation in getting his players ready. In 1917 he took his team on a 10-game tour against southern colleges in preparation for the upcoming season.

Piez was a gas heater salesman and lived at 31 East Illinois Avenue in Absecon with his wife, the former Helen Middleton, when he met his sudden demise. On December 29, 1930, Piez was a passenger in a car driven by his friend, John M. Bewley, a former Internal Revenue Service agent and Secretary of the Atlantic City Hospital. Having just left his house, Bewley attempted to pass a car as they drove over the Absecon Boulevard Bridge. The car skidded on some ice, crashed through the guardrails, and landed in 15 feet of water in Absecon Creek.

Bewley climbed out of the sinking wreck and made his way to shore through the freezing water. Piez was not so lucky—his body was pinned in the rear seat. It took more than two hours for rescue teams to pull the car from the water.

The official cause of Piez's death was drowning. He was buried at Atlantic City Cemetery in Pleasantville, New Jersey.

Lewis "Snake" Wiltse

The older brother of George "Hooks" Wiltse, Lewis "Snake" Wiltse was noted for having one of the best pickoff moves to first base in all of baseball. Still, he never was able to achieve the fame or success of his baby brother, and he bounced around from team to team in the minors and the pros.

At the turn of the century in the pros, he made stops with the Pirates, the Athletics, and the Baltimore Orioles, who would become the New York Highlanders. He was part of the Highlanders original Opening Day roster. Wiltse only appeared in four games for New York, starting in three of them.

After he hung up his spikes, he settled in Harrisburg, Pennsylvania, where he worked in the service department of the Underwood Typewriter Company, fixing office machines and typewriters. On Sunday, August 25, 1928, Wiltse was trimming the hedges on his property with a heavy-bladed pruning knife and somehow accidentally cut the femoral artery in his left leg. Before help could arrive, he died as a result of a massive loss of blood. He was only 56 years old.

After his death, his brother George said, "If Lew had cut himself anywhere else, he would have made it. It was just terribly bad luck, I guess."

Snake Wiltse was buried at the Paxtang Cemetery in Harrisburg.

Bert Myers

A journeyman pro who accrued a lifetime average of .253 with no homers and 52 RBIs in 160 games, Myers' final stop in life came soon after stepping on a rusty nail.

An energetic third baseman who never lacked hustle, Myers retired and settled down in Washington, D.C., after seeing time in the majors with the St. Louis Browns, the Milwaukee Brewers, the Washington Senators, and the Phillies.

The native of Frederick, Maryland, was originally signed by Chris Von der Ahe at St. Louis in 1896 and brought in for the purpose of taking over for Captain Arlie Latham at third base. Myers became one of the more popular players on the team due to his upbeat approach, and newspaper accounts of the day described his play at the "hot corner" as brilliant.

Fifteen years out of the game and living in retirement in the northeast corner of the nation's capital, Myers died on Tuesday, October 12, 1915, at 10:20 PM. His death was the result of traumatic tetanus and cerebral edema due to a foot injury. He apparently received a wound to his foot from a rusty nail, the resulting complications leading to his death at the age of 51.

He left his wife, Martha Healey Myers, and was buried at the Rock Creek Cemetery in Washington, D.C.

Jim McKee

Jim McKee made his major league debut for the Pittsburgh Pirates on September 15, 1972, in a 10–4 loss to the Cardinals. Coming in to relieve battered starter Bruce Kison, he pitched two innings of no-hit ball—walking one and striking out two. McKee appeared in two games total that September and was sent back to Charleston.

He was called up again by Pittsburgh in 1973 when he went 0–1 with 15 appearances and one start. His final appearance came on September 29 in a 6–4 loss to the Expos.

McKee retired and became a phys ed/health teacher at Sedalia Elementary School in Columbus, Ohio, and later at Groveport Madison High School in Groveport, Ohio, where he was coach of the girls' track team. He was known among his students for his pleasant demeanor and was well liked by his coworkers and students.

On September 14, 2002, McKee was killed in a car accident on Route 23, just south of the Franklin/Pickaway county line in Pickaway County, Ohio. McKee, only 55, was cremated, and his ashes given to his family.

Roberto Clemente

One of the all-time greats in major league history, Roberto Clemente lost his life doing what he cared about most—helping people.

A true humanitarian, Clemente died in a plane crash while attempting to deliver medical supplies, food, and clothing to Nicaragua, which had been stricken by an earthquake in 1972. He was in the twilight of a stellar career and had just knocked out his 3,000[th] hit the previous September.

Clemente's fateful plan was to personally oversee the distribution of the supplies, making sure they got into the hands of the civilian population. Supplies he had sent on an earlier date never made it to the victims, infuriating Clemente and giving him the incentive to accompany the next shipment himself.

The plane, a four-engine DC-7, crashed just moments after takeoff from the San Juan International Airport at 9:22 PM. The wreckage was found the next day at about 5:00 PM, in 100 feet of water. Clemente, pilot Jerry Hill, and two other crew members were killed.

In the tragedy, baseball lost one of its great players and humanity lost a true friend of the common man.

The sad episode has been well-chronicled, and there is little to add beyond a bizarre postscript. Years after the crash, two pieces of wreckage, including a gray steel propeller from the plane, were to be auctioned off by Lelands.com. Bidding may have gone thorough the roof on the items if the Clemente family had not threatened legal action—like a piece of one of the airliners that hit the World Trade Center on 9/11 being auctioned on eBay, consider it a sign of the times.

Diving anywhere near the site of the wreckage of Clemente's plane is now prohibited in order to keep scavengers from picking through what is rightfully considered a grave site.

Thurman Munson

Like Roberto Clemente, Thurman Munson died in a plane crash. Unlike Clemente, Munson was at the controls, and his career was arguably still very much on the rise when his jet went down.

Born on June 7, 1947, in Akron, Ohio, Munson grew up in a lower-middle-class family. He became a multi-sport star in high school and earned a baseball scholarship to Kent State University, where he became an All-American catcher.

Munson married his childhood sweetheart, Diane Dominick, in 1968—three months after he was drafted as the number-one pick, and fourth overall, by the New York Yankees in the amateur draft. After 99 minor league games, the young Munson joined the Yankees for good near the end of the 1969 season.

Brash and self-assured, Munson's confidence was contagious to his teammates. He smacked his first major league base hit on August 8, 1969, off of Oakland's Catfish Hunter in the second game of a twi-night doubleheader at Yankee Stadium.

The next season he took over as the Yankees' starting catcher. On the field, Munson immediately established his ability to handle veteran pitchers, eventually calling his own game. But at bat, he got off to a terrible start as a rookie. Manager Ralph Houk stuck with him, telling him that he could win more games with his catching then he ever could with his bat. Houk's faith in the young catcher paid off when Munson went on to have an outstanding defensive season, hitting .302 and capturing AL Rookie of the Year honors.

Munson's power was hindered at first by Yankee Stadium's gigantic left-field dimensions—the infamous "Death Valley." He did hit for average, but was often not utilized properly in the second slot in the order in his early years. Due to the fact that he could drive the ball for power, particularly to the opposite field, he was much better suited lower in the lineup, particularly in the third slot.

During the Yankees' rebuilding years, Munson and Bobby Murcer were the stars around whom the team was constructed. The two established a lifelong friendship and remained close, even after Murcer was traded for Bobby Bonds in 1974.

With Murcer's departure, Munson became the star of the team and hit his peak during the Yankees' mini-dynasty from

1976 to 1978. The Yankees had gone from a mediocre team to back-to-back world champions, and Munson rivaled Johnny Bench as the best catcher in baseball.

During that three-year stretch, Munson piled up his career-best offensive statistics (even a surprising 14 stolen bases in 1976). He hit over .300 with 100 or more RBIs three years in a row

Photograph from Frank Russo's private collection.

(1975–1977), won the MVP Award in 1976, and hit .529 in the 1976 World Series and .320 in the 1977 and 1978 Fall Classics.

In 1998 *The Sporting News* selected him as its all-time starting American League catcher for the '70s.

Over the course of his career, he was a six-time All-Star with Gold Glove Awards from 1973 to 1975. He injured the thumb on his throwing hand in the spring of 1974 when Dave Schneck of the Mets hit it with his bat after a follow-through on a swing. The injury indirectly led to a shoulder injury that would plague him for several seasons. Munson adapted and began throwing sidearm to second base to cut down runners. The technique gave him the quickest release in baseball in throwing out base-stealers. He was fearless behind the plate, and was given the nickname "the Wall" due to his effectiveness in preventing opposing runners from scoring. Catfish Hunter credited Thurman for his late-season come-back during the Yankees' 1978 pennant run.

A devastating clutch hitter, he was toughest when the chips were down. His most famous home run came in the 1978 ALCS off Kansas City pitcher Doug Bird. With New York trailing the Royals 5–4 in the eighth inning, Munson hit a 430-foot blast into the Yankees' bullpen that gave the Bombers a 6–5 win.

Munson had taken up the hobby of flying in early 1978 so he could fly home after games and spend more time with his family. In 1979 Munson had moved up to fly a jet, a Cessna CE 501 "Citation." Moving up to jets after flying prop planes is a huge step and requires experience, something Munson lacked at the time.

On the afternoon of August 2, 1979, Munson met his friend, Jerry Anderson, and flight instructor David Hall at the Akron–Canton Airport. The two joined him while he practiced touch-and-go landings. Thurman made the first three approaches from a left pattern with no problem, but on the fourth attempt, he was instructed to use runway 1-9 by the air traffic controller.

This touch-and-go would be attempted from a right pattern.

At this point, Munson's lack of experience with his new jet showed in the form of several deadly mistakes. First, Munson's air speed was not sufficient, causing the jet to fly at too slow a speed for the maneuver he was performing. The National Transportation Safety Board stated in its report that the jet also descended too quickly, and that neither the landing flaps nor the landing gear were down. The pilot errors caused the jet to stall, and although Munson tried to correct the problems, it was too late.

Munson fought in vain to control the jet, which clipped the tops of trees as a wing was ripped off. The craft hit the ground 870 feet from the runway, skidding into a ditch before slamming into a tree stump near Greensburg Road.

Munson yelled to his friends, "Are you guys okay?" They were, but Munson wasn't. He couldn't move from his severe injuries, which included a broken jaw and a broken rib. He was bleeding from his nose, and an autopsy revealed he had sustained a bruised heart and broken neck.

Munson lost consciousness as smoke and flames began to fill the cockpit. Anderson and Hall escaped through an emergency exit and both suffered second- and third-degree burns.

Munson was pronounced dead at the scene at 4:02 PM that afternoon. He was 32 years old. The official cause of his death was "asphyxiation, due to acute laryngeal edema and due to inhalation of super heated air and toxic substances." The NTSB ruled the cause of the crash as pilot error.

News of his death brought shock and grief throughout baseball and the sporting world in general. When Munson's longtime rival Carlton Fisk heard of the tragedy, tears streamed down his cheeks. The game betweens the Mets and Phillies at Shea Stadium was temporarily stopped for a moment of silence when the scoreboard flashed the news of the cross-town hero's death.

Lee Mazzilli of the Mets, who was up at bat, stepped from the batter's box and wiped his eyes.

The next day, a stunned and devastated Yankees team stood on the steps of the dugout for a moment of silence that turned into a nine-minute standing ovation. The Yankees honored him by retiring his uniform number (15) and placing a memorial plaque on the center-field wall at Yankee Stadium in 1980. A huge No. 15 is engraved onto the back of his monument. Munson's widow, Diane, requested that the number be added to the back of the monument because that is the way, she said, she always saw him when she watched him play—squatting in the catcher's position, facing the play with No. 15 showing.

Munson was buried on August 6, 1979, at the Sunset Hill Burial Park (Section 1, Lot 6) in Canton, Ohio.

Although not a member of baseball's Hall of Fame, Munson established himself, during his brief 10-year career, as one of the premier catchers in the game's history. He left a legion of adoring fans. A bronze recreation of his locker, spikes, glove, and jersey has been preserved in Cooperstown.

John Kane

John Kane played four seasons in the major leagues with the Cincinnati Reds and the Chicago Cubs before leaving the majors because the warm weather of the Pacific Coast League suited him just fine.

It didn't hurt that, in 1911, he was offered a contract worth $1,000 a month by manager Happy Hogan to stay with the California-based Vernon Tigers of the PCL.

Cash and climate now to his liking, Kane became everything and more to Hogan's minions, as he turned out to be one of the best players of the PCL. Using a heavy bat, which he choked up on, he sprayed the ball evenly all over the field, at times with power. He also played the outfield with equal ease, becoming the team's center fielder. Kane was so good during his second stay in the PCL that in 1912 he came in second behind Oakland third baseman Gus Hetling in the league's MVP vote.

Kane had other fine attributes, namely character and compassion. A case in point occurred on February 1913, when he came to the defense of Jack Tiedemann, a hulking first baseman who played for Oakland. The previous season, Tiedemann had muffed a play trying to block Kane off first base. Tiedemann then became the butt of jokes dealing with his size and coordination by fans and opposing players alike. He was booed so vociferously that he thought of quitting the game for good.

But "Little Johnny" spoke eloquently in the big man's defense.

"Tiedemann has had a tough deal here, and a good deal more than he deserves," said Kane. "A lot of people have him down as a roughneck. There is not a better man at heart in baseball than Tiedemann. His size and awkwardness are his worst sins. This thing of trying to take a man's means of living away from him is bad. Drive Tiedemann out of baseball and you not only do that, but you ruin a most promising young player. Be good sports and give the big fellow a chance."

Kane wound his career down with several clubs in quick succession before taking up residence in St. Anthony, Idaho, where he became a successful businessman, operating a pool hall and then a cigar store for the last 11 years of his life.

He was killed on January 28, 1934, when his car skidded on an icy patch of road and flipped, causing Kane, 51, to sustain a broken neck. He left his wife, Ruby, a son, five sisters, and two brothers, and was buried at the Riverview Cemetery in St. Anthony.

It should be noted that there were two John Francis Kanes who played baseball in the major leagues. Both were born in

Chicago, 18 years apart, and both passed away before their times.

Also of note is that, while playing with the Vernon Tigers, Kane was a teammate of two other ill-fated players: catcher Drummond Brown and Dick Bayless. Brown took his own life with a pistol, and Bayless died from asphyxiation in a copper mine explosion in New Mexico in December 1920.

Clap for Your Heroes

Dementia. Paresis. General Paralysis of the Insane. Locomotor Ataxia. The death certificates don't lie, and they document the same mortal disease: syphilis.

Yes, it is different from "the clap"—another sexually transmitted disease known as gonorrhea. But it's harder to fit in a catchy headline (Revenge of the Syph?).

In the days before penicillin, syphilis was an ailment as insidious as it was ruthless. Classically manifesting itself in three stages, a long incubation period was often followed by a merciless ending where the organism, Treponema pallidum, a type of bacterium called a spirochete, frequently attacked the cardiovascular and central nervous systems of its victims. The mixed bag of potential results was not pleasant: heart valve disease, aneurisms, and gradual softening of the brain tissue leading to progressive paralysis and insanity.

For centuries, mercury, taken orally or applied as an ointment to lesions caused by the disease, was the earliest, preferred, and largely ineffective chemical treatment. It gave rise to the old adage, "A night in the arms of Venus leads to a lifetime of mercury."

It should be emphasized that the disease, while normally transmitted through sexual contact, could also be contracted from the child through the mother in utero (congenital syphilis).

History is dotted with famous personages alleged to have had the disease (French King Charles VIII, French author Guy de Maupassant, German philosopher Friedrich Nietzsche, and French painter Paul Gauguin), and some who had it for sure (Al Capone).

Baseball's history is no different.

The discovery of penicillin in 1928 and its widespread availability by the mid-1940s made it the effective treatment of choice for syphilis. It remains so today with other antibiotics.

George Davis

Posthumously elected to the Baseball Hall of Fame in 1998, George Stacey Davis was one of the game's all-time greats whose body of work went overlooked long after his death when he succumbed to paresis due to tertiary syphilis on October 17, 1940.

Davis' career numbers touch most of the standard indicators of greatness. He batted .300 or better nine times, had 2,660 hits, and drove in 1,437 runs. He did all that while only hitting 73 homers, which is a testament to his clutch performance. He wound up with a lifetime average of .295. Had there been an All-Star Game during his playing career, he would have been preferred material for at least 15 times during his 20-year career.

He was also the first true superstar shortstop during the American League's infancy.

Starting out as an outfielder with the Cleveland Spiders in 1890, Davis was traded to the Giants in 1893 for future Hall of Famer Buck Ewing. He played third base for his first four years in New York before taking over at shortstop in 1897, where he played for most of the remainder of his career. He became the

Giants' player/manager for part of 1895 and again from mid-1900 through 1901. During his second tour of duty as leader of the Giants, he was Christy Mathewson's first major league manager, even naming Mathewson's most famous pitch: "the fadeaway." When Davis took batting practice against the rookie pitcher for the first time, Mathewson threw the veteran Davis his "freak ball." After Davis took several hacks at it, he told the rookie to "keep throwing that pitch, it sort of fades away."

After Davis' career ended, not a lot was documented about his life. At one point he was found to be selling cars in Philadelphia. He died at the Philadelphia State Hospital, where he had been confined for several years. He left a widow, the former Jane Holden. The couple had no children. In fact, when Davis died, his death went virtually unreported. He lay in an unmarked grave in Philadelphia's Fernwood Cemetery (Section 34, Lot 85), forgotten, until 1998, when he was enshrined in the Hall.

Members of the George S. Davis Chapter of the Society for American Baseball Research raised funds to have a proper headstone placed upon his grave the summer he was inducted. The long wait for recognition was finally over.

Adam Comorosky

A lifetime .285 hitter, Adam Comorosky played 10 seasons in the majors, eight of them for the Pittsburgh Pirates. He was born in the mining town of Swoyersville, Pennsylvania, on December 9, 1904. He said he acquired his first name in a most unusual way: "My older sister's name is Eve, so when I came along, Dad said that since we had an Eve in the family we might as well have an Adam. We do like our names, too, even though they lead to a lot of joking."

There was no joking when it came to the kind of athlete the bowlegged Comorosky was. He played all positions on his high school baseball team, including pitcher, where he amassed a 27–0 record. He also worked in the mines, where his job included breaker, mule driver, and nipper, which called for him to open and close doors in order to allow toxic gases to escape. After high school, he attended Wyoming Seminary of Pennsylvania, where he helped pay for his tuition by playing with the Luzerne Stars of the independent Sunday League. His seminary days were over for good when he was signed by Waynesboro of the Blue Ridge League in 1925 at the tender age of 20.

Converted to an outfielder by the Waynesboro brain trust, he then moved on to Williamsport of the New York–Penn League in 1926. Before the season was even over, he signed a contract with the Pirates who brought him up for an eight-game stint. Pittsburgh then sent him to play with Wichita of the Western League for the 1927 season, where he hit an amazing .398. As a September call-up, he played in 18 games but missed out on playing in the World Series against the Yankees. Optioned by the parent club to Indianapolis of the American Association for 1928, he was called up to stay in August of that year. Never much of a power threat, he nonetheless twice batted over .300 for Pittsburgh, and was a steady influence in the outfield where he teamed with the Waner brothers—Paul and Lloyd—for four years. A guitar and banjo player, he enjoyed entertaining his teammates, and was considered to be a kind and generous friend by all who knew him.

He was traded by the Pittsburgh Pirates on October 17, 1933, along with Tony Piet to the Cincinnati Reds for Red Lucas and Wally Roettger. After his career in the majors, he made minor league stops with Indianapolis once again, Minneapolis, Toronto, Wilkes-Barre, and Hazleton. Even after his retirement from the pros in 1939, he continued to play semi-pro ball, often supplementing his income by playing as a ringer for hire.

He opened a store in his native Swoyersville, Pennsylvania, where he lived with his wife, Helen, at 390 Main Street. Unfortunately, the always-smiling Comorosky's retirement proved to be a short one, as he passed away from acute myocardial failure due to syphilitic cardiovascular disease on March 2, 1951, at the age of 47. He was buried in the St. Ignatius Catholic Church Cemetery in Pringle, Pennsylvania.

James B. "Chippy" McGarr

Third baseman/shortstop Chippy McGarr was only 5'7", 168 pounds, but he had the heart of a lion and was as fearless as any player of his time.

The son of James and Margaret McGlinchy, McGarr played with seven teams during the course of his career, but it wasn't until his final stop—a four-year stay with the Cleveland Spiders of the National League—that the always-game McGarr found a style of play that suited him.

McGarr started out with the Chicago/Pittsburgh franchise of the Union Association. "Chippy" was a perfect nickname for the win-at-all-costs Worcester, Massachusetts, native whose style of play was in the mold of the legendary John McGraw. A decent fielder and hitter, McGarr bounced around during the first part of his career. The highlight for him was in 1888 when he played 25 games for the pennant-winning St. Louis Browns of the American Association. The Browns went on to lose the World Series to the National League Giants, 6–4 (McGarr did not appear in the Series.)

He then hooked up with Denver of the Western Association in 1891 and Milwaukee of the Western League in 1892. While at Denver, the pugnacious McGarr was thrown out of a game for hitting an umpire in the back with a baseball. Fines and a suspension were assessed, but they didn't change the way McGarr played.

Signing with Cleveland in 1893, McGarr felt right at home with the Spiders, one of the roughest and dirtiest teams of all time. McGarr was adept at the "trip play." When a runner was rounding the bases, McGarr would kick his back foot to upend a player. His dirty work on the base path did not go unnoticed, and he drew the ire of fans around the league. On more than one occasion, he had to be escorted from the field by police due to threats from fans.

The rowdy Spiders, along with the Orioles, were baseball's biggest attractions due to their exciting and suspect styles of play. McGarr flourished under Spiders manager Patsy Tebeau, who encouraged his players to use fists, elbows, or any other part of their bodies for that matter, in order to impede opposing base runners. The Spiders finished in second place the last two seasons McGarr played there and were beginning to emerge as a real powerhouse in the league. Unfortunately, McGarr's arm went bad, and he was sent out by Cleveland before the 1897 season started.

His career totals were more than credible: a lifetime .268 average, 872 hits, 388 RBIs, with 267 stolen bases. Not bad at all for the pugilistic half-pint. After his career was over, he turned to umpiring. After so many brawls and disagreements with the men in black over the years, one could hardly believe that the rough-hewed McGarr could do well as an arbiter. McGarr umpired in the minors for two seasons until he signed on with the National League staff in 1899. His contract was not renewed by the NL, though, mostly because of the erratic behavior that he displayed during his brief tenure that season.

Depression set in when he could not find a job umpiring in 1900—so much so that his family had him committed to an asylum. Reports of the time stated that he was suffering from melancholia, but in truth, it was third-stage syphilis. He spent his last remaining years under doctors' care before passing away from general paralysis of the insane and exhaustion at the Worcester Insane Hospital on June 8, 1904.

Only 41 at the time, McGarr was buried at the St. John's Cemetery in his hometown.

Bill Moriarty

Talk about holiday spirit, William Joseph Moriarty literally became one when he gave up the ghost on Christmas Day, 1916, from general paralysis of the insane due to syphilis.

His motor functions diminishing and his mind feeble, he had been confined by his family to the Elgin (Illinois) State Hospital for the last 10 months of his life. But that was a far greater period than his stint in the majors, which lasted less than a week—five days, six games, and 20 at-bats as a shortstop with the 1909 Cincinnati Reds to be precise.

Moriarty came from a baseball family. The Chicago native was the brother of George Moriarty, who not only played 13 seasons in the majors with four teams but managed the Detroit Tigers for two years and served the American League as an umpire for 22 years.

But Bill was nowhere near the heavy-hitter George was, and after his brief cameo in the Big Show, he headed back down to the minors, where he originally played with the San Francisco Seals of the PCL and Stockton of the "Outlaw" California League before getting signed by the Reds on February 4, 1909. Before his contract was signed, Moriarty had to be reinstated by the National Commission due to his stint with Stockton.

Moriarty's health deteriorated at an alarming rate after getting sent back down to the bush leagues. A lifelong bachelor, it was never brought to light whether he sought treatment for the disease that would eventually claim him. Likely not. His body was taken back to Chicago for burial at the Mount Olivet Cemetery.

His brother George, whose grandson is the accomplished actor of stage, screen, and television, Michael Moriarty, survived him until 1964.

Bill Moriarty is listed on his death certificate as being 31 years old. According to records in the Baseball Encyclopedia, he was born in 1883, making him 33.

Bill Phillips

Handsome, broad-shouldered Bill Phillips made his mark playing first base with the Cleveland Blues of the National League in 1879. The infield combine, which included Jack Glasscock at shortstop and Fred "Sure Shot" Dunlop at second, was considered one of the best of the era.

Although he batted more than .300 and drove in 100 runs only once during his career, Phillips was a consistent hitter who could always be counted on when needed. After six seasons in Cleveland, he followed Blues manager Charlie Hackett over to Brooklyn of the American Association. Changing leagues did not bother Phillips as he continued to shine in the field and at the plate. His final major league season came with the Kansas City Cowboys in 1889, when he batted only .236 and had an on-base percentage of just .284. He did, however, drive in 56 runs.

Phillips, also known as "Silver Bill," was the first Canadian-born player to play in the majors. During his tenure in the big leagues, there was but a handful of players from north of the border. Phillips was born in St. John, New Brunswick, Canada, in 1857. His family moved to Chicago when he was a teenager, and it was there that he made his home for the rest of his short life. Chicago was also the place where he honed his skills playing with amateur teams. Phillips played with the Winona, Minnesota, club in 1878 and Rockford, Illinois, in 1878, before latching on with Cleveland.

Phillips returned to his birthplace in 1890 to play one final pro season with Hamilton, Ontario, of the highly competitive

International League. After batting only .245, he retired from ball for good.

In 1891 rumors circulated that Phillips, along with former players such as Silver Flint, Tony Suck, Rudy Kemmler, and Billy Taylor, were to be signed to a team headed by former pitcher and Chicago native Emil Gross. The plan was to move the team out West to Tacoma, Washington, and become the backbone of a new league. The plan never materialized.

Healthwise, Phillips went downhill toward the end of the Gay Nineties when the lifelong bachelor found himself in the throws of the third and final stage of syphilis. He was living at 393 Orchard Street in Chicago when he died on October 7, 1900, at the age of 43 from locomotor ataxia due to advanced syphilis. He is buried in Graceland Cemetery in Chicago.

Butch Rementer

More than 16,000 players have stepped onto the field at major league ballparks, and among those, a little more than 900 have seen action in one game. You could say Butch Rementer was one of these one-hit wonders.

The son of Charles Rementer and Eunice Baker, Willis J. H. Rementer was given the nickname "Butch" as a child while growing up in his hometown of Philadelphia. It must have been quite a thrill for Rementer when he finally made good with his dream of playing in the major leagues, making a cup-of-coffee appearance with the Phillies on the last day of the season, October 8, 1904. Butch went 0–2 with three putouts. Although that was it for his major league career, it did not end his pro career—he went on to play with the Holyoke, Massachusetts, team in 1905.

It was from there that he gained a reputation as an "outlaw player" when he jumped to Lancaster, Pennsylvania, of the Tri-State League. Contract jumping to so-called outlaw leagues was a common practice at the time, and the National Commission actually had to review the contract of not only Rementer's but dozens of other players who had jumped to the Tri-State League.

On January 13, 1907, Charles F. Carpenter and the rest of the executive board of the National Association decreed that Rementer and most of the outlaw players who had violated their reservations were to stay with their clubs in the Tri-State League, which was not a member of the National Association.

Rementer stayed with Lancaster until being purchased by Memphis of the Southern League on November 10, 1909. At Memphis, Rementer saw exhibition action against major league clubs such as the A's and Tigers. Memphis sold him to York, Pennsylvania, of the Tri-State League on June 4, 1910, after which his career in the bushes slowly wound down.

Butch finally hung them up for good to settle down in his home town of Philadelphia. With his wife Hanna, he made his residence at 3200 South 10th Street, which was located in the 39th ward. His occupation was listed as engineer. He died on September 23, 1922, at Philadelphia General Hospital. The cause of death was listed as general paralysis of the insane, which was due to tertiary syphilis, which he apparently acquired during his long stay in the minors. He was laid to rest in Holy Cross Cemetery in Yeadon, Pennsylvania (Section Y, Range 13, Lot 33, Grave 4).

Bobby Mathews

Baltimore native Bobby Mathews had plenty of firsts during his brilliant playing career.

In one fell swoop on May 4, 1871, the son of "Monumental City" became the first pitcher to win and throw a shutout in a professional league game. He started the National Association's first game, a 2–0 win by the Ft. Wayne Kekiongas over the Cleveland Forest Cities. He also became the first man to pitch 100 professional league games, and supposedly he was the first pitcher to ever throw an out-curve and spitball, though other players have also laid claim to those feats.

In the days of one- and two-man rotations, Mathews was a typical iron man on the mound. He pitched 400 innings or better in five of his first six seasons, with a career high of 626.7 for the 1875 New York Mutuals of the National Association. The Mutuals joined the newly formed National League in 1876, and Mathews went 21–34 that season, accounting for all his team's wins and losses except for one game. That season, he pitched a 15-inning 5–5 tie against his friend, Jim Devlin, and the Louisville Grays. The 15 innings set a National League record (the game was called on account of darkness). Although he had a very good out-curve, he considered his best pitch to be his in-curve to a right-handed hitter.

Known for his wonderful demeanor and temperament, Mathews was never a pushover, especially when it came to money. He sued the Philadelphia Athletics for pay that he was supposedly owed for coaching duties, which at the time was unheard of. The lawsuit persisted even after the Athletics went under in 1890. Mathews actually did the best pitching of his career for those very same Athletics, winning 30 games three years in a row from 1883 to 1885. His 30–13 mark in 1883 led the Athletics to the American Association pennant.

He retired with a lifetime record of 297–248, with a very creditable 2.98 ERA, surely more than enough to include him among the great pitchers of all time and certainly good enough to be considered for election to the Hall of Fame. His retirement years should have been happy and productive ones, basking in his former glory. Unfortunately, his days were numbered, as his mind and body gradually deteriorated from the syphilis that he had contracted years earlier. He died on April 17, 1898, at the young age of 46 and is buried in the New Cathedral Cemetery in his beloved Baltimore.

Upon his death, his long-time friend Nick Young, National League president, said of him, "Mathews was the paragon of honesty, a fast friend, frank almost to bluntness, never given to the 'can't' and hypocrisy we often encounter in this world."

John "Jiggs" Donahue

A typical "good field, no hit" dead-ball-era player who averaged around .250 most of his career, Jiggs Donahue put up his best numbers in 1905 with the Chicago White Sox "Hitless Wonders," batting .286 with a career-high 76 RBIs. The following season, he led all players batting in the 1906 World Series (.333).

Baseball card image courtesy of the Library of Congress.

The Ohio native got his name from his clog dancing to Irish jigs. He started out as a left-handed catcher/outfielder in the minors with the Dayton, Ohio, club managed by Bill Armour before breaking in with the Pittsburgh Pirates in 1900. Dexterous and adroit, he eventually found the first-base position much more to his liking.

Donahue, whose brother Pat was a catcher with three major league teams from 1908 to 1910, played with Pittsburgh briefly in 1901 before going to Minneapolis of the Western League. It was from there that Donahue "jumped" his contract and signed to play with the Milwaukee Brewers of the American League on July 6. Donahue was subsequently suspended by Western League president Hickey. Donahue played for the Browns in 1902 and the Milwaukee Brewers of the American Association in 1903 when he was purchased by Charlie Comiskey in August with the intent of using him in 1904. Donahue was injured at the time of the purchase. It was in Chicago that he made his mark as part of an infield that included stalwarts like Frank Isbell, Billy Sullivan, and future Hall of Famer George Davis. Tim Murnane, the former player and great baseball writer, called him a "baseball genius at first."

Off the field, Donahue was a quiet, unassuming owner of several billiard and bowling establishments. On the field, however, he flashed a colorful vocabulary, a quick Irish temper, and a never-say-die attitude. Known for cheering his team on to the very last out, the one word that best described him would be "scrappy." As his manager Fielder Jones said of him, "Jiggers is all about the winning."

Donahue's stay in Chicago ended with a trade on May 16, 1909, when he was sent to the Washington Senators along with Gavvy Cravath for "Sleepy" Bill Burns. Finishing out the season, Donahue obtained his release from Washington in early 1910 and then became owner of a semi-pro team called Jiggs Donahue's Red Sox.

There was speculation that Donahue might return to his old team in Chicago for the 1911 season, but he didn't make the roster in spring training and headed to Hot Springs, Arkansas, to open up a billiard business. His health was starting to take a slow but steady turn for the worse and, by 1912, he was falling apart at an alarming rate, physically and mentally. He was then sent by family to the state hospital at Columbus, Ohio, where he spent the last year of his life. He died there as a result of general paralysis of the insane due to syphilis and was buried at the Calvary Cemetery in Springfield, Ohio.

One newspaper reported that "domestic trouble" had hastened his demise. If that's another way of saying "syphilis," then political correctness has a whole new dimension.

Danny Clark

Some speculated that 18-year-old Danny Clark's hustle and ability caught the eye of the great Ty Cobb when Clark was showing his wares with a minor league club in Augusta, Georgia, in 1914. And it remains unclear whether Cobb, as manager of Detroit seven years later, had anything to do with Clark's minor league contract being purchased by the Tigers.

What is clear is that Clark was short on staying power in the big leagues and had to settle for a long career in the bush leagues dotted with three brief stints in the majors.

It's also clear that Clark did not disappoint "the Georgia Peach" when he got the chance to play for the Tigers in 1922. In 83 games, he batted .292 with three homers and 26 RBIs in 185 at-bats. He played second, outfield, and even made one appearance at third. But his stay in the Motor City would be short—he was traded with Carl Holling, Howard Ehmke, Babe Herman, and $25,000 to the Boston Red Sox in exchange for Del Pratt and Rip Collins on October 30.

Clark would be sent to Birmingham again and then Atlanta before his second shot at the major league level with the Red Sox in 1924. In 104 games that season, he batted a steady .277 with two homers and 54 RBIs, and was the starting third baseman for the majority of the season for the seventh-place Bostonians. Once again, his performance was still not good enough to keep him at the major league level. He was released to San Antonio of the Texas League at season's end. In 1925 San Antonio sold him to the Cardinals, who immediately sent him to Syracuse for the 1926 season.

Clark's last hurrah in the majors came in 1927, when the Cardinals recalled him. He appeared in 58 games and batted only .236 with no homers and 13 RBIs before being sold to Houston. From there, it was two seasons with Baltimore before he finished his career in 1930 as manager of the Springfield, Illinois, club.

After he hung up his spikes, he became an oil dealer and was living with his wife, the former Mildred Cox, on 8th Street in his hometown of Meridian, Mississippi, when he died on May 23, 1937, at the age of 43. His death resulted from tertiary neural syphilis, which apparently he had contracted during his stay in the minors. He was buried in the Magnolia Cemetery in Magnolia, Mississippi.

Charlie "Hoss" Radburn

Cocky. Self-assured. Defiant. Charlie "Hoss" Radburn was a rabble-rouser with a passion for hunting whose claim to fame was one great season in which he won an astounding 59 games.

Radburn's season for the ages with the Providence Grays in 1884 almost never occurred—he was suspended several times and came close to getting kicked off the team on multiple occasions. Yet he still went out and pitched every day, no matter how tired he was and no matter how badly his arm hurt. He took to the practice of using a cast-iron ball to stretch with before each start. He credited that and, of course, his perseverance, for how he was able to accomplish what he did.

Radburn was initially part of a two-man rotation in 1884 that included the hot-headed Charlie Sweeney—winner of 17 games for the Grays when he was thrown out of the National League permanently for leaving the field in the middle of a game (Sweeney found work immediately with the Union Association's St. Louis Maroons). So it was left to Radburn to pitch his team home in first place. (By the way, it's important to note here that most pitchers threw underhanded back then when the rules were very different.)

In all, Radburn went 59–12 in 1884 with a 1.38 ERA. He started 68 games that season, completing 66 of them, logging an absolutely mind-boggling 678⅔ innings. Too bad for him they didn't have performance clauses in the contracts at the time. After his greatest of seasons, Charlie continued to be a great pitcher, winning 20 games or more five more times. At his retirement, his record showed a lifetime 309–195 record with a 2.67 ERA and 4,535⅓ innings pitched.

On top of this, Radburn was a lifetime .235 hitter with nine homers and 259 RBIs.

An extremely frugal individual, Radburn saved his money and invested well. He was the proprietor of a successful saloon/pool hall in his native Bloomington, Indiana, after his retirement. This allowed him to enjoy the one thing he loved to do most—hunt. While on one of his outings, his face was disfigured by an accidental shotgun blast during which he lost an eye. It left him disfigured and he spent many of his last days huddled in the back room of his business. Truth be told, even before the accident, he was not the picture of health—he had been showing signs of tertiary syphilis. One could speculate that at the time of the accident, the syphilis was affecting his motor functions.

In any event, Radburn went downhill fast and by 1896 was feeling the full effects of the insidious disease, including convulsions, paralysis, and locomotor ataxia. Mercifully, he died on February 5, 1897, and was buried in the Evergreen Cemetery in Bloomington (Section 17, Lot 4). His plot is near that of his younger brother, George, who followed him almost seven years later, in 1904.

John Hinton

John "Red" Hinton's place in the Baseball Encyclopedia is marked with a four-game stint with the Boston Beaneaters in 1901. Records show that he had one hit and two walks in 13 at-bats.

He was a lifetime .077 hitter.

In the minors, though, Hinton was a star—especially for his hometown Altoona, Pennsylvania, team of the Tri-State League. The son of John and Mary Ann Lindsey, Hinton was born in Pittsburgh but, at age three, moved to Altoona where he grew up playing sandlot ball. He decided to make a go at a career in baseball when he experienced success as a third baseman at the Bellefonte Academy. He went on to become captain of the minor league team in Altoona, where he lived until about 1910 when he moved to play in the Ohio and Pennsylvania Leagues.

After his playing days were over, he moved back to Pittsburgh, where he worked as a bartender until syphilis slowly and thoroughly incapacitated him. He died as a result of general paralysis of the insane due to syphilis on July 19, 1920, at his sister Harriet's home on Talbot Street in Pittsburgh.

A widower, he was survived by two sons ages 16 and seven, and three sisters. He died on the sixth anniversary of his wife's death, and he was buried next to her in Braddock, Pennsylvania.

Icicle Reeder

The son of John and Lena Bieler Reeder of Cincinnati, Ohio, James Edward "Icicle" Reeder had the potential to be a fine player at the major league level, if not for one major character flaw: Reeder loved to go out on the town and light the candle at both ends.

Reeder himself cited his lack of discipline for his poor career, which saw him appear in only six games for two teams, in two leagues, in the span of two months. The games were split evenly, with the National League's Cincinnati Red Stockings and the Union Association's Washington Nationals.

He batted only .154 with four hits in 26 at-bats.

In March 1890 Reeder, in a newspaper interview, talked about the tough luck he had getting his act together and his hopes for the future: "I have not seen one of 'the gang' this winter. They never did me any good, and I don't want to get back in 'society.' I'd like a chance to get on with Indianapolis or Washington. Jack Glasscock wrote me the other day. I've a good place now, but of course prefer to play ball. When I left Toledo, I led the Tri-State League in batting. There was never any question about my ability as long as I took care of myself. I've learned a lesson at a bitter cost."

Despite flashing signs of real brilliance in the minors, Reeder would never get another chance at the majors and fell back into old habits. One of those habits was said to be women of ill repute. He was living at 1620 Mansfield Street in Cincinnati when he passed away from dementia paralysis due to syphilis on January 15, 1913, at the age of 54. He was laid to rest in the Spring Grove Cemetery (Section 121, Grave 519).

John Valentine

John Gill Valentine, a native of Brooklyn, New York, is another brief footnote in the history of baseball. He was a career minor leaguer except for one season in the majors in 1883 when he pitched for the Columbus Buckeyes of the American Association, twirling to a miserable 2–10 mark with a 3.53 ERA in 132 games.

After his playing career, he decided to try to call strikes from behind the plate instead of throwing them from the mound. He became an umpire in both the American Association and the National League. He steered games in the AA from 1884 to 1887 and the NL from 1886 to 1887. (His yearly salary in the American Association was $1,000.)

When in the National League, it was noted that he had a rather rough relationship with Cap Anson, who tended to be less than polite to the men in black behind the plate. It got rather testy between the two, so much so that once, right before a series between Chicago and New York, Valentine proclaimed that he would "stop Anson's kicking," even if he had to fine him every game.

When his contract was not renewed, he umpired in the minors, most notably in the Atlantic Association, where former superstar pitcher Larry Corcoran also worked. He also umpired semi-pro and industrial league games until just a few years before he died at the state hospital in Central Islip, New York, on October 10, 1903. Cause of death: paresis. He was 47 at the time of his death and was buried in the Greenwood Cemetery in Brooklyn.

As a point of interest, Valentine became the second member of the Buckeyes to meet his demise as a result of "the Pox." Columbus teammate Harry Wheeler succumbed to locomotor ataxia three years earlier in 1900.

Pat Duff

Rhode Island native Pat Duff had his number called only once in the majors. That was when Washington Nationals manager Jake Stahl brought him in to pinch hit for catcher Mike Heydon in the ninth inning of a 5–3 loss to the Athletics.

It was Monday, April 16, 1906—the second game of the season at Columbia Park in Philadelphia. Duff had the misfortune of having to face the fire-balling future Hall of Famer Rube Waddell, who retired him. Waddell had come in to pitch in relief of starting pitcher Jimmy Dygert.

Duff had all the pedigree to succeed in the majors. He was a star backstop for Manhattan College from 1901 to 1904. He was on two of the greatest teams in Jaspers' history. The 1903 team went 18–2, and the 1904 team did even better at 32–4, setting a record for single-season victories. Duff captained the 1904 squad and batted cleanup for most of his career there. He was inducted into the Manhattan College Hall of Fame in 1993.

After his playing career was over, he turned to coaching and became the first baseball coach of Providence College. That stint lasted two years. Unfortunately for Duff, his health had slowly begun to deteriorate over time and, by his late forties, he was noticeably going downhill. Duff died at the state hospital in Providence on September 11, 1925, from syphilis-induced paresis. Duff, a bachelor, was 50 years old. He was laid to rest at the St. Ann Cemetery in Cranston, Rhode Island.

Harry Betts

Harry Betts made a most forgettable debut in the majors on September 22, 1903, when he took the mound for the Cardinals against the Boston Beaneaters. He went nine innings, gave up 11 hits and 10 runs in a 10–1 mashing by the hometown nine. To add icing to the cake, he also hit three Boston players.

On the bright side, he struck out two.

St. Louis newspapers at the time mentioned that Betts was a "local amateur" who had been given a tryout by Cards' management. Betts' battery mate, Jack Coveney, made his major league appearance just three days earlier on September 19. St. Louis was not exactly fielding a pennant-winning team, and when Betts made his first-ever start, he was shelled for three runs in the first inning.

His next appearance in the majors would not come for another 10 years.

At the time of his next call-up, Betts was a semi-pro pitcher and was also working as a typewriter salesman in Cincinnati. His second—and last—appearance, on May 13, 1913, was much better than his first. Reds Manager Joe Tinker threw Betts to the wolves to finish out the game after starter Art Fromme was bombed for six runs in the second inning and was still struggling in the fifth. Betts came in and allowed one hit, one earned run, and three walks in 3⅓ innings of relief.

Not a bad way for the bush leaguer to finish out his big-league career.

Betts, who was born in Alliance, Ohio, on June 18, 1881, moved to Texas and worked for the San Antonio Express as a bill collector. A widower, he spent the last 16 months of his life at the San Antonio State Hospital, where he died from the effects of general paralysis of the insane due to syphilis on May 22, 1946, at the age of 64. His body was cremated at the Mission Burial Park in San Antonio, the same resting place of Hall of Fame players Ross Youngs and Rube Waddell.

Jake Aydelott

North Manchester, Indiana–native Jacob Stuart "Jake" Aydelott played in 15 games over the course of two seasons in the majors. His 5–7 mark for the 1884 Indianapolis Hoosiers of the American Association was a good enough mark to make him second in wins behind Larry McKeon's 18.

The Hoosiers were a dreadful club, finishing with a 29–78 record, good enough for 12th place in the 13-team AA. Fans had plenty to grumble about that season at Seventh Street Park in Indianapolis, the Hoosiers' home park. Aydelott also appeared in one game in the outfield that season, which would be the only year that Indy would have an entry in the American Association.

Aydelott went back to the minors for 1885 but came back to pitch in two games for the 1886 Philadelphia Athletics of the American Association. With his final appearance on July 14 of that year, his major league career officially came to an end.

He went back to twirl in the minors, most notably in the Southern Association where he played for New Orleans and Atlanta, to name two. After his career was over, he worked in construction and did odd jobs. He was living in Detroit, with his wife Emma, when he died from general paralysis of the insane due to tertiary syphilis, on October 22, 1926.

Interestingly, there was no mention of his baseball career on his death certificate—his profession was listed as "laborer." He was buried in the Motor City on October 22, 1926.

John Bates

There were two John William Bates who played in the major leagues. One was a nine-year major leaguer, and the other was a one-game, cup-of-coffee player from the 1880s. The latter made his only major league appearance with the American Association's Kansas City Cowboys on Sunday, August 25, 1889, in the second game of a doubleheader with the Philadelphia Athletics.

Bates, who was signed out of the Texas League by Cowboys manager Bill Watkins, started on the mound and was blasted for 14 runs on 15 hits in a 14–3 loss. (KC also lost the first game 5–2.)

It didn't help that the Cowboys made four errors in the field behind Bates, but it didn't matter in the long run. From his lone appearance in the box, Bates wound up having a lifetime 0–1 record with a 13.50 ERA. He struck out three and walked five.

He was never given another chance to show his wares in the bigs and was retired and living at 3900 Broadway in Oakland, California, with his wife, Adaline, when he died on the morning of March 24, 1919, at the age of 50. The cause of death: locomotor ataxia due to advanced syphilis. He was cremated at the California Crematory and his ashes returned to his family.

Charlie Morton

Charles Hazen Morton had a dual career in the majors. As a player, he toiled with the Pittsburgh Alleghenies, St. Louis Brown Stockings, and Toledo Blue Stockings of the American Association, and the Detroit Wolverines of the National League, batting a lifetime .194. As a manager, he was a bit more successful, guiding the Wolverines in the NL and two different Toledo clubs in the AA, the Blue Stockings and Maumees.

Morton, who normally went by the moniker C. H. Morton, was born in Kingsville, Ohio, in 1854. As manager of the Savannah club of the Southern Association, he made sure that the teams he guided played major league clubs in exhibition games in order to ready them for the season. As was his wont, he would always keep his eye open for the best possible talent to fill his roster, never going on the cheap like so many other bush-league clubs often did.

He represented Toledo's interests when the American Association held its meeting and 180 league executives met with their National League counterparts in November 1890. Toledo was one of the teams designated to be dropped from the financially troubled league. Morton had just guided the club to a fourth-place finish, and many felt that since the team was still in good standing, it had a chance to stay in the league. It was not to be, and eventually Toledo was dropped before the 1891 season, which, as it turned out, would be the final year of the AA.

With the close of his major league career, his lifetime won-loss record as manager stood at 121–153. He quickly found work as manager in the Eastern League with Erie and later managed in the Ohio-Pennsylvania League. As is the case with most people who suffer from long-term, untreated syphilis, Charlie Morton's health deteriorated as the disease went into its third and final stage. He passed away at the Massillon State Hospital in Massillon, Ohio, on December 9, 1921, as a result of general paralysis of the insane. His remains were taken to Akron, Ohio, a place he had made his home since the 1880s, for burial.

Harry Wheeler

The son of Robert and Jane Wheeler played in three different leagues and nine cities during his six-season major league career. And that's not counting all his minor league stops.

Breaking into the majors with the National League's Providence Grays at the age of 20 in 1878, Wheeler was only a .229 lifetime hitter. Still, he did have one shining season in the majors as a member of the 1882 Cincinnati Red Stockings of the American Association. That team just so happened to be the first Reds team to win a pennant, and also the Reds team that has a franchise-best .688 winning percentage. That season Wheeler appeared in 76 games and batted .250 with one homer and 29 RBIs. He even pitched in four games with a 1–2 record.

An outfielder by trade, he also logged time as a second and first baseman. He appeared in 50 games or better only twice during his career, with a high of 82 for the 1883 Columbus Buckeyes of the American Association.

A true ramblin' man, he eventually settled down in Cincinnati after he hung up his spikes and was living at 425 Park Street when he died at the age of 42 from syphilitic locomotor ataxia on October 9, 1900. He is buried in the Spring Grove Cemetery in Cincinnati, Ohio (Section 110, Lot 325).

Frank Pears

But for a four-game, major league cameo with two teams from the Show Me State, pitcher Frank Pears played the majority of his pro career in the minors. The Kentucky native played three games with the Kansas City Cowboys in 1889 and capped off his career four years later in the Show with a solitary outing with the NL's St. Louis Browns in 1893.

After Kansas City left the American Association, Pears stayed in town and continued to play ball for the local nine. While there, he played with one of his old Kansas City teammates, John Sowders. Pears played in the time when players came and went, turning contract-jumping into an art form. If a player couldn't make it in the big leagues, he had his choice of going at it in literally hundreds of leagues throughout the country. These leagues were by no means up to snuff with the majors in caliber of play or conditions, but it was still competitive baseball, and the players took it seriously. The Tri-State League, International League, Pennsylvania State League, Atlantic League, Eastern League, and Southern Association were just a few of the places that a player like Pears could ply his trade if he chose to and had the talent.

After his stint with the Browns, Pears played and umpired in the Western League, where he went up against the likes of former major leaguers Perry Werden and Egyptian Healy. Pears remained on good terms with the St. Louis organization and recommended several Western League players to the Browns' brain trust. Pears also managed the Paducah, Kentucky, franchise of the Central League for several seasons.

In his later years, he worked for the Riverview Clark Company as a yardman until serious health issues began to overtake him. A resident of St. Louis for more than 40 years, Pears lived in the city's Sixth Ward, until his health deteriorated to a level where he no longer could care for himself. He was moved to the city sanitarium, where he passed away from dementia paralytica due to advanced syphilis on November 29, 1923, at the age of 57. He was buried in the Calvary Cemetery (Section 5, Lot N, Grave 1357).

Frank Siffell

Frank Siffell had the misfortune of being a back-up catcher behind the talented Jocko Milligan and Jack O'Brien with the

Philadelphia Athletics. His career lasted a total of 10 games, spanning two seasons from 1884 to 1885. Siffell played in the era of no shin guards, when the catcher was usually the only player on the field to wear any kind of glove at all (and even they tended to be inadequate at best). His career totals were a .140 average with four hits, including a double with three RBIs in 27 at-bats. He also scored three runs.

After his playing career was over, Siffell, who was born in Germany, took up roots in Philadelphia and was living at 1310 North 3rd Street when he died on October 26, 1909. A bachelor, he succumbed to locomotor ataxia due to advanced syphilis and was buried at the Greenmount Cemetery (Section R, Single, Grave 2929).

Apparently, his family was aware of his approaching demise. Albert Siffell, possibly a brother, had purchased the burial plot four years earlier, in 1905, when Frederick, another relative, had passed on and made arrangements to have Frank buried in the same family plot.

Ezra Sutton

Known as "Sut" or "Uncle Ezra," Ezra Ballou Sutton was an early star at third base in baseball's formative years—the days of gloveless play. Born in Seneca, New York, on September 17, 1850, Sutton is considered by many experts to have been the finest third baseman of the 19th century.

Sutton joined the Forest City team of Cleveland in 1869 and stayed with that team when it joined the National Association in 1871. He joined the Philadelphia

Athletics in 1872, staying with them until 1876. Ironically, on April 22, 1876, Sutton made the first error in the first-ever National League game in which Boston defeated Philadelphia at Athletic Park, 6–5.

In 1877 he joined the Boston Red Caps, where he was part of pennant winners in 1877, 1878, and 1883. He stayed until 1888, when the Beaneaters released him to Rochester after the 1888 season. He was later assigned to Milwaukee before his last playing stint with Auburn, New York, in 1897.

Sutton had a cannon for an arm, and first basemen often had problems catching his throws. He never had a great fielding percentage, but that was due more to the fact that he played without a glove. He manned every position during his career and had a lifetime .860 fielding average. A good hitter, he originally batted cross-handed and averaged .300 or better seven times with a lifetime .294 mark.

John Morrill called him "a good steady fellow." Soon after his career, he was seized with the onset of locomotor ataxia and was sent by his family to the Homeopathic Hospital in Rochester. The disease progressed rapidly, and not only caused him great suffering, but also prevented him from saving the life of his wife. On the evening of November 26, 1905, Sutton was having dinner with his family. A lamp exploded, and the resulting flames lit Sutton's wife's dress on fire. Sutton was unable to move to help his wife, due to his disease. She lingered in a hospital for six weeks, eventually passing away on January 6, 1906.

Many of Sutton's friends felt that the tragic death of his wife was punishment for the hedonistic lifestyle that caused his physical ailment. Despite the death of his wife, he managed to keep his spirits fairly cheerful, but his body continued to go downhill. Sutton had to apply to the state to help him with care for his disease. Even though he had made very good money playing ball, several financial reverses and his disease had drained him of his resources. (He invested in an ice plant in Palmyra, New York, in 1886 and lost a huge amount of money.) His many friends gathered together to set up a financial account for him so he could be better cared for.

At first, he was admitted to the state hospital also called "the State Farm" at Bridgewater, Massachusetts, but was subsequently removed to a private hospital on Middle Street in Braintree, Massachusetts. His disease was reported at various times as paralysis and spinal trouble. Sutton passed away on June 20, 1907, as a result of locomotor ataxia due to tertiary syphilis.

His old friend, "Honest" John Morrill, took charge of the body and made arrangements to have it sent back to his relatives in Rochester. He was laid to rest at the Palmyra Village Cemetery, in Palmyra, New York.

Bill Popp

The son of German immigrants, William and Josephine Popp, William Peter "Bill" Popp was a career minor leaguer except for a nine-game stint with the 1902 St. Louis Cardinals.

Photograph courtesy of Connie Nisinger.

Popp pitched for Little Rock of the Southern League in 1901. There were reports that Popp would jump to the American League when in April of 1902 he chose to sign a contract with Patsy Donovan and his hometown team rather than several other offers from minor league franchises.

One wonders what kind of feeling the 170-pound right-hander had when he stepped onto the mound for the first time representing his home town on Saturday, April 19, 1902. He appeared for the Cardinals in a 10–4 loss to Pittsburgh at St. Louis before a crowd of 10,000. Popp could have used a bit more support as his team committed 11 errors in the game.

Popp was sent down to Columbus of the American Association in mid-June due to his record but pitched himself back to the parent club in mid-July for one final tryout. St. Louis management ran out of patience after Popp got blasted by the Phillies on July 14, 9–2. Popp's career lasted a little less than two months, with his final appearance coming on Monday, July 21, 1902, in a 7–2 loss to the Reds. In between, he accrued a lifetime 2–6 record in nine games, of which seven were as a starter. He completed seven of his starts and pitched to a 4.92 ERA in 60⅓ innings.

After that it was back to the minors, where he pitched for Terre Haute, Indiana, among other clubs. On August 13, 1902, he struck out 12 Cedar Rapids players, with the opposing pitcher striking out 15 Terre Haute strikers.

Popp was married and living at 2817 Nebraska Avenue in St. Louis when he died on September 5, 1909, at the age of 32. His death took place at an insane asylum in St. Louis, his family having moved him into the facility sometime before that. The cause of his demise was the result of dementia paralytica due to advanced syphilis.

He is buried in the Popp family plot at the Calvary Cemetery in St. Louis (Section 20, Lot 904, Grave 2). He left a wife, a mother, and a few lines in the Baseball Encyclopedia by which he could be remembered.

Chick Evans

Chick Evans pitched just under 53 full innings in the major leagues. Yet, growing up in his native state of Vermont, he showed the kind of early promise that he'd have a much longer stay in the bigs.

A high school phenom at Burr & Burton Seminary, Evans signed on to play minor league ball with Hartford in the Connecticut League where he hurled a perfect game on July 21, 1908, against Bridgeport. Evans struck out nine and no Bridgeport player managed to get a ball out of the infield.

Evans won 13 games in his rookie season and 10 the next before he was sold to the Boston Doves on July 19, 1909. That year, he appeared in four games and went 0–3. He made the squad the following season when he got his only big-league victory, coming on in relief in the opening game of the season against the New York Giants.

All told, Evans pitched in 13 games that season, going 1–3.

He later pitched with Montreal of the Eastern League in 1911 and Syracuse of the New York State League in 1912. Arm problems, which he developed while in the minors, eventually ended his career.

Evans settled in Schenectady, New York, where he worked for General Electric in the munitions department and pitched on the company baseball team. By the summer of 1916, his health had deteriorated due to the effects of gonorrhea which he had contracted some years earlier.

He entered the Ellis Hospital in Schenectady on July 30, remaining there until the end of his life on September 2 at 5:30 in the evening. His official cause of death was listed as "generalized septicemia and acute gonorrheal endocarditis compounded by a cerebral embolism."

Evans, who was only 27 years old, was laid to rest at the Vale Cemetery in Schenectady a few days later.

With his demise, he became one of the few major leaguers to die as a direct result of gonorrhea.

Bronx Cheer

The 1927 Yankees were one of the best teams of all time. They were also one of the most cursed. Cursed because four of their starters, as well as batboy Eddie Bennett, died before the age of 50. Eleven of the dozen mentioned in this chapter never reached the age of 60, and Mike Gazella punctuated the string of either early or hard-luck demises with the exclamation point of a fatal head-on collision in 1978.

As for the on-field endeavors, the names are immortal—start with Babe Ruth and Lou Gehrig. Throw in Earle Combs, Tony Lazzeri, Waite Hoyt, Herb Pennock, and manager Miller Huggins, and you have seven Hall of Famers altogether.

The 1927 Yanks went 110–44 and swept the Pittsburgh Pirates to win the World Series. It was a team that could hit for power, hit for average, and steal bases. They had the two most feared back-to-back hitters the game has ever known in Ruth, batting third in the lineup, followed by Gehrig. Ruth hit 60 home runs that season, Gehrig 47. They were the heart of what became known as "Murderers' Row," which also included leadoff man

Combs, who hit .362 that season with an on-base percentage of .414.

The team batting average was .307.

The four-man rotation on the mound was equally as formidable. That year, Hoyt won 22 games, Pennock 19, and Urban Shocker 18. Dutch Ruether was 13–6. A 30-year-old rookie, Wilcy Moore, wound up collecting 19 wins and 13 saves.

Cancer and heart failure were the most common eventual causes of the deaths here. Then there was the cruel disease that was subsequently named after the man whose life it took, Lou Gehrig. With blood poisoning, a gastric ulcer, a cerebral hemorrhage, and a house fire, you're left with unhappy and untimely endings to what were unparalleled days of glory.

Urban Shocker

Cleveland-born Urban Shocker was one of the better spitball pitchers during his time in the majors. (The spitball wasn't outlawed until 1920, when Major League Baseball finally put a rule into effect. Interestingly, a group of pitchers who depended on the pitch were officially listed by MLB, which allowed them to continue throwing it for the rest of their careers. Shocker was among them.)

Shocker was considered one of the best arms in the Yankees organization when he first pitched for New York from 1916 to 1917. But the Yanks needed a shortstop, so they traded Shocker along with

Les Nunamaker, Joe Gedeon, Nick Cullop, and Fritz Maisel to the St. Louis Browns for shortstop Del Pratt, pitcher Eddie Plank, and $15,000 cash. (Plank retired instead of reporting.)

With the Browns, Shocker was a four-time 20-game winner. On December 17, 1924, the Yankees got him back in the midst of an overhaul of their pitching staff. They traded Joe Bush, Milt Gaston, and Joe Giard to get him. Shocker became one of the mainstays of the rotation for three seasons, winning 12, 19, and 18 games.

In early 1928 he was diagnosed with a heart condition and retired to Colorado. He succumbed to pneumonia as a complication of heart disease on September 9, 1928, at the age of 38. As a final gesture, his widow was voted a share of the 1928 World Series bonus money by the Yankees players and management. He was buried in Calvary Cemetery in St. Louis, Missouri (Section 24, Lot 3313, Grave 2).

He was the first member of the 1927 Yankees to die.

Miller Huggins

Miller Huggins was born on March 27, 1878, although some baseball reference books list the year as either 1879 or 1880. Known as "Hug" or the "Mighty Mite," his entire 13-year career as a player in the National League was spent with the Reds and Cardinals. A steady, nuts-and-bolts second baseman with great speed, he was also known for his heady play and how he got the most out of his modest 140-pound frame.

Before baseball, Huggins went to the University of Cincinnati, where for a time he thought about becoming a lawyer. Legend has it that a professor influenced his decision to make baseball a career. It turned out to be a good one for Huggins, who accrued 1,474 lifetime hits with 318 stolen bases and a .265 average. He spent the last four years of his playing career as player/manager for the Cardinals.

On the suggestion of American League president Ban Johnson, Yankees owner Jacob Ruppert hired Huggins to manage the Yanks

in 1918. He did so even though there was a divide between New York's two owners—Ruppert and Cap Huston, who wanted Wilbert Robinson to manage the team.

Still, Huggins took over and continued on at the helm of the Yanks through the 1929 season, winning six AL titles and three World Series in all. A respected leader of men, he even won over the Babe, although they battled tooth and nail. Lou Gehrig and Tony Lazzeri might have been the two closest players to Huggins on the Yanks, and upon his death in 1929, both were devastated. Huggins believed in a straightforward managing style, quiet and patient in his belief in his team. "Hug" was the type who believed that the manager should be in total command of the baseball club and that no one was above the team.

Years after Huggins' passing, ex-Yankee Waite Hoyt remarked, "I believe we took 20 years off that man's life. He always had to worry about something one of us was up to. Sure, we were a rowdy bunch who never meant any harm, but I think that sometimes we took things a bit too far. Poor Hug always seemed to get the brunt of it."

On September 20, 1929, Huggins arrived late for a game at the stadium with Boston. He was weak and pasty-looking with a very nasty red boil on the side of his face. He left the dugout after the third inning, and after an examination by a doctor, checked into St. Vincent's Hospital. Various newspaper reports suggested that Huggins was suffering from influenza, as his temperature varied to as high as 105 degrees. Despite four blood transfusions, he died five days later as a result of erysipelas (blood poisoning), on September 25, 1929, at the age of 51.

The Yankees were at Fenway Park the day he died, and flags were lowered at half mast when the announcement was made. Tears flowed that day in both dugouts.

Many in baseball attended the funeral at the Church of the Transfiguration, also known as "The Little Church around the Corner" on 1 East 29th Street in New York City. John McGraw, Johnny Evers, Hans Lobert, and Tris Speaker were just some of the baseball celebrities who paid their respects. Huggins' two coaches, Art Fletcher and Charley O'Leary, were pall bearers along with Pennock, Ruth, Gehrig, Lazzeri, Combs, and Bob Shawkey. Lazzeri was so devastated that he went home to California after the funeral in Cincinnati.

Huggins was a lifetime bachelor, and his body was accompanied by his sister Myrtle and brother Arthur back to his hometown for burial. He was laid to rest in the Spring Grove Cemetery in Cincinnati (Section 53, Lot 172).

Eddie Bennett

The hunchbacked mascot for the Yankees, Eddie Bennett served in that capacity from 1920 until May of 1932, when he was involved in a serious car accident that brought an end to his batboy days.

Bennett was a beloved figure in the Yankees' clubhouse—known to take losses as hard, or harder, than the players. He was often seen shedding both tears of joy or grief in times of triumph or defeat.

Bennett loved to have a good time when the team was on the road, where he often roomed with pitcher Urban Shocker. Bennett was not the most camera-friendly of people due to his hunchback condition, and it was very rare that he posed for the camera with a smile on his face. Born an orphan, Bennett served time with the White Sox and Brooklyn before joining the Yankees.

After his accident, which resulted in a severely broken leg and other broken bones, doctors advised him not to go back on the field. The pain from his injuries led Bennett into severe depression and drinking to ease the pain. His alcohol abuse became excessively worse, eventually causing his death on Wednesday, January 16, 1935. His landlady discovered his lifeless body amidst the memorabilia he had collected throughout the years. Bennett was in his early thirties.

Yankees management paid for all funeral and burial expenses for "Little Eddie" in St. John's Cemetery in Queens. Strangely, newspaper reports of the day showed that not a single Yankees player showed up for the funeral.

Of note, a coroner's attendant who picked up Bennett's body tagged him with a piece of paper that said "heart," to indicate the cause of death. In reality, that might have been the truth, because without baseball, Bennett's heart had broken.

Lou Gehrig

Lou Gehrig's life and subsequent death from a fatal illness has been well chronicled. A quiet man with the smile and air of self-

assurance, he was arguably the finest first baseman of all time. Still, to this day, his legendary consecutive-game streak (2,130) along with his formidable career stats, place him among the crop of baseball's immortals. He had a .340 lifetime average, 493 home runs, 1,990 RBIs, and a slugging average of .632.

What is ironic is that he most likely played during the early stages of the dread disease that eventually caused his demise. His name lives on in that disease, amyotropic lateral sclerosis, which will be forever more be known as "Lou Gehrig's Disease."

Gehrig died one-third of the way through Joe DiMaggio's 56-game hitting streak, succumbing to his disease on the evening of June 2, 1941, 17 days before his 38th birthday. His body was cremated, and his ashes placed in the facing of his headstone in Kensico Cemetery in Valhalla, New York (Section 93, Lot 12686).

He became the fourth member of the 1927 Yankees to meet an untimely demise.

In an interesting note, Gehrig's final resting place at Kensico is literally surrounded by the graves of his family members and associates from his professional life. Buried within a long line drive of his grave are: father, Henrich; mother, Christina; wife, Eleanor; college baseball coach at Columbia, Andy Coakley (a former major league pitcher); Paul Krichell, the Yankees scout who signed him (a former major league catcher); Yankees owner, Jacob Ruppert; and Yankees president, Ed Barrow.

Charley O'Leary

Chicago native Charley O' Leary was a coach for the 1927 Yankees, serving under the leadership of Miller Huggins from 1920 to 1930. Huggins credited O'Leary for developing infielders Mark Koenig and Tony Lazzeri. O'Leary took the two youngsters under his wing, schooling them on the intricacies of play and making them into solid major league infielders. O'Leary stayed with the club for one season after the untimely death of Huggins in 1929.

When Joe McCarthy was named manager of the Yanks, O'Leary was let go in order to allow McCarthy to bring in his friend, "Sunset" Jimmy Burke. O'Leary coached for the St. Louis Browns and later the Cubs, serving under Rogers Hornsby.

The son of Timothy and Ellen O'Connell O'Leary, O'Leary played three seasons with Des Moines, Iowa, before joining the Detroit Tigers in 1904, where he became the regular shortstop for the next four seasons. By 1908 he became the club's utility man, serving time at shortstop, third base, and second base. He appeared in three straight World Series for Detroit from 1907 to 1909.

A heady fielder but never a great hitter, he only batted .226 lifetime.

At the time of his death, O'Leary was living at 7615 South Morgan Street in Chicago and working as a security guard for the Sanitary District of Chicago. On January 6, 1941, O'Leary died as a result of peritonitis from a chronic penetrating gastric ulcer and was buried at the Mount Olivet Cemetery (Section 11, Lot 60) on January 9, 1941. He was 58 years old.

O'Leary was the fifth member of the 1927 Yankees to die young.

Johnny Grabowski

Johnny Grabowski's claim to fame in the majors was being the back-up catcher for the 1927 Yankees, sharing the duties with Pat Collins and Benny Bengough. He chipped in with career highs of 25 and 21 RBIs in 1927 and 1928, respectively. All told, he played for three big-league teams in his career, and he was noted more for his defense than his hitting. He started out with the

White Sox in 1924, and after his stint with the Yankees, he went to the minors in 1930 with St. Paul of the American Association. His last stop as a player in the majors was with the Tigers. He played with Montreal of the International League for three years before he eventually turned to umpiring, becoming a competent minor league arbiter in the Canadian-American, Eastern, and International Leagues.

On May 23, 1946, a fire broke out at Grabowski's home in Guilderland, New York. Inexplicably, he ran back into the inferno in order to save his car and suffered second- and third-degree burns. He lingered in the hospital for five days before succumbing. He was just 46 years old and was laid to rest in the Park View Cemetery in Schenectady, New York (Section B, Lot 112, Grave 3).

Tony Lazzeri

Tony Lazzeri was one of the players who helped to make the Yankees popular with the Italian American population which would chant "Poosh 'em up, Tony" whenever he came to bat. The most amazing thing about Lazzeri is that he played his entire 14-year career with epilepsy.

As a rookie in 1926, he batted .275 with 18 home runs and 114 RBIs. His confrontation with Grover Cleveland Alexander in the seventh inning of Game 7 of the 1926 World Series, in which he struck out with the bases loaded, is considered one of the greatest moments in the history of the game. (Interestingly, Alexander was also an epileptic.)

Lazzeri went on to have a Hall of Fame career, collecting 1,191 RBIs on 178 home runs—a remarkable feat for a right-handed hitter in Yankee Stadium considering that, when he broke in, the left-center-field fence was 460 feet away from home plate with the center field wall at 490.

After his career, Lazzeri opened a tavern. He was a fairly successful businessman at the time of his death from a coronary occlusion (a massive heart attack) on August 6, 1946, at the age of 42. His wife had been away on a trip, and his body was found at the foot of the steps that led down to his basement. He had actually been suffering from acute cardiovascular disease for several years.

He was buried in the Sunset Mausoleum (Sunset Terrace, West Corridor, Section 32–28) in Kensington, California.

Herb Pennock

Herb Pennock was probably the best left-handed pitcher in the American League during the 1920s. Hailing from historic Kennett Square, Pennsylvania (the "Mushroom Capital of the World"), Pennock had a silky smooth delivery and used a variety of pitches and speeds.

Photograph from Frank Russo's private collection.

Babe Ruth considered the crafty southpaw one of the all-time best pitchers, noting, "If I had to use one word to describe Pennock, it would be 'class.'"

Pennock's knowledge of each hitter was extensive, and Miller Huggins always had as much faith in him as any pitcher he ever managed.

He started his career with the Philadelphia Athletics, but Connie Mack felt that Pennock would never put in the time to be a great pitcher because he came from a rich family. In June 1915, he was put on waivers by Mack and picked up by the Boston Red Sox. He was traded by Boston on January 30, 1923, to the Yankees for Camp Skinner, Norm McMillan, George Murray, and $50,000 cash.

With the Yanks, Pennock became a full-blown star—playing on five pennant winners and appearing in four World Series, where he compiled a 5–0 record.

After his career, he worked in various capacities in the game, culminating with a GM position with the Phillies in the 1940s, where he helped build the foundation for the 1950 "Whiz Kids," signing such soon-to-be stars as Granny Hamner.

Pennock was in New York City for league meetings when he passed away from a cerebral hemorrhage on January 30, 1948, at the age of 53. He was buried in the Union Cemetery in Kennett Square, Pennsylvania. His grave (Section C-C) is just a few yards from the final resting place of movie star Linda Darnell.

Babe Ruth

"The Bambino" needs no introduction. The records of George Herman Ruth speak for themselves. Considered by many to be the greatest player of all time, "the Babe" also had one heck of a good time—cramming enough fun and excitement into his 53 earthly years to last 20 lifetimes.

Obviously, Ruth would have had a much better shot fighting the throat cancer that took his life had he lived in a more modern

era. The "Sultan of Swat" died after a painful, two-year bout with the disease on August 16, 1948.

He is buried in Westchester County, just about 25 minutes away from Yankee Stadium, at the Cemetery of the Gate of Heaven in Hawthorne, New York (Section 25, Lot 1115, in the center of Graves 3 and 4).

His final resting place is the most visited of all baseball players, adorned with gifts and notes from people from all walks of life, from all over the country and the world.

A Kiss for the Babe

The most striking token of remembrance adorning Babe Ruth's grave site that day was not the unopened bottle of Ole Slugger Pale Ale, the one cigar, the two wooden bats, the eight small American flags, the seven baseballs, the dish of pennies, or any of the scattered ticket stubs from Yankee Stadium—most from victories over the Red Sox.

There was something that left a more heartfelt impression on the façade of the 10-foot-tall granite marker, which depicts Ruth as a small boy walking side by side with Christ, who is looking down, resting a hand upon his shoulder.

On Ruth's cheek that day was a lipstick mark from a kiss.

There is a palpable feeling of love and reverence at the site for a man who, though long dead, is still larger than life. It's more of a shrine than a grave—a bona fide destination for an old-fashioned pilgrimage to the Gate of Heaven Cemetery.

And what is to be found here for so many? Ruth was no saint, and this site is a long way from Lourdes. But people still believe in him—in what he was as much as what he did. They perceive an endearing goodness in him and come here to revel in it.

What else would possess a parent from a town in north Jersey to trek out to Westchester and leave laminated novelty baseball cards of young twin boys standing on the lower ledge of the tombstone? There was also a little league trophy left there. And what motivates a person to write "God bless you, Babe" on one of the baseballs?

Several years ago a letter written in a child's hand was left at the grave site. The letter was from a kid who wrote that his father told

him what a great player Ruth was, and it asked the Babe to say hi to his grandpa and grandma in heaven.

There is an inscription of a quote from Cardinal Spellman down the left side of the slate-gray headstone that reads:

"May the divine spirit that animated
Babe Ruth to win the crucial game of life
inspire the youth of America!"

This is a pure benediction. You get the feeling that some people believe they can get a little closer to God by getting a little closer to the Bambino, resting beneath their feet at the Gate of Heaven.

Joe Giard

The son of Albert and Girilia Thibodeau Giard, Joe Giard was originally signed by the Yankees who traded the port-sider to the St. Louis Browns on December 17, 1924, along with Joe Bush and Milt Gaston for former Yankees spitball pitcher Urban Shocker.

Giard proved to be a good pickup for St. Louis, going 10–5 his first year for the Brownies. After a 3–10 record in 1926, he was traded back to the Yanks on February 8, 1927, along with Cedric Durst for "Sad" Sam Jones. Giard did not have a win-loss record in 1927—he appeared in only 18 games, all in relief. He compiled 27 innings of work that season, with an 8.00 ERA. Giard was released to the St. Paul Saints of the American Association in December of 1927 along with Ray Morehart. Giard also pitched for San Antonio of the Texas League as property of the Washington Senators.

After his career, he settled in Worcester, Massachusetts, where he lived at 604 Main Street. He died at the Worcester City Hospital as a result of metastasized lung cancer on July 10, 1956, at the age of 57 and is buried in the Mount Carmel Cemetery in Ware, Massachusetts.

Walt Beall

Walter Beall possessed one of the best curveballs in all of baseball during his time in the majors, yet he could never harness his skill to make himself a winning pitcher.

He first burst onto the baseball scene in 1924 with Rochester of the International League, winning 25 games—second best behind Lefty Grove (26). In August 1924, Beall was acquired for $50,000 by the Yankees. He

appeared in four games, going 2–0 before getting sent to St. Paul of the American Association.

Beall would take the New York–St. Paul shuttle several times over the next few years, and he went 0–1 in 1925 and 2–4 in 1926. He only appeared in one game for the 1927 Yankees, pitching one inning and giving up one run. Beall pitched for Chattanooga and Montreal in 1928, going a combined 3–9. He made his last major league appearances for the Washington Senators in 1929, going 1–0 in three games.

Beall died on January 28, 1959, in Suitland, Maryland, the official cause listed as acute congestive heart failure due to cardiovascular renal disease. He was living at 4714 Huron Avenue in Suitland at the time of his death and is buried in the Cedar Hill Cemetery in Suitland, Maryland.

Upon his death, Bucky Harris, his manager with Washington, said, "He possessed one of the best curveballs I have ever seen, if not the best."

Mike Gazella

At the time of his death at age 82, in 1978, Mike Gazella was the second-oldest living member of the famed 1927 Yanks. He was enjoying a happy retirement in Odessa, Texas, when he was killed in a head-on collision while driving his pick-up truck.

Gazella was a utility man with the Yankees for four seasons in the 1920s. After an eight-game stint with the parent club in 1923, he went back to the minors for two years, sticking with New York for its championship runs from 1926 to 1928. It was after the 1926 season ended that Gazella found out that he had been voted only a quarter share of the World Series money by his teammates, even though he had appeared in 62 games for New York that season. This infuriated Gazella, who was known for having a bit of a temper. He went straight to Commissioner Kenesaw Mountain Landis for help, and Landis decreed that he get the full share

The college-educated Gazella once told the entire Yankees team off at a dinner for not playing up to their capabilities. After he left the Yanks, he made stops in the American Association, the Eastern League, and the Pacific Coast League, and later scouted for his old ballclub in the late 1940s.

Murderers' Row

The majority of the players here wound up on the wrong end of a gun—shot by friends, shot by foes, shot by family, shot by total strangers for no apparent reason whatsoever.

Some were killed as bartenders. Another was killed by the bartender.

Some were innocent, upstanding citizens who met their violent fates by simply being in the wrong place at the wrong time. Others were playing a little closer to the edges, so to speak, and paid the ultimate price in more venal circumstances.

In a most bizarre episode, Dodgers pitcher Len Koenecke had his head bashed in with a fire extinguisher by a commercial airline pilot when he tried to wrest controls of the plane in mid-flight. Another was fatally hit over the head while he was sleeping. Another got hit over the head with a keg.

There were brave police officers killed in the line of duty after their playing days were over. There was a stabbing at a fish fry.

By far the most exotic case of the bunch was that of ex-Boston pitcher Gordon McNaughton, gunned down by a jealous lover.

It was the stuff movie screenplays are made of.

But in the end, like all the other cases, it was still murder most foul.

Gordon McNaughton

Gordon Joseph McNaughton's career was nothing to shout about—six appearances on the mound for the 1932 Boston Red Sox with a record of 0–2.

His death, however, was the stuff Hollywood screenplays are made of—gunned down in a jealous rage by a "dice girl" who was his jilted lover.

McNaughton's life was never the same the day he cast his eyes upon the sweet figure of a platinum-blonde beauty by the name of Eleanor Williams. Williams, 22, worked as a dice

girl in one of the games the pitcher ran in local taverns in Chicago.

It was the preferred occupation for McNaughton, who had been released to Reading of the International League for 1933. When his contract was purchased by Boston after that season, he quit the game to become a postal clerk. An average working stiff by day, the ex-chucker and former pro basketball player frequented Chicago's many clubs at night, becoming a lucrative dice concessionaire.

Born in Canada, Williams was married with a young child when she met the handsome ex-athlete. She completely fell head over heals in love and, against the warnings of her family and friends, immediately left her husband and child.

Thus began their tumultuous three-year relationship. The two became a well-known item in the Chicago nightlife scene. McNaughton eventually got Williams pregnant, but she had a miscarriage, which caused the relationship to go south. McNaughton often beat her, mostly in jealous fits when he suspected her of cheating with other men.

In late July 1942, McNaughton decided to cool things off between them. He did this primarily by heating things up with another pretty blonde by the name of Dorothy Moos.

Moos had her own troubles. She also came from a broken marriage, although she had the good sense to get divorced first. Moos fell for McNaughton, who treated her well. But while he was seeing Moos, McNaughton was still in contact with Williams, even talking romantically with her and giving her hope that the two might get back together. Williams felt that he still loved her and that he was only after Moos for the money she supposedly had.

Williams wanted her boyfriend back at all costs. McNaughton had been seeing Moos for only about three weeks when Williams took matters, and a gun, into her own hands. She stole the service revolver from a Chicago policeman she was having a fling with—35-year-old Barney Towey. Armed, dangerous, and possibly hung over, she headed for Moos' room at the New Lawrence Hotel on the morning of August 6, 1942, looking for her man.

Williams banged on the door. A scantily clad Moos opened it as McNaughton hastily got dressed. Moos let Williams in so that she would not draw attention by making a scene. Once inside, Williams argued with McNaughton, going on about their relationship and everything it meant to her.

All the while she kept making threats that she would shoot him.

Moos tried to calm Williams down, saying that "no man was worth killing."

Williams fired a shot but missed. McNaughton grabbed her wrist, and the gun fell onto the couch. Moos grabbed the gun and ran into the bathroom in a vain attempt to hide it. When Moos came out of the bathroom, she began arguing with Williams, who told her to mind her own business. Meanwhile, Williams was still rambling about her miscarriage, about not wanting to become a bum and a street walker, and about how "Gordie" needed to make up his mind and choose between them.

As McNaughton remained silent, Williams ran into the bathroom and came out with the pistol in her hand. In a bizarre dare, McNaughton, according to Williams, spoke the following fateful words: "I am a coward. Go ahead and shoot me. I deserve it." (According to Moos, McNaughton's last words were: "Go on, shoot me; I'm tired of arguing.")

Williams fired one fatal shot at point-blank range, hitting him in the chest. Then, she ran into the hall and began yelling that she had just killed a man. Hotel officials held her in the lobby until police arrived. At the Racine Avenue station she was booked on suspicion of murder.

The official cause of death on McNaughton's death certificate read: bullet wound through the chest. Williams was eventually found guilty of manslaughter that October and sentenced to one to 14 years. Sadly Towey, whose revolver was used in the murder, committed suicide two months later, days after being let go from the Chicago police.

McNaughton left behind his father, a successful tavern owner, his mother, his ex-wife Caroline, whom he had divorced in 1937, and an eight-year-old daughter, Patricia. He was buried at the Calvary Cemetery in Evanston, Illinois, on August 10, 1942.

When she was first questioned by police, Williams declared, "I just had to kill him. I had to do it. I couldn't bear to let somebody else have him."

Gus Polidor

Gustavo Adolfo Polidor Gonzalez played for parts of seven seasons in the majors. An exceptional utility infielder, he only batted .207 lifetime.

The Venezuelan native signed with the California Angels as an amateur free agent on January 5, 1981. After several seasons with Holyoke, Massachusetts, of the Eastern League, Polidor made his major league debut with the California Angels on September 7, 1985. With the bases loaded and the score tied 3–3 in the bottom of the ninth against the Orioles, Polidor was inserted as a fifth infielder, stationed between second baseman Rob Wilfong and first baseman Bobby Grich.

Unfortunately, manager Gene Mauch's defensive strategy failed as Mike Young lined a single down the right-field line to give Baltimore a 4–3 win.

Polidor became a utility specialist for the Angels over the next three seasons, playing second, third, and shortstop with equal adroitness. He was traded from the Angels to the Milwaukee Brewers on December 7, 1988, for Bill Schroeder. His salary with the Angels in 1987 was $67,000. He earned $125,000 with the Brewers in 1989.

His final major league appearances came with the expansion Florida Marlins in 1993. He headed back to Venezuela to play shortstop for the LaGuaira Sharks team.

On Friday, April 28, 1995, Polidor left his home with his wife and one-year-old son, Gustavo Adolfo. Waiting outside were two men who approached him, demanding that he give them the keys to his car. Polidor complied, but when the two men attempted to kidnap his baby, Polidor made his stand. The heroic Polidor was shot twice in the head at point blank range and died at a hospital a short time later.

Polidor was remembered by most as a genuinely nice, easy-going soul who loved his family and loved the game. Players like Steve Finley and Andres Galarraga expressed outrage at what happened. But no one was more shaken by his murder than White Sox shortstop Ozzie Guillen.

Guillen and Polidor had been friends since childhood, and when the tragic news reached him, the grief-stricken Guillen left immediately for Venezuela to attend the funeral. Guillen not only took over for the financial welfare of Polidor's family, but he also put his widow, son, and two daughters in a second house that he owned.

Hiram "Hi" Bithorn

The first Puerto Rican to play major league baseball, Hiram "Hi" Bithorn became a hero to the people of his native island. He was well on his way to becoming a good, if not great, pitcher until military service and a bad arm ended his pro aspirations.

After a disappointing 9–14 season with the Chicago Cubs, he seemed to finally fulfill his promise with an 18–12 record and a 2.60 ERA in 1943. He was looked upon by management to be one of the future stars of the rotation but, like many players of the time, had his career interrupted by service in World War II. He rejoined the Cubbies in 1946, after two years in the Navy, but was

never the same pitcher again due to arm trouble, which he claimed was because he was out of shape. He was purchased by the Pirates in 1947 but never played a game for them—the Pirates put him on waivers in spring training. The White Sox picked him up, and it was with that club that his major league career ended after a two-game stint.

Bithorn was normally quiet and good-natured, and seldom

lost his temper, but he did get unhinged once when Leo Durocher said some unflattering things at him from the dugout. Bithorn whipped a ball at him and told his team after the game he was going to get "the Lip." Even after getting fined by league president Ford Frick, Bithorn planned revenge. The next time the Cubs were at Ebbets Field, Bithorn lurked near the Dodgers dugout before the game. Cubs manager Jimmy Wislon asked Bithorn what he was doing, to which Bithorn replied, "I wait for that Durocher. If he come out of dugout, I kill him."

It's a good thing Durocher didn't surface.

After his playing days, Bithorn opened a tavern in Puerto Rico called The Tenth Inning. He also did some umpiring in Puerto Rico and Mexico.

On December 30, 1951, Bithorn was in the process of selling a car in El Mante, Mexico, when a policeman named Juan Cano asked him to produce the vehicle's ownership papers. When Bithorn couldn't come up with them, the policemen got in the car with Bithorn and asked him to drive down to the stationhouse to sort the matter out. According to Cano, Bithorn struck him and attempted to flee, prompting Cano to shoot him once in the stomach with his service revolver.

The nearest hospital was 84 miles away, in Ciudad Victoria. During the ride there, Bithorn passed away from internal hemorrhaging. He was 35 years old.

Bithorn was buried at the civil cemetery in Ciudad Victoria. He left a wife, Virginia, a mother, and a brother. After his death, Cano was held at the station on open charges, and questions about Bithorn's death lingered. Why, for example, was Bithorn selling a car he needed to get around with? And how was he shot in the stomach as he fled from the officer?

In 2003, 52 years after his death, Bithorn's name came to the forefront when the Montreal Expos played a home game at Hiram Bithorn Stadium which was built in 1962 and named in his honor.

Howie Fox

In 1943 jug-eared Howie Fox was attending the University of Oregon when he was discovered and signed to a contract by the Cincinnati Reds. Fox, who was playing basketball on a scholarship, was then sent to Birmingham of the Southern Association that April. In 1944 he went 19–7 for the Barons, causing the Reds to take notice. He was recalled on September 4 and made his major league debut with a brief appearance on Thursday, September 28, 1944, in a 10–6 win over Brooklyn. The game was noted for Reds catcher Ray Mueller breaking the major league record of 151 games caught in a season (the record had been held by Ray Schalk since 1920). Fox pitched sub-500 ball for his career except for one season, 1950, when he went 11–8. This came on the heels of the worst season of his career, 1949, when he lost 19 games.

In December 1951 he was sent to the Philadelphia Phillies, along with catcher Smoky Burgess and second baseman Connie Ryan, for catcher Andy Seminick, Eddie Pellagrini, Dick Sisler, and Niles Jordan. The deal was very unpopular in Philadelphia.

For Philly, Fox appeared in 13 games for the Phillies, going 2–7. His last year in the majors was 1954, when he made 38 appearances, all in relief. He pitched in the Texas League with the San Antonio Missions in 1955 and, while there, opened his own tavern. On October 9, 1955, young men entered the bar and began making trouble with the bartender, Hubert Callahan. A brawl ensued, and Fox stepped in to help. Fox was getting the better of the three thugs when one of them, 19-year-old John Strickland, pulled a knife and stabbed Fox to death. Police later charged the cherubic-looking Strickland with murder.

In 248 major league games, Fox accrued a lifetime 43–72 record with six saves and a 4.33 ERA.

He is buried at Laurel Hill Cemetery in Eugene, Oregon.

Ivan Calderon

Originally signed by the Seattle Mariners as an amateur free agent in 1979, Ivan Calderon burst upon the big-league scene in 1985 when he made a strong start for American League Rookie of the Year honors. A hand injury in August took him out of the running.

Calderon was not considered to be a great player in the field due to an average arm and limited range. The Mariners also felt that he was too slow to play consistently on the slick artificial turf of the Kingdome. On July 1, 1986, he was sent to the Chicago White Sox as the "player to be named later" in a June 26 trade for catcher Scott Bradley. Calderon, who was batting only .237 at the time, found the South Side much more to his liking. The following season, 1987, he smacked 28 homers (a career best), while driving in 83 RBIs.

After an injury-plagued 1988 campaign, he rebounded nicely with two strong seasons, batting .286 with 87 RBIs in 1989 and .273 with 74 RBIs in 1990, although each year he was never able to push his home-run total past 14.

He was sent by the Sox along with pitcher Barry Jones to the Expos for a "player to be named later," Tim Raines, and a minor leaguer on February 15, 1991. Calderon had his last good season in the majors in 1991, as he finally batted .300 and showed some of his old power, cracking 19 out of the yard. He also made the All-Star team.

After one more season in Montreal, he was traded to Boston in exchange for Mike Gardiner and Terry Powers on December 8, 1992. He was released by Boston on August 17, and re-signed with Chicago, playing out the rest of the year with them.

Calderon finished his career as a .272 lifetime hitter with 104 homers and 444 RBIs.

On December 27, 2003, he entered a store in his hometown of Loiza, Puerto Rico. Two people entered with him. Apparently, they had been trailing him. Without a word, they opened fire and shot the former outfielder multiple times in the back. Rumors spread that it was a gang-related hit. Ivan Calderon was just 41 years old.

Dan Leahy

Dan Leahy never dreamed that his friend, Frank Ragan, would ever be the one to cause him physical harm. Yet, an argument between them over a somewhat trivial matter was the provocation that caused Leahy's death—a former major leaguer who appeared in two games for the 1896 Philadelphia Phillies.

A promising ballplayer in the Knoxville, Tennessee, area, Leahy began his pro career with Lynchburg, Tennessee, of the Virginia State League in 1894. Leahy was also the day bartender at the Butt Inn Saloon, located in the southwest corner of Knoxville. On December 30, 1903, Leahy opened the place as usual. Ragan entered the establishment, along with a gentleman named Fitzgerald and an African American boy.

Ragan apparently did not like the presence of the boy and slapped him. This did not sit well with Leahy, who told Ragan to stop. After this, Ragan began to simmer. Charles Ammana, Leahy's brother-in-law, was also present. According to various accounts, Ragan left the bar after Leahy reprimanded him but returned a short time later. Another account describes Ragan as being in the saloon the whole time.

Several patrons, including Ammana, warned Leahy that Ragan was going to kill him, but the always jovial Dan laughed it off. Ragan, who had a revolver in his possession, wanted to know why Leahy reprimanded him and also wanted to know if the bartender was sore at him.

Leahy stated that he wasn't sore at him or anyone else.

Ragan ordered a whiskey but, still seething, didn't drink it. Leahy even offered a steak to his friend to set him right. It was to no avail; Ragan slapped the young man in the face once again. After being reprimanded by Leahy once more, Ragan slapped his friend in the face in an attempt to provoke him.

This prompted Leahy to say, "That's all right, Frank, you know I am your friend and you are only funning with me." The non-aggressive response seemed to make Ragan even angrier, and with that, Ragan pulled out the pistol and fired it into Leahy's side. Leahy, stunned, and with a look of hurt and betrayal in his eyes, said, "Frank, you have got me this time," and crumbled to the floor.

Ragan ran out a side door and down the street as Leahy struggled to hang on. By the time help arrived, Leahy had breathed his last breath.

Ragan, who allegedly killed two other men before Leahy, was followed by police to the Southern Hotel, where he was arrested and later charged with murder. Leahy, who was single and living at Central and Park at the time of his death, was laid to rest a few days later in the Calvary Cemetery in Knoxville.

Friend or no friend, Leahy would have done better that day to steer clear of the racist murderer.

Never trust a man who just passed up a whiskey and a steak.

Monroe "Dolly" Stark

Not to be confused with the umpire, Albert "Dolly" Stark, Monroe "Dolly" Stark was a minor leaguer except for parts of four seasons he spent in the majors with Cleveland and the Brooklyn Robins.

The son of William and Olivia Stark, he played for Little Rock and then San Antonio of the Texas League before making his debut for the Cleveland Naps on September 12, 1909. He replaced Neal Ball in the infield during a 1–0 loss to the Chicago White Sox. (Ball had loafed a bit on a play, and manager Nap

Lajoie inserted Stark in the game.) After his stint with the Naps, he played a year for Dayton, Ohio, of the Central League. It was from there that he signed a contract with "Uncle Robbie's Minions" in Brooklyn.

A below-average hitter at best, he outdid himself in 1911 when he batted .295. Stark always showed a lot of moxie when playing, which endeared him to the fans in Brooklyn. Used mostly in a utility/backup role, the most games he ever appeared in were 70 in 1911.

Stark's career was almost cut short in April of 1911 when he was involved in an auto accident in Knoxville, Tennessee, with several other Brooklyn players. The car they were riding in swerved to avoid a carriage and ran into a street car. The three players in the car, Stark, Larry Lejeune, and Al Burch were on a scenic ride of the Knoxville suburbs on invitation from one of Stark's friends. Stark and Burch escaped uninjured, while Lejeune suffered minor cuts to the forehead and a bruised knee.

Stark's major league career ended on May 29, 1912, when he was traded by Brooklyn along with Bill Schardt to Newark of the International League for Bob Fisher and Bill Kay. Stark still had plenty of baseball left in him, making minor league stops both as a player and manager.

During World War I, Stark served with the YMCA overseas. A fine all-around athlete, he also toured with Al Schacht's barnstorming basketball team for a time.

He was the owner of a roadhouse saloon in Memphis, when he was involved in a fight with a man named A. S. Atkinson, on December 1, 1924. Atkinson, who may have been drunk, apparently came up on the short end of the stick with a badly broken nose and wanted revenge. He ran to a room where Stark kept a revolver, came back, and confronted Stark before shooting him once in the chest. By the time police arrived, it was too late. Stark was pronounced dead on arrival at St. Joseph's Hospital.

Stark had recently been married and was just 39 years old. He was laid to rest at the Elmwood Cemetery in Memphis, Tennessee.

Ed Morris

Born in Alabama, Morris attended Palmer College and signed with Bradenton immediately upon graduation in 1920. He hurled for the Chattanooga Lookouts in 1921 and then played a five-game stint with the Chicago Cubs in 1922. He was sold to Cincinnati and then sent down to Mobile, Alabama.

His trek through the minor leagues ended when he was purchased by Boston in 1927. The following season he became the ace of the last-place Red Sox, winning 19 games. Hot-tempered and fearless, Morris once injured his arm during a scuffle in a St. Louis hotel elevator. In 1929 he broke even with a 14–14 record, but arm injuries relegated him to 4–9 and 5–7 records the next two seasons, respectively.

Morris was feeling healthy and looking forward to the Red Sox 1932 spring training camp at Savannah, Georgia. He attended a farewell fish-fry in Century, Florida, held in his honor, on Monday, February, 29, 1932. At the party was Joe White, a gas station operator from Brewton, Alabama. The two apparently got into a heated discussion, and Morris wound up decking White. But Morris tripped and fell, and as he lay on the ground, White stabbed him twice, one wound narrowly missing the big pitcher's heart.

Morris was taken to the Tuberville Hospital in Century where he remained for the next three days. At first doctors gave him an even chance of recovery, and for a time, he held his own. Gradually though, his condition weakened, and he was put on oxygen during his third night at the hospital. He finally succumbed to his wounds on Thursday, March 3, 1932, and was buried at the Oak Grove Cemetery in Flomaton, Alabama, the next day.

Morris was 32 years old and was survived by his wife, two children, and his mother.

Frank Grube

There are conflicting reports on the details surrounding Grube's death. It is known, however, that he died from gunshot wounds in New York City in the wee hours of the morning on Sunday, July 1, 1945.

The *New York Herald-Tribune* reported that he was shot to death in the basement of his apartment building after a session of heavy drinking with his friends. *The Sporting News* reported that he was shot to death outside his apartment building by a prowler.

What is known of the incident is that one of the men drinking that night was Jose Medina, a merchant marine, who evidently took umbrage to racist remarks being passed about him. Medina got into a fistfight at the gathering and left. A short time later, it is believed several friends of his showed up with a shotgun and killed Grube.

It was a sad ending for the catcher who was only 40 years old at the time—retired and living in the Big Apple with his wife, who worked as a nurse.

Grube played mostly as a back-up catcher for seven seasons in the major leagues for two teams, the Chicago White Sox and the St. Louis Browns. In 1931, his first year in the majors, he backed up catcher Bennie Tate.

Grube took over the primary catcher position in 1932, back-stopping 94 games. In 1933 he was again the reserve catcher behind Charlie Berry. On December 15, 1933, he was purchased by the Browns. After just one season with St. Louis, he was sent back to Chicago for cash on September 20, 1935. After the 1936 season, he returned to the minors for a four-year stint. He came back for an 18-game stay with St. Louis in 1941.

Over the course of his career, Grube accrued a .244 lifetime average with one home run and 41 RBIs.

Frank McManus

It's tough when a person can't even bunk down for a while and get some shut-eye without having to worry about getting clocked over the head. That is exactly what happened to former major league catcher Frank McManus—found dead in his room at the City Tavern in Syracuse, New York, on September 1, 1923.

Autopsy results showed that he had a suffered a severe skull fracture and hemorrhage caused by a blunt instrument. The coroner ruled his death a homicide.

McManus had been complaining of being ill just a few hours before his death and asked acquaintances of his take him to a hospital. After they declined, McManus went back to his room to lie down. He never got up. Police eventually pegged the motive for the killing as a robbery and arrested and charged the owner and two employees of the inn.

McManus began his baseball career in 1899 with the Washington Senators of the National League. He also appeared for the Brooklyn Superbas, Detroit, and the Highlanders, to whom he was traded on July 25, 1904, for Monte Beville.

Over parts of four seasons he appeared in 14 games, batting a lifetime .229.

He played for several teams in the minors, most notably with Jersey City and Buffalo, both of the Eastern League. In 1905, while playing with Buffalo, McManus, his manager George Stallings, and teammate Edward Murphy were all arrested in Providence after a brawl with police. They had just come in from a night out on the town and had a confrontation outside the hotel in which they were staying.

A bachelor, McManus' occupation at the time of his death was plumber, but he also worked in construction as well. On his death certificate, his residence was listed as the Boone Hotel in Syracuse.

His was buried in Massachusetts just 20 days shy of his 48th birthday.

George Craig

George McCarthy Craig was just beginning to develop into a fine southpaw pitcher when he was struck down by an unknown assailant while playing in the minor leagues at the tender age of 23.

Craig went to the Mineral Springs Resort in Indiana for spring training in 1911, anticipating a big year for himself. The previous season, he had pitched so well for Trenton, Ohio, of the Tri-State League that Indianapolis of the American Association purchased his contract.

But just a few minutes before midnight, on April 22, 1911, Craig was awakened by a burglar who was rummaging through the clothes in his hotel room. A struggle ensued, and the fight between Craig and his assailant spilled into the hall. A shot rang out, and Craig fell to the floor. He was shot in the abdomen.

The assailant made his escape through a side door. Other players and hotel guests were awakened by the shot and made their way out into the hall. There they found Craig, struggling to hold onto life until medical help arrived. Craig was able to tell police what had happened and allowed them to begin a manhunt (in vain) for the killer.

Craig was taken to City Hospital, where he died a short time later due to blood loss. He left a wife, a child, and a mother. He was buried at the Fernwood Cemetery in Pennsylvania.

A native of Philadelphia, Craig first gained notice playing with many of the local amateur nines throughout the City of Brotherly Love. Connie Mack gave him a two-game trial in 1907 at the age of 19. He made his pitching debut on Wednesday, July 19, 1907, in a 6–1 loss to the Detroit Tigers. Craig walked two in the game for the "Mackmen."

He pitched in one more game, on September 17, in an 11–3 loss to the New York Highlanders before heading back to the minors where he toiled for Reading and Trenton of the Tri-State League before his big break, which was tragically cut short.

Johnny Ryan

Johnny Ryan played in the early days of professional baseball, logging time in both the National Association and the National League with the Philadelphia Whites, Baltimore Canaries, New Haven Elm Citys, Louisville Grays, and Cincinnati Reds

The native of Philadelphia played shortstop, first base, outfield, catcher, and even pitcher in 12 games. He finished a lifetime .207 hitter with 125 hits in 156 major league games.

After his playing days, Ryan became a member of the Philadelphia Police Department. Sworn in on March 1, 1891, he became popular and well-respected among his fellow officers. While on duty, a meeting with a gentleman named Charlie Hemple, who had been arrested several times prior for assault and battery, would end his life.

On the evening of Saturday, March 22, 1902, Hemple was involved in a brawl in a saloon near Girard Avenue. The trouble started when Hemple, prone to viciousness when drinking, began blowing the froth from his beer at his friends. A gentleman named Joseph Duffy took exception to being drenched, and a fight ensued.

The saloon keeper went outside and flagged down Ryan, who interceded and arrested Hemple. On the way to a call box, on 29th and Flora Streets, Hemple managed to attack Ryan, punching and kicking him in the stomach. Hemple broke away from the injured Ryan and found himself pursued by another patrolman and about a dozen civilians.

Hemple ran into a room at 29th and Thompson, locked himself in, and refused an officer's order to open the door. A struggle ensued after police broke it down, and a blackjack over the head put an end to Hemple's hope of a second getaway.

By the time the battered thug was packed into the paddy wagon, shouts of "Murderer!" and "Lynch him!" filled the air. Meanwhile, Ryan was carried to the office of Dr. H. W. Mindil on Girard Avenue, where he was pronounced dead just a few minutes later. The kicking Ryan suffered caused internal damage to his stomach and spleen.

From the doctor's office, Ryan's body was carried to his home at 2228 Master Street. He was buried two days later in a private ceremony at the New Cathedral Cemetery in Philadelphia.

Thomas "Mox" McQuery

Ex-ballplayer William Thomas "Mox" McQuery was working as a police officer in his native Kentucky when he was mortally wounded in a shootout with assailants at the Cincinnati–Covington suspension bridge on Friday, June 8, 1900.

In a scene straight out of an old western, McQuery and fellow officer Lieutenant Schweinfuss were in pursuit of two men who had just killed a transient when a gun battle erupted.

Two men, Wallace Bishop and Thomas Mulligan, had met a homeless man at the Ludlow Lagoon Saloon in Kentucky. They gave the transient money to buy a keg of beer. When he came back and refused to divvy up, Bishop shot him dead.

The men fled by trolley to Covington, Kentucky, where they were intercepted at the bridge by McQuery and Schweinfuss. McQuery was shot in the chest by Bishop, who had received a leg wound before leaping off the 90-foot-high bridge to the river below with a gun in each hand. Schweinfuss quickly climbed down to the banks of the Ohio side of the bridge in pursuit of Bishop, who began a swim toward a barge.

Schweinfuss climbed onto the barge and caught a break when Bishop's attempt to fire at him was thwarted by a water-logged cartridge.

Both assailants were arrested and tried. Bishop was later hanged for the murders, while Mulligan got life in jail.

As for McQuery, he was brought to Cincinnati and treated for his wound. In the days before antibiotics, with only rudimentary surgical techniques on hand, McQuery only managed to last through the weekend.

He died on Tuesday, June 12, 1900, four days after he was shot.

McQuery played parts of five seasons in the major leagues. "Moxie," as he was known to his friends, began his pro career with the old Kenton Ball Club of Covington. He also played for Terre Haute of the North Western League in 1884 before being obtained by the Cincinnati Outlaw Reds of the Union Association. He debuted in the big leagues on August 20, 1884, in a 19–5 win over Chicago.

Overall, he appeared in 417 games for five teams in three leagues during his major league career. In the minors, he also played for Indianapolis of the Western League; Hamilton, Ontario, of the International League; Syracuse, New York, of the American Association; Troy, Michigan, of the Eastern Association; and Evansville, Indiana, of the Illinois-Iowa League. He batted an astounding .399 in 1887 for Hamilton and Syracuse. After his final big league appearance with the Washington Senators in 1891, he was released and signed with Syracuse, eventually becoming team captain.

McQuery was remembered at the murder trial as a good man, a talented player, and a fine officer who gave his life in the line of duty. He was buried at the Linden Grove Cemetery in Covington.

Pat Hynes

Many felt Pat Hynes was a good enough ballplayer to make a run at a successful major league career. His main professional shortcoming, as one newspaper writer at the time put it, was his "convivial propensities."

In other words, the young man was no stranger to fast women and hard liquor, and his undisciplined approach toward living is what ended up getting him killed on March 12, 1907—his 23rd birthday.

Out and about with friend Michael Hessian, many happy returns were not in the future for Hynes, who walked into a saloon located at 6116 Easton Avenue and ordered two beers from bartender Louis Richardson.

Hynes and his friend downed their drinks, and Richardson asked for payment. Hynes replied, "I know Harry," referring to the saloon's owner, Henry Von Stein Grover, by his nickname. Hynes assumed the beers would be either free or put on a tab, but when told he had to pay up, he became enraged.

First Hynes threw a bowl of pretzels at the bartender. Then he threw a spice holder. Finally, he grabbed a mop and began whacking Richardson about the face and head, hitting him in the eye. When Hynes attempted to go behind the bar, Richardson had had enough. He reached for a revolver, pointed it at the oncoming Hynes, and fired twice. One bullet struck Hynes, the other missed. Hynes immediately slumped to the floor.

According to newspaper reports, Hynes was shot in the head at point-blank range. The death certificate, however, states that Hynes died from a "gunshot wound of lungs."

Either way, Hynes was dead. Noted for having a bit of a temper, especially when he drank, Hynes was preparing to leave for spring training with Milwaukee, which had just signed him to a contract.

His manager in the minors, Joe Cantillon, lamented the death: "I don't believe the story his assailant had to kill him in self-defense, for Pat never carried a weapon of any kind in his life and was anything but a trouble hunter."

Hynes made his major league debut with the St. Louis Cardinals on September 27, 1903, starting the first game of a doubleheader against the Phillies. Philadelphia won the game 6–3, with Hynes going the distance and surrendering 10 hits.

The next year he was sent down to the Vicksburg club of the Cotton States League, where he was suspended and then released. The St. Louis Browns, under manager Jimmy McAleer, picked up his contract while he played local minor league ball. He did most of his work in the outfield for the Brownies, playing there in 63 games. He did start two games as a pitcher, going 1–0. His name often was listed in box scores as "Hines."

In the end, the price of two beers cost him his life.

Hynes, who lived with his parents at 6123 Ridge Avenue in St. Louis, was buried at Calvary Cemetery in St. Louis (Section 12, Lot 1851, Grave 1).

Arthur Lawrence "Bugs" Raymond

All-time great Christy Mathewson once said of Arthur "Bugs" Raymond: "After a night out, don't get too close to Bugs, his breath will stop a freight train."

Another one of John McGraw's reclamation projects, Raymond had a reputation as one of the most difficult players to manage in the National League. Besides his drinking ability, Bugs also had a bit of a temper, too.

Despite using the tool of suspension and fines and even coming to blows with him on several occasions, McGraw made every attempt to save the man. He prided himself on his ability to turn Raymond around. He even offered him cash to stay off the booze. The legendary manager was indeed able to coax one great season out of him, and Raymond went 18–12 after being obtained from St. Louis, where he had logged a 2.03 ERA in 1908 but led the National League in losses with 25.

When asked about his drinking habits, Raymond once said, "If anyone should ask me to have a drink, I'd be so plum mad that I'd have to take it."

Axed midway through the 1911 season, Raymond returned to his hometown of Chicago where he did a little pitching and some umpiring in semi-pro circles.

On Saturday, September 7, 1912, Raymond was found dead in his room at the Hotel Veley in Chicago. Originally, a heart attack was given as the cause of death, but after some investigation by authorities, it was discovered that he had a fractured skull and died of a cerebral hemorrhage.

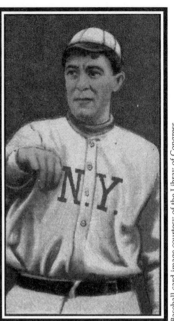

Baseball card image courtesy of the Library of Congress.

Chicago native Frank Cigranz confessed that he had gotten into an argument with Raymond at a baseball game several days earlier. The argument escalated into a fight that saw Cigranz pummel Raymond with head shots, including a whack with a baseball bat. It was later revealed that Raymond had also gotten into a brawl with several men three weeks earlier and had been rapped in the head several times.

When first questioned by police, Cigranz never fully admitted to the beating, saying he didn't think it was enough to cause the death of his old friend. When he was brought in for questioning a second time, he saw Raymond's funeral cortege headed to Chicago's Montrose Cemetery and broke down in tears before confessing to his part in the slaying.

When news of Raymond's death reached McGraw, "Little Napoleon" snapped, saying, "That man took seven years off my life."

Sam Parrilla

Retired from pro ball for some 20 years, Sam Parrilla was driving his car in Brooklyn in the winter of 1994 when he was rammed from behind by a Jeep that contained several passengers. Both he and the other driver decided not to report the accident to their insurance companies, agreeing instead to meet a few days later when Parrilla would collect the money for the damage to his car.

On the afternoon of February 9, Parrilla showed up to get his money at the corner of Hoyt and Pacific Streets. An argument ensued, and at approximately 5:45 PM, Parrilla was shot once in the chest by a 15-year-old assailant at point-blank range. He was taken to Long Island College Hospital in Brooklyn, where he died from his wound.

Parrilla only played 11 games in the majors for the 1970 Philadelphia Phillies, who signed him as a free agent on June 1, 1969. The Phillies first sent him to Raleigh-Durham of the Carolina League. There, he had a great season. In just 95 games he led the league in grand slams (3), was second in homers (28), and third in RBIs (85). Parrilla finally got to the Big Show, making his debut on April 11, 1970. Parrilla pinch hit in a 4–0 loss to the Pittsburgh Pirates, which ended a Philadelphia three-game win streak.

In his last game, on May 11, 1970, a 3–0 loss to the Cardinals, he played right field and went hitless in three at-bats.

Samuel Parrilla Monge was born in Santurce, Puerto Rico, in 1943. An outfielder, he was of half–Puerto Rican and half-Italian decent. He graduated John Jay High School in 1961, where he played both baseball and football. He worked as a construction worker before getting spotted and signed by Cleveland scout Jose "Pepe" Seda.

He started his pro career with Dubuque of the Midwest League in 1963 before getting traded to the Phillies later that year.

The tragic and unnecessary death of Parrilla was not even carried by most daily newspapers at the time. *New York Newsday* had a brief blurb on the shooting, and the *Sports Collectors Digest* ran a short story about it two months later.

Parrilla's daughter, actress Lana Parrilla, never saw him play, as she was born in 1977. Parrilla was also related to actress Candice Azzara.

Bill Wilson

Bill Wilson was marginally talented and saw limited time in the majors at the turn of the century—the stints separated by seven years in the minors.

He was also a petty criminal and a drunk—police believe he was most likely stabbed to death by shady cohorts in a dispute over how to split up stolen cash.

Born William G. Wilson in Hannibal, Missouri, in 1867, he made his major league debut with the National League Pittsburgh Alleghenies on April 30, 1890, in a 6–1 loss to the Chicago Colts. Wilson went 0 for 3 at bat with a passed ball in the field. His second go-round in the majors began with the Louisville Colonels in 1897 and lasted until June 16, 1898, when he was released along with reserve outfielder Josh Clarke in a cost-cutting measure.

After hanging up his spikes, he immersed himself in illicit activities. He became an adept pickpocket and eventually moved on to more elaborate forms of larceny. In 1909 he was arrested for the first time by postal inspectors who charged him with forging postal money orders.

Wilson was broken out of captivity by underworld friends, though, and evaded authorities for some time before finally being captured. Wilson had a fairly extensive rap sheet, yet he did not serve as much jail time as one who was in a shady profession might have under normal circumstances.

On Friday night, May 9, 1924, Wilson's body was found in a soft drink parlor located at 418 Wacouta Street in St. Paul, Minnesota. The establishment was owned by a gentleman named John Murray, although it was still named for and run by its old owner, Billy O'Connor.

Acting on an anonymous tip, police found Wilson lying in a pool of his own blood. He had been stabbed 10 times. At first, investigators thought the motive for the killing was revenge; Wilson had gotten into a drunken brawl with a few of his drunken cohorts, and some suspected payback. Slowly, police began gathering information that suggested that the killing may have stemmed from an old grudge concerning the division of loot. Wilson, it seemed, had been warned by other outlaws to skip town or die.

The two suspects sought in the killing were never apprehended.

Wilson's wake and funeral only brought 13 mourners. Reports of the day say no one was shedding tears for Wilson. The majority of those who passed his bier were from his palmy days—leaching around the fringes of society. On his death certificate, his occupation was listed as retired baseball player, and his residence as "unknown transit."

Wilson was buried at the Calvary Cemetery in St. Paul on May 16, 1924.

Bob Schultz

Bob Schultz was a rarity who played for the love of the game, and he never cared for fame, publicity, or glory. To him, baseball was baseball, whether it was in the majors or the sandlots.

Born in Louisville, Kentucky, in 1923, to Albert and Dora Schultz, he served in the United States Marine Corps as a private during World War II. Upon returning home in 1948, he hooked up with the Greenville club of the Cotton States—an affiliate of the Chicago White Sox. The Chisox put him on waivers in March 1950, and the Cubs' farm team at Nashville, owned by Larry Gilbert, picked him up for the minimum $2,500.

It proved to be a wonderful investment. The 1950 season would be the best of Schultz's pro career. He went 25–6 for the Vols—18 of those wins coming in succession at the home ballpark. Four of them were shutouts. He became only the third man since 1928 to win as many as 25 games in the Southern Association. He also fanned 202 and ran up a 2.68 ERA.

Legendary manager Branch Rickey rated Schultz as one of the top pitchers in the Cubs farm system. Schultz made his major league debut against the Cardinals in relief of Johnny Schmitz. The southpaw retired every Cardinal he faced in his one-plus inning of work. The Cubs lost the game 5–1, which also happened to be St. Louis' home opener.

Schultz stayed with the Cubs organization through June 4, 1953, when he was traded in a multi-player deal that also sent Bob Addis, Toby Atwell, George Freese, Gene Hermanski, Preston Ward, and $150,000 cash to the Pirates for slugger Ralph Kiner, Joe Garagiola, Howie Pollet, and Catfish Metkovich.

He spent time with New Orleans of the Southern Association and Buffalo of the International League before retiring in 1955.

After his career he became a house painter. In the early morning of Saturday, March 31, 1979, between 1:00 and 1:30 AM, Schultz was shot and killed during a fight at a VFW Hall in Nashville. The assailant was charged with first-degree murder.

Schultz was survived by his second wife Blanche, a daughter, Debbie Lynn, and a son, Robert D. Jr. He was buried at the Nashville National Cemetery (Section X, Grave 87) on April 4.

Dernell Stenson

Major league baseball lost not only a good player but also a good man when Dernell Stenson was brutally and senselessly murdered on Wednesday, November 5, 2003. Police found his body at about 1:45 AM on the 2200 block of West Butler Drive in Chandler, Arizona. He had been shot in the chest and head and run over by his own SUV. Eventually four men were arrested, two of them, Reginald Riddle and David Griffith, were charged with six felonies, including armed robbery, first-degree murder, and kidnapping.

Shock and dismay over his death spread quickly. The Arizona Fall League suspended play for two days in his memory and eventually inaugurated the Dernell Stenson Sportsmanship Award, given annually to the player in the league who displays the values of perseverance and humility.

The native of LaGrange, Georgia, toiled in the minor leagues for Boston and then Cincinnati, which called him up for his big-league debut on August 13, 2003. Three days later, he doubled twice and singled against Houston in his first big-league start.

Considered to be one of the Reds' most promising young players, on the next-to-last day of the season, Stenson made three outstanding catches in left field to preserve a win over Montreal. On the final day, he homered in a 2–1 loss. Overall, he batted .247 with three home runs in 81 at-bats and played stellar defense.

Stenson's kind streak was felt by many. While playing with the Trenton Thunder in 1998, he hit a home run against Portland at the Sea Dogs' home stadium. The ball left the park and landed on railroad tracks near a young homeless man who picked it up. He walked to the outfield fence and was told it was hit by Stenson.

After the game, the man met Stenson, who offered to autograph the ball. The young man asked if he wanted it back and complimented him on the tape-measure shot. The two struck up a conversation, and Stenson was moved by the indigent's story—how he was down on his luck and had given up all hope of ever achieving his dream, which was to make it in the music industry. Stenson walked with the man to a pizzeria, bought him two slices, and sat with him for more than an hour. Dernell told him that he could achieve his dream of playing music, and he inspired him to pursue it. As they parted company, Dernell returned the ball to the man, signed. The pep talk had an effect, and the young man reportedly moved to California and found work in his own field of dreams.

Dernell Stenson was laid to rest in the Restlawn Memory Gardens in his hometown of LaGrange, Georgia. He was only 25 years old.

Don O'Riley

Shaking off some minor cuts and scrapes suffered in a car accident a few days earlier, Donald Lee O'Riley made his major league debut with the Kansas City Royals on June 20, 1969.

Used mostly as a reliever, he won his first big-league game against the White Sox on July 11 as the fifth pitcher of six used that day. He faced two Sox batters in the seventh and picked up the "W."

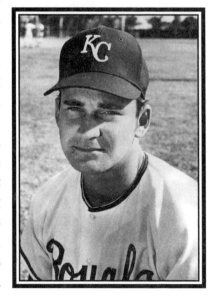

Most of O'Riley's time with the Royals' organization was spent with their farm club at Omaha. His last big league outing came on August 1, 1970. He was traded from the White Sox and then released that year and was contemplating a comeback with the Atlanta Braves before an elbow injury in a motorcycle accident ended his career for good.

Retired, O'Riley loved to play golf and took a job as the night manager at a Fast Stop convenience store so he could pursue his hobby by day.

The store was located in the 3500 Block of Independence Avenue, in one of the worst neighborhoods of Kansas City. But O'Riley, considered by those who knew him to be fearless and tough as nails, had grown up in the area and wasn't worried.

On Friday, May 2, 1997, at around 10:30 PM, a man named Robert Muse entered the store and attempted to rob it. O'Riley pulled a weapon to protect himself, and a brief gun battle ensued. According to police reports, the two men struggled behind the counter. O'Riley was able to get a round off, hitting Muse in the back. Muse fired at point blank range and hit O'Riley in the head, killing him almost instantly.

Muse fled to a house just a few blocks away, where police found him a short time later. He was charged with second-degree murder and sent to a local hospital under guard to have his wound treated.

O'Riley was laid to rest at the Floral Hills Memorial Gardens (Section 33, Lot 23a, Space 4) in Kansas City.

Ed Irvin

If not for one of the most famous on-field incidents in baseball history, the incident that saw Ty Cobb beat on a heckler named Claude Lucker, William Edward Irvin would never have seen the light of day on a major league ball field.

Lucker, who was a page in the office of Tammany Hall Chief Thomas F. Foley, had been heckling Cobb since the first pitch of a contest between the Highlanders and the Tigers at Hilltop Park on Wednesday, May 15, 1912.

In the fourth inning, Cobb blew a gasket and went after Lucker, beating him but good.

The fact that Lucker was handicapped due to a printing press accident and basically had only half a hand to defend himself with didn't matter to "the Peach." Lucker had been baiting Cobb, using a variety of adjectives, racial slurs, and unmentionables, and it was only a matter of time before the fiery southerner exploded. After hearing of the altercation, American League president Ban Johnson suspended Cobb indefinitely.

As soon as Cobb was suspended, Detroit players began talking about a strike. The feeling was that Cobb was unfairly suspended without a hearing, and he had been in the right to go after the loudmouth Lucker. Stories ran in newspapers nationwide about the possibility of a strike, and there was even a rumor that the Athletics would join in and refuse to play if Cobb was not reinstated.

The Tigers moved on to Philadelphia for a four-game series against the Athletics. After a Thursday rainout and 6–4 loss on Friday to the A's, the Tigers were ready to walk. With the news that Cobb was still not reinstated, Tigers players handed in their uniforms and equipment.

After manager Hughie Jennings was informed that his players would not be playing, he and his assistant coaches, Deacon Maguire and Joe Sugden, began a search for any and all local talent. Faced with a possible $5,000 fine if they did not field a team, Jennings was desperate. Word spread quickly that Detroit needed men. Irvin, a semi-pro player who grew up on the sandlots of Philadelphia, was one of the men picked to be a sacrificial lamb.

Along with Irvin, Jennings picked several members of the St. Joseph's College team and several other local amateurs. Among Irvin's teammates were future priest Al Travers, who was the starter and loser of the game, and boxer Billy Maharg (real name William Joseph Graham), who was later implicated in the Black Sox scandal. Irvin was the hitting star of the day for the replacements, as he smacked two triples and played catcher and first base.

The game, which was laughable, saw the Tigers get smashed 24–2. The appearance for Irvin, (some newspapers reported his name as Irwin) would be the only one of his major league career. He went back to playing semi-pro and three years later would end up losing his life in a most unrefined fashion.

On February 2, 1916, Irvin was involved in a brawl at a saloon in Philadelphia and was thrown through the front window. He died from his injuries a short time later.

Had he lived to a ripe old age, he might have been able to tell his grandchildren about his only major league appearance, his .667 lifetime average, and his 2.000 slugging average.

Fleury Sullivan

Not a lot is known about Fleury Sullivan's life before or after the majors.

Florence P. Sullivan made his debut in a 9–8 victory over the Philadelphia Athletics by the Pittsburgh Alleghenies. The game, played on May 3, 1884, was a sloppy affair in which each team made nine errors. Sullivan's stay in the majors lasted a total of just one season, but he did make it count. He and Jack Neagle were part of a two-man rotation for the Pittsburghs, as the team was often called, and they led the team in games pitched—Sullivan started and completed all 51 contests he pitched in. He also made three appearances in the outfield as well.

Hurling to a 16–35 record that season, he accumulated 441 total innings pitched. After his career, Sullivan met a rather unpleasant demise when he was shot during a political argument on February 15, 1897, in East St. Louis, Illinois. He was just 34 years old.

He was not the only member of Pittsburgh to die young. The 1884 Allegheny club was one of the most snakebitten of all time, as no less than 14 players who were on the roster that season passed away before the age of 59—now considered a young age.

Frank Bowes

Brooklyn native Frank Bowes' only stint in the majors came with the 1890 Brooklyn Gladiators of the American Association. Bowes, who was talented enough to play all infield and outfield positions, made his debut in a 3–2 loss to the Syracuse Stars, starting at catcher.

Overall, he appeared in 62 games that season, batting .220 with 24 RBIs. After one year in the AA, Bowes opted to stay close to home and play ball with several semi-pro teams, including the Long Island City Stars and the local Greenpoint nine.

Bowes had been employed at a box factory located at 420 Oakland Street in Brooklyn for about five years when, in 1895, a violent disagreement at work wound up getting him killed.

The trouble started when Bowes went to pick up his paycheck on Saturday, January 19, and discovered that he had been docked several hours' pay by the foreman, William H. Snow. An argument between them ensued. Bowes wanted his pay, which came to about half a day's work, and Snow told him to take the matter up with the factory's owner, Edward C. Smith. Bowes knew that going to see Smith was nothing more than a canard, believing that the owner would not ever overturn a decision by his foreman, especially when it came to saving money.

When the argument got too heated, Snow discharged Bowes, who simmered the whole weekend before showing up at the factory on Monday afternoon to demand his half-day's pay.

Denied again, Bowes left in a huff and lingered outside, looking for Snow, who left the factory later that night at about 7:00 PM. Bowes walked along Greene Street toward Manhattan Avenue and spotted Snow, who had stopped at a corner to speak to a friend of his, Jim McKeegan. As the two conversed, Bowes came out of a cigar store and walked up to Snow, again demanding the money. "It's a half day's pay and I want the money," Bowes said angrily. Once again, Snow told Bowes that he should go speak to the owner of the factory on the matter. Bowes, tired of being jerked around, finally let loose, reportedly striking Snow several times.

Snow then pulled a revolver from his pocket and fired three shots, two of which found the mark. Bowes slumped to the ground, having been hit in the chest and the stomach. Snow dropped the handgun, mumbled something to a crowd of people who had gathered, and walked away. The wounded Bowes was taken to, of all places, an undertaking establishment, where he was then taken by ambulance to his home. He died a short time later, having never regained consciousness.

Snow was later arrested and held at the Raymond Street Jail. There was worry about retaliation and revenge for Bowes' murder—Bowes' father was a New York City policeman, and there was talk that Snow might be in extreme danger.

In the long run, it didn't matter since Snow would eventually be released from jail in March due to failing health. He died from heart disease at the Brooklyn Hospital on March 10.

Bowes, who lived with his wife and two children at 181 India Street at the time of his death, was laid to rest at the Calvary Cemetery in Brooklyn (Section 18, Range 29, Plot E, Grave 7).

The half-day's pay over which Bowes lost his life was 80¢.

John "Larry" McLean

Lean and lanky at 6'5", 225 pounds, Larry McLean was one of the tallest catchers of all time. He played 13 years in the majors, making a big target for pitchers.

Unfortunately, he also made a big habit of drinking. So-called "demon rum" was the fuel for most of his escapades on and off the field, and it seemed that no matter how hard he tried, the monkey on his back got the best of him.

Born John Bannerman McLean on July 18, 1881, in Fredericton, New Brunswick, Canada, he was supposedly given the nickname Larry due to his resemblance to Napoleon "Larry"

Lajoie. That was about the only similarity between the two. While Lajoie was a standup citizen, McLean was just the opposite. Although never intentionally mean-spirited, drink often turned McLean nasty.

He started his drinking habits at a fairly young age, and they continued on through his short life, which saw him get into more and more scraps and situations due to his addiction. McLean played in places such as St. John and Fredericton in Canada before he made his debut with the

Boston Americans on April 26, 1901. After a short stint in Beantown, he returned to Canada to play for Halifax. In 1903 he played with the Cubs for one game, staying with that organization until he was sent to the Cardinals in a rather historic trade.

On December 12, 1903, McLean was part of a two-for-two swap of players. He and Jack Taylor were sent to the Cardinals for Mordecai Brown and Jack O'Neill. What the Cardinals were thinking when they made the trade, one can only surmise. Brown went on to Chicago and an eventual Hall of Fame career. McLean lasted 24 games and was soon sold to the Portland Beavers of the Pacific Coast League.

McLean did fairly well in Portland, helping to lead them to a pennant. He stayed with Portland through mid-September of 1906, when his contract was purchased by Cincinnati. With Cincinnati he became one of the better receivers in the National League. Though his stay in Cincinnati would not be a smooth one—as it would not be in any place he played—he still played a good game of ball despite his demons.

Throughout his career, managers and executives tried everything to get him on the wagon. At times, their efforts seemed to work, but he always reverted back to bad habits. Still, he was one of the more popular players in the majors, always well received by friends and opposing players alike.

Suspended for not playing an exhibition game in September 1912, Mclean was offered to several minor league teams by Manager Hank O'Day. But there were no takers. In October rumors circulated that McLean would box former major league catcher Charlie "Boss" Schmidt in a 10-round bout during the World Series. Nothing came of it, luckily for McLean. "Long Larry" might have gotten his clock cleaned by Schmidt, who was a hard-as-nails catcher—he once sparred with Jack Johnson and once pummeled Ty Cobb, although the two would become good friends later on.

Finally, McLean was sold to the Cardinals, signing a contract on January 23, 1913. Before he even got a chance to play a game in St. Louis, he broke his arm breaking up a fight. He and his brother were at a billiard hall when the fight started. Larry attempted to intercede when he was hit below the elbow on the left arm by a pool cue. His brother and several other men were taken downtown and arraigned. McLean's arm took a bit of time to heal, but he was still able to play in 48 games for St. Louis, where he batted .270.

The power of liquor strengthened its vice grip on McLean. Frank Bancroft, business manager of the Reds, once asked McLean, "Have you had any lunch?" to which Mclean replied, "Not a drop."

Reds manager Miller Huggins, an old teammate and friend of his from the Cincinnati days, invested a bit of time in McLean early on while his arm was mending. He convinced McLean to take up the practice of drinking water, lots of it. Huggins knew that the notoriously hot and humid St. Louis summers could be murder on a ballplayer, especially one that loved to imbibe.

Though not a cure, the drinking of water did help for a while, until he supposedly got an upset stomach from the practice.

Still, Larry played a good game of ball for his old teammate and was no trouble in the clubhouse. On August 6, he was traded to the Giants for Doc Crandall. John McGraw obtained him as a backup to Chief Meyers. The trade soon proved to be a very fruitful one for New York—McLean batted a lusty .330 in the 30 games he appeared in. He was called into emergency service before Game 2 of the World Series to replace Chief Meyers, who had broken a finger in practice. Mclean did not disappoint, batting .500 for the series and going 6–12 with 2 RBIs. Though the Athletics beat the Giants in five games, McLean could be proud of his work in the Series. He stayed with the Giants until June of 1915, when he was involved in an altercation with several members of the club. McLean had been involved in a drinking episode in Chicago and was suspended on June 8. Originally, McGraw issued a suspension for the remainder of the season, but he cut it down to 10 days. During that time rumors flew that Larry would sign a contract with a Federal League team. The Giants then moved on to St. Louis. McLean, accompanied by a few companions, entered the lobby of the Buckingham Hotel and began voraciously accusing scout Dick Kinsella of recommending him for suspension.

A full-scale brawl ensued, with McLean getting two chairs broken over him as McGraw, Kinsella, and six of his teammates joined in the fray. In the end, McLean ran out of the lobby into an auto filled with women and begged for protection. Afterward, McGraw stated: "I'm done with Larry McLean. He'll never play with New York again." He was, of course, true to his word. McLean was released on July 21.

Later that season McLean played in an exhibition game between New Jersey's Bergen County All-Stars and the Brooklyn Robins. On December 19, it was reported in the newspapers that he had signed a contract with the Reds for the next season. But

McLean would never play again in the majors, unfortunately—manager Christy Mathewson had little tolerance for the out-of-control catcher.

In March 1917 the *Chicago Daily Tribune* reported that McLean was hired as an extra to work in a new Fox film starring Valeska Suratt, who was known as "the Vampire Woman." In January of 1919, newspapers reported that McLean had fallen asleep in a Turkish bath in Newark, New Jersey, and as a result received severe burns about the back and legs.

On March 24, 1921, McLean was out drinking with a gentleman by the name of John F. "Jack" McCarthy at a near-beer saloon in the south end of Boston. The two men had been there the previous night and had caused considerable trouble with the bartender, chasing him away. McCarthy, who was out on parole, had a fairly extensive rap sheet. The two men became involved in an argument with a bartender by the name of James J. Connor.

Apparently, McLean asked Connor for some cigarettes, and when Connor refused, "Big Larry" got abusive. Threatening to beat up Connor, he made a move for the bar with McCarthy in tow. As McCarthy began helping McLean climb over the bar, Connor pulled a revolver and shot both men in the stomach at point-blank range. McLean, mortally wounded, staggered out the door and fell to the sidewalk. McCarthy made his way out of the saloon, traveling about 100 yards up the street before he collapsed.

McLean was taken to a local hospital where he was pronounced dead on arrival.

McCarthy was taken to the hospital by auto where he remained in critical condition. Connor was arrested and charged with murder and assault with attempt to injure. McCarthy received several blood transfusions from his mother and brother, allowing him to live long enough to marry his 19-year-old fiancée. He died five days later, on March 29.

As for James Connor, he got off relatively easy. Pleading to a lesser charge of manslaughter, he was sentenced to a year in jail.

McLean, who was married, was buried at the Cedar Grove Cemetery in Dorchester, Massachusetts.

Len Koenecke

Was it a severe Jekyll-and-Hyde reaction to alcohol? Maybe it was a case of temporary insanity brought on after being sent home by the Dodgers for the remainder of the season. Did extreme depression turn into a determined death wish? Whatever the case, Len Koenecke wound up getting his head smashed in by a pilot as he tried to grab controls in the cockpit of a commercial airplane flying from Detroit to Buffalo on September 15, 1935.

Big things were expected from Koenecke and his teammates in the 1935 season. The left-handed–hitting Koenecke, recently acquired from Buffalo, stood out for the Dodgers in 1934, batting .323 with 14 homers and 73 RBIs. Brooklyn was expected by many to rise to first place in their division. But the Dodgers tanked, finishing fifth at 70–83. Except for Van Mungo, Watty Clark, and Ray Benge, the pitching faltered and the hitting was inconsistent. Koenecke slumped to .283 with only four homers and 27 RBIs in 100 games.

On that fateful day in September 1935, while the club was in St. Louis to face the Cardinals, Koenecke, Les Munns, and Bobby Barr were all sent home for the remainder of the season by Dodgers manager Casey Stengel. The move was supposedly made in order to bring in some younger talent.

Koenecke, naturally, was depressed. He and his two teammates took an American Airlines flight first to Chicago. From there they switched planes. Their new pilot, Joseph Hammer, had his hands full with Koenecke, who had tried a bit of self-medicating and, once inebriated, fought with members of the crew and challenged another passenger to a fight.

Both Munns and Barr tried to control Koenecke, who was ordered off the plane in Detroit, part of his fare refunded. Koenecke then booked a flight to Buffalo. Halfway through the trip, Koenecke, sitting in the front seat, made the bizarre move of grabbing for the controls.

The pilot, William Mulqueeney, convinced Koenecke to trade places with his assistant, Irwin Davis. Koenecke then began trying to grab Mulqueeney from behind, causing the plane to veer. At only 2,000 feet, it was a combustible situation. Davis tried to calm Koenecke down but he again started up after about 10 minutes. Davis finally was forced to grab a fire extinguisher to beat back Koenecke. Eventually, Mulqueeney got a hold of it and fatally battered Koenecke.

The plane flew off course and had to be landed at the Long Branch Race Track near Toronto. When police arrived, they found Koenecke dead, his skull fractured and face smashed in. The cabin of the plane was splattered with blood.

Davis and Mulqueeney were initially charged with manslaughter. The coroner reported that Koenecke died from a brain hemorrhage. Of the incident, Mulqueeney said, "If he's dead, then I am the one who killed him. My God, I wish I could take those blows back."

Mulqueeney and Davis were both freed on September 20 by Magistrate Douglas Keith, who ruled that the two of them acted in self-defense.

When news of his death reached the Dodgers, the team went into shock. Sam Leslie, one of Koenecke's good friends on the club, was most shaken and wept openly. Casey Stengel was shocked and ordered the team to wear black arm bands for the remainder of the season.

Koenecke's body was sent back to Friendship, Wisconsin, where it was laid to rest in the Repose Cemetery. He left a wife and a young daughter.

Luis Marquez

Luis Marquez played in the Negro Leagues with the Homestead Grays and Baltimore Elite Giants before finding himself at the center of a contract dispute between Cleveland Indians general manager Bill Veeck and New York Yankees general manager George Weiss.

Both claimed they had signed him along with Negro Leaguer Art Wilson.

In 1949 league commissioner Happy Chandler split the difference in the protest, awarding Marquez to Cleveland and Wilson to the Yanks.

Marquez was never able to harness the potential he flashed in the Negro and minor leagues. He was eventually recommended by Braves scout Johnny Moore, and picked up by Boston on November 16, 1950. He made his major league debut on April 18, 1951, when Braves manager Billy Southworth sent him in to pinch run for Jim Wilson in the top half of the ninth inning. Marquez would later score on a three-run homer by Sam "the Jet" Jethroe later in the inning off Giants pitcher Dave Koslo.

It was an eventful rookie debut in an otherwise disappointing season for Marquez, who went on to bat only .197 in 68 games. After two more years in the minors, he was picked up by the Chicago Cubs on November 30, 1953, and later traded to Pittsburgh for Hal Rice the following season, where he appeared in only 31 games that season, batting .095.

He toiled in the minors from 1955 to 1961, most notably in the PCL with his old team, the Portland Beavers, becoming one of the team's leaders, playing outfield and first base and showing off his power and speed.

After his career was over, he became a Caribbean scout for the Montreal Expos in 1969 and 1970. On March 1, 1988, Marquez became involved in an argument with his son-in-law, Luis Ramos, 45, at his home in Aguadilla, Puerto Rico. Ramos pulled a handgun and shot the 62-year-old Marquez twice, killing him.

Ramos fled, but was later apprehended and charged with first-degree murder and violation of firearms laws.

Luke Easter

If not for his race, which confined him to the Negro Leagues until he was all but past his prime in his mid-30s, Luke Easter would have enjoyed a long and fruitful major league career. Still, in all, Easter wowed fans with his tape measure home runs during his brief five-year stint in the majors.

"Likeable Luke," as he was sometimes called due to his genial personality, spent most of his playing days as an outfielder for the Homestead Grays, becoming one of the Negro Leagues' established stars. He batted .376 his final season there in 1948.

By the time Cleveland Indians general manager Bill Veeck purchased him from the Grays, Easter was nursing two bad knees. He made his debut on August 11, 1949, in a game against the Chicago White Sox. He pinch hit for Indians pitcher Sam Zoldak in the eighth inning and grounded out with the score tied 5–5 with a runner on third. The Indians won the game 6–5 in 12 innings.

From 1950 to 1952, the left-handed hitting Easter slugged out 27, 27, and 31 homers, respectively, and twice drove in more than 100 RBIs during that span. Playing mostly first base, he was named the American League Player of the Year by *The Sporting News* in 1952. Injuries caught up with the big fellow in the 1953 season, when he broke his foot, and he was limited to only six appearances in 1954.

In mid-October of 1954 his contract was sold by the Cleveland Indians to the Indianapolis Indians of the American

Association. Cleveland also sold the contract of catcher Mickey Grasso. The Indians, in return, bought the contracts of three Indy players, including the soon-to-be star Rocky Colavito. Easter did not play any games for Indianapolis—he was sold to Charleston of the American Association in early January of 1955.

While at Charleston, Luke was suspended two times, the second time due to four counts of insubordination, including throwing baseballs to kids in the stands from the bullpen in St. Paul, Minneapolis. Easter left the club for a while as a result of the suspension. Even with all the trouble he got into, he still smashed 30 homers and drove in 101. The Buffalo Bisons of the International League bought his contract in October 1955. Easter gladly accepted the move and, over the next three seasons, he clocked another 113 homers for the Bisons.

As always, wherever he went, he became a fan favorite. Buffalo released him in mid-season of 1959, but he immediately found work with the Rochester Red Wings. He played several

seasons with the Wings, occasionally showing his old flashes of power.

On August 17, 1963, the Red Wings held Luke Easter Night. Before 7,434 fans, Easter confessed to being 10 years older than his listed birthday of August 4, 1921. "I'm really 52," he told the crowd.

In his retirement, Easter dabbled in politics and coaching. In 1965 he ran for supervisor in Rochester's Third Ward on the Republican ticket.

In 1969 he became a batting coach for a season with the Cleveland Indians.

Easter was employed by TRW Inc. for almost 15 years, working as a steward for the Aircraft Workers Alliance, a union at the TRW plant in Euclid, Ohio. On Thursday, March 29, 1979, Easter, as he did every Thursday, went to a local bank to cash payroll checks. Usually he had a policeman accompany him, but on this day, for some reason, he did not. After he cashed the checks, he was accosted in the parking lot of the Cleveland Trust Company by two men who had been stalking him and were well aware of the bounty that Easter was carrying. They proceeded to rob him, shooting him in the chest with a sawed-off shotgun and .38 caliber revolver and fleeing with about $40,000 in cash. The two thugs led police in a high-speed chase and were eventually captured after a brief gun battle.

Easter was pronounced dead on arrival at the hospital—a tragic and useless end to a truly nice man who was able to hit balls as far as anyone in major league history.

Likeable Luke was buried at the Highland Park Cemetery (Section 16, Lot 297, East Half, Grave 1) in Cleveland, Ohio.

Lyman Bostock

Lyman Bostock was one of the major up-and-coming stars when he was tragically shot to death in September of 1978 while visiting family in Gary, Indiana.

Born in Birmingham, Alabama, and raised in Los Angeles, he was the son of former Negro Leagues player Lyman Bostock Sr. He attended Manuel Arts High School and then Cal State–Northridge University. Bostock originally signed with the Minnesota Twins, batting over .300 in his three seasons in the Twin Cities, finishing with a .336 batting average in his final year while challenging for the batting title. Playing out his option with the Twins, he signed a lucrative deal with the California Angels.

Bostock got off to a terrible start with the Angels in 1978, going 2 for 37. He was so disappointed in his performance that he asked Angels owner Gene Autry not to pay him his salary for April, feeling he didn't deserve it. Autry paid Lyman anyway, and the thoughtful Bostock donated the money to charity. In an age where many ballplayers were looked upon as selfish, Bostock's gesture was an incredible rarity.

Bostock liked to spend his summers with family in Gary, Indiana, and would often visit with his uncle, Tom Turner, whenever the Twins or Angels played in Chicago.

Coming off of a 2 for 4 day at the plate against the Chicago White Sox, Bostock was at Turner's place on Saturday, September 23, 1978, when he decided to arrange a visit with an old family friend, Joan Hawkins, who was Turner's godchild. Bostock used to read to Hawkins and her sister when they were children. Turner, who hadn't seen them in years, set up what was an enjoyable reunion that day.

As they were leaving Hawkins' home, Joan and her sister asked Turner if he could drop them off at a friend's house. Joan was only 22 at the time. She was estranged from her husband and was going by the name Joan Smith. As the car came to a halt at the corner of Fifth and Jackson Avenues, Joan's husband stepped out of a car and pointed a .410 gauge shotgun at the open window of the car and fired. Bostock was hit in the side of the head. Hawkins was also hit, but less seriously. Bostock's uncle immediately rushed the mortally wounded Bostock to St. Mary's Medical Center. He died about two and a half hours later. His body was taken back to California for burial at the Inglewood Park Cemetery (Parkview Section, Lot 342, Grave D).

Miguel Fuentes

Miguel "Mickey" Fuentes was on the verge of a promising big league career when he was shot and killed at age 22 during a bar fight in Puerto Rico.

Fuentes made his major league debut for Seattle against the Chicago White Sox on September 1, 1969. He defeated the Chicago White Sox and starter Gary Peters by the score of 5–1. In eight games he was 1–3 with a 5.19 ERA, and Mariners' management felt that he only needed more experience. They had plans to move him to either Double A or Triple A the next season.

But there would be no next season.

Fuentes played with Caguas of the Puerto Rican League that winter, pitching mostly in a relief role. Seattle was toying with the idea of making him a reliever, hence his work from the bullpen. Fuentes was just a few weeks away from leaving for spring training when he went to a bar located in his hometown of Loiza Aldea, about 20 miles east of San Juan. He was hanging out with several teenagers when a fight broke out. Shots were fired, and Fuentes was struck three times, once in the abdomen, once in the right hand, and once in the left thigh close to the femoral artery. He went into shock. He was taken to the Fajardo District Hospital, where emergency surgery was performed, but he didn't make it.

A suspect was arrested and held on open charges of murder in the case.

Tim McKeithan

Emmett "Tim" McKeithan pitched in 10 games over parts of three seasons for the Philadelphia Athletics. After starring at

Duke University, he signed with the Philadelphia Athletics in 1932. Starting out with Albany, he made his major league debut on July 21, 1932, in a 5–3 loss to the St. Louis Browns. The win by St. Louis ended an 11-game losing streak.

McKeithan was among a host of young pitchers Philly manager Connie Mack was putting his faith in to bring the A's back to prominence. McKeithan never panned out. Control issues were the main reason he failed in the bigs, where his short life-time record was 1–1 with a 7.20 era.

In the minors, McKeithan pitched for the Montreal Royals of the International League, Syracuse, and Albany, among others. In his later years, he operated a rest home in Forest City, North Carolina, and was also a salesman. He resided at 300 Morgan Street in Forest City. On August 20, 1969, McKeithan was fatally shot in the stomach with a .32 caliber pistol by a man named Britt Carroll Teseniar. The incident occurred at an office building in Forest City.

McKeithan was 61. He was buried on September 9 at the Concord Baptist Church Cemetery in Bostic, North Carolina.

Tony Solaita

Tolia "Tony" Solaita was the fourth of seven children born to Tulafono and Lilia Solaita, in the village of Nu'uuli, on the main island of Tutuila in American Samoa. He grew up playing a Samoan version of cricket called "kirikiti," which used a three-sided bat.

At the age of eight, Solaita moved with his family to Hawaii, where he was introduced to baseball. His father, who was a marine, then moved the family to the U.S. mainland, eventually settling near San Francisco around 1960. An all-around great athlete, Solaita blossomed into an exceptional football and base-ball player in high school. He went on to attend Mira Costa College, where he was signed to a contract by Yankees scout Dolph Camilli for $1,000 a month with a $500 bonus.

"He's built like a fireplug," noted Camilli, who suspected that the stocky, powerfully built left-handed hitter would be a good fit for Yankee Stadium's short right-field porch. After several years in the minors, Solaita had his breakout season in 1968, batting .322, with 49 homers and 122 RBIs for the High Point–Thomasville club of the Carolina League. The gaudy numbers helped him garner the Topps Minor League Player of the Year award.

He made his major league debut with the Yankees on Monday, September 16, 1968, stepping in for Mickey Mantle at first base against the Detroit Tigers in a 9–1 loss. The win by Detroit stopped a 10-game winning streak by the Yanks and also clinched a tie for the American League pennant for the Tigers.

Solaita played the last four innings and went 0 for 1, a strike-out. He was sent back to Triple A the next year, spending the next four seasons there. Always feeling like he never got a fair chance to play at the big-league level while with New York, he was finally traded on February 28, 1973, to the Pirates for George Kopacz. Solaita played for the Charlestown Charlies of the International League until he was drafted by the Kansas City Royals on December 3, 1973, in the Rule V draft for a sum of $25,000. With the Royals, he became John Mayberry's back-up at first base and excelled under the leadership of manager Jack McKeon.

He stayed with the Royals even after McKeon was replaced by Whitey Herzog, although his playing time slowly diminished. He was finally put on waivers in July 1976, eventually being picked up by the California Angels on July 14. Kansas City won the American League West just two months later. For the rest of his major league career, which saw him make brief stops with Montreal and Toronto, he was relegated to a pinch-hitting and backup role.

He began a new career in Japan in 1979, signing a deal with the Nippon Ham Fighters. As the Ham Fighters' designated hitter, he displayed amazing power, once hitting four homers in a game and breaking the club record for single-season home runs. After four successful and often alienating years in Japan— foreign players frequently did not feel at home there—Tony retired at the age of 37. He moved back to American Samoa, where he eventually worked as head of the American Samoan Parks and Recreation Department and kept his hand in the game, coaching youth baseball.

In 1990 he was living in Nu'uuli when he began having problems with a man named Harry "Tapu" Taylor. Taylor, who had migrated from San Francisco, was a transient who had claimed that land that Solaita owned was rightfully his. Solaita had established a meat market business some years earlier on a plot of land that was granted to him by Samoan chiefs. Taylor asked the chiefs to intercede in his favor and give him the land, which was originally communally held. When the decision went against him, Solaita was allowed to keep the land and building that was on it.

Taylor turned malicious and began vandalizing the property. The good-natured Solaita was not inclined to have a fight with a total stranger, yet things came to a head one Saturday night on February 10, 1990. After discovering that lumber he owned behind his store had been vandalized, Solaita confronted Taylor. The two men argued. As Solaita turned to walk away, he was shot in the back by Taylor with a .38 revolver. Solaita was found a short time later and was pronounced dead on arrival at the LBJ Tropical Medical Center. He was just 43 years old.

News of his death brought sadness to the people of American Samoa. Solaita had become a bit of a folk hero on the island. He had achieved something no one in their nation had ever done before—he played major league baseball. His killer, Taylor, plea bargained and was released after serving only seven years of his sentence.

Solaita was buried outside his home in his native village.

Mother Watson

Mother Watson's brief lifetime record is in dispute. *The Baseball Encyclopedia* lists him with a 0–1 record with two games started over a nine-day stay in the majors with the 1887 Cincinnati Red Stockings of the American Association.

But two box scores in the *Chicago Tribune,* one from May 20, 1887, and another eight days later, show Walter L. Watson winning his debut outing against the Brooklyn Grays before dropping a 9–5 loss to the Philadelphia Athletics.

So, maybe he was 1–1.

One thing is certain about Watson: he was involved in an argument in a saloon in his hometown of Middleport, Ohio, on November 23, 1898, and was shot and killed. He was buried at Middleport Hill Cemetery.

TB or Not to Be

Perhaps the most famous ballplayer to succumb to tuberculosis (TB) was the legendary Christy Mathewson. Sadly, he was close to controlling his first bout with TB after going to a "cure house" in Saranac, New York, where the pristine, oxygen-rich air of the Adirondack Mountains was thought to have healed him.

His premature return to Boston to take a job caused his demise.

Another Hall of Fame pitcher, Rube Waddell, and prolific umpire Hank O'Day were among the many others taken by the cruel and insidious disease.

During the 19th and early 20th centuries, TB—also called "consumption" and "phthisis" (Greek for consumption)—was the leading cause of death in the United States. In its victims, TB usually progresses from a dry, persistent cough to fatigue, night sweats, and finally a general wasting away, with acute hemorrhages of blood from the lungs. Typically, but not exclusively, TB is a disease of the lungs caused by the bacillus *Myobacterium tuberculosis.*

Tuberculosis is the most common infectious disease in the world today. Luckily, 90 percent of the nearly two billion infected on the planet carry only a latent form of TB that is controlled by the body's immune system and is not contagious.

Still, active TB strikes down 2–3 million annually worldwide.

Prior to the 1940s, there were no reliable drugs available for the treatment of TB. Most often, doctors advised their patients to rest, eat well, and exercise outdoors. Those who survived their first bout with the disease were often haunted by severe recurrences that destroyed any hope for an active life. It was estimated that, at the turn of the century, 450 Americans died of TB every day, most between ages 15 and 44.

At that time, the vast majority of the victims were the poor in urban settings, where crowded and often filthy living conditions provided a fertile environment for the airborne spread of the disease. In the days before treatment, victims of TB were often stigmatized and ostracized. They were called derisive names such as "Lunger," and the terrifying threat of the contagion made the tubercular invalid an "untouchable"—a complete outcast. Many lost their jobs because of the panic they created among coworkers. Some landlords refused to house them. Hotel proprietors, forced to consider the safety of other guests, turned them away. All but rejected by society, TB victims gathered in secluded TB hospitals and headed for treatment to sanatoriums, where large percentages of them died.

Doctors today can successfully treat TB with a combination of antibiotics, provided the medicine is administered for a prolonged period.

Christy Mathewson

Perhaps the most famous baseball player to ever die of the dread disease, Christy Mathewson was the game's first 20th-century idol.

Winner of 373 games, holder of numerous records, and arguably the best pitcher of his era, Mathewson was a man of

great character. Smart and handsome, he was adored by fans. His
teammates and opponents respected
his competitive edge.

In the end, his incredible drive
and will to succeed may have caused
his demise when he prematurely
returned to work when convalescing
from TB.

Many people have surmised that
Mathewson's accidental exposure to
poison gas during a training exercise
in France during World War I weakened his lungs to a point where they
became more susceptible to the

Baseball card image courtesy of the Library of Congress.

disease. In the army, he served in the chemical warfare unit with
his buddy, Ty Cobb.

Upon his return from the war, he went back to the game as
a coach for the Giants but had to retire from the game after just
one season when he learned that he had contracted TB—
the same disease that killed his brother Henry a few years
earlier. Mathewson went for treatment at Saranac Lake, New
York, where Dr. Edward Livingston Trudeau had set up the
famous Adirondack Cottage Sanatorium in 1885 to help treat
consumptives.

Known to many as the "Adirondack Cottage Cure," a
regimen of diet and exercise was prescribed amid the pristine,
oxygen-rich mountain air. Mathewson's health improved greatly
during his long stay there, and had he continued on with his
course of treatment, he most surely would have been able to
enjoy a long and healthy life.

Unfortunately, his competitive baseball juices got the best of
him, and he took the position of president of the Boston Braves in
1923. Working in the dirty air of an urban area in cramped and

much more stressful conditions, TB took hold of him again. By the spring of 1925, his health had begun to take a step backward, and he returned to Saranac Lake in early July in the hopes of once again finding a miracle in the mountain air.

It was too little, too late.

By that fall, Mathewson was bedridden and died on Wednesday night, October 7, 1925, with his wife Jane by his side.

News of his death spread like a somber cloud, enveloping the baseball world that should have instead been celebrating the World Series between Washington and Pittsburgh. "Matty" was mourned like no player before him. When news of his passing reached two of his closest friends in the game, Walter Johnson and Ty Cobb, both men were driven to tears. Cobb spoke the following poignant words: "He was my friend and I shall miss him dearly. You couldn't help but love Matty."

Mathewson was laid to rest at the Lewisburg City Cemetery in Lewisburg, Pennsylvania, in the area known as the Path of Love.

Alex Farmer

New York City native Alex Johnson Farmer appeared in 12 games for the 1908 Brooklyn Dodgers, batting only .167. In his final game on September 29—a 5–2 loss to the Boston Doves at Boston's South

Photograph from Frank Russo's private collection.

End Grounds—seven Boston players stole bases, prompting the hometown paper, the *Boston Globe,* to note, "The home team won on its base running; Farmer, the catcher, showing wretched form in throwing to bases." Not the most memorable swan song in baseball history, although Farmer did smack a double during the game.

After his career, he took up the occupation of plumber and was living at 2189 Morris Avenue in the Bronx with his wife, Charlotte, when he died from pulmonary tuberculosis on March 5, 1920.

His body was taken to Kensico Cemetery (Section 47, Lot 5856, Grave 2) in Valhalla, New York.

Amos Cross

The oldest of the three baseball-playing brothers, Amos Cross caught for the American Association's Louisville Eclipse club from 1885 to 1887 before his promising career was cut short by consumption in 1887.

In June of that year, Cross was already showing signs of the disease—he began suffering from hemorrhages. Due to his sickness, he was only able to appear in eight games total.

He accrued a lifetime average of .268 with one home run and 56 RBIs in 117 career games.

His brother, Lave, was a star for 21 major league seasons and played with four Philadelphia teams in four different leagues, while his other brother, Frank, had a one-game cup of coffee with the Cleveland Naps in 1901.

Both Lave and Frank felt that Amos was the most talented baseball player in the family and was sure to have a long career had he lived longer.

Amos wound up having a rather embarrassing public break-up with his live-in fiancée, Cora, also known as Viola Pauline Floyd, after having an affair with the sister of a friend. Amos met Cora in Memphis, Tennessee, in 1885, and they engaged and eventually moved to Cleveland. When Cross went to Memphis in the spring of 1887, he stayed at a boarding house with a friend who, it just so happened, had a young, attractive sister. Cross became smitten by the young girl.

When Cora came down to Memphis to join her man, she found out soon enough that he had taken a liking to someone else. This prompted Cora to demand he return a diamond ring she had given him. When Cross refused, Cora sued him in magistrate's court. Cora also demanded back money that she had loaned him to buy a horse. The suit was eventually dropped when Cross was unable to get a refund back for the animal.

After the mess, Cross went back to his residence at 668 Clark Street in Cleveland, which was located in the 39th Ward. He died there on July 16, 1888, and was buried in the Joseph Cross Plot in the Riverside Cemetery in Cleveland.

It is not known whether Cora showed up at the funeral.

Michael "Bub" McAtee

Born in March of 1845 in Troy, New York, Michael James "Bub" McAtee was one of the original members of the Haymakers baseball club of Troy, a collection of stars who competed against other top-flight baseball teams throughout the East.

McAtee joined them in 1866, where he gained a reputation as a top-rate infielder. He played first base so well that a New York paper wrote that "he played the position better than it had been filled hitherto."

Over the course of his career, he accrued a lifetime average of .246 on 65 hits. He collected 11 doubles, three triples, and 25 RBIs in 264 at-bats.

Cross retired from pro ball after the Haymakers dropped out of the recently formed National Association at the end of the 1872 season. McAtee continued to play local ball, enjoying the game almost up to the time of his death. He became a successful saloon keeper.

He was stricken with consumption and died on October 18, 1876, at the age of 31. At his death, he was lauded as "a generous and warm friend, and his early death is deeply regretted."

He was laid to rest at the St. John Cemetery in Troy, New York.

Cy Bentley

Clytus G. "Cy" Bentley had the dubious distinction of becoming one of the first professional league players to die from consumption.

A native of Connecticut, Bentley was primarily a pitcher who twirled in 18 games for the 1872 Middletown Mansfields of the National Association, posting a 2–15 record. He also appeared in seven games in the outfield.

In late 1872 he contracted pulmonary tuberculosis, eventually dying at his home in Middletown, Connecticut, on February 26, 1873.

Hugh Campbell

Born in Ireland and a resident of New Jersey from the age of four when his father, Patrick, and mother, Mary, emigrated to the United States, Hugh Campbell played for Jersey's entry in the National Association, the 1873 Elizabeth Resolutes.

Joining them from the nearby Irvington club, Campbell, originally a right-handed pitcher, made the transition to outfielder with relative ease. The Resolutes' number-one man in the box for their only professional season, Campbell sported a dreadful 2–16 mark for a club that went 2–21.

Campbell also made appearances in the outfield, at second base, and at shortstop. After the Resolutes closed up shop, Hughey, as he was known to his friends, continued to play ball for a time, eventually giving up the profession to take on a trade.

Campbell was residing at his brother's home on North Avenue in Elizabeth when he passed away as a result of pulmonary TB on March 1, 1881, at 3:00 in the morning.

He had been confined to his bed the last three months of his life. Campbell's brother was Mike Campbell, who also played on the Resolutes. Interestingly, both brothers debuted in the majors on April 28, 1873, and played their final games on July 23, 1873.

Hugh Campbell was laid to rest at the Holy Sepulchre Cemetery in East Orange, New Jersey.

Mike Chartak

Bad luck seemed to follow Mike Chartak during his career.

Born in Brooklyn to Russian-immigrant parents and raised in Carbondale, Pennsylvania, Mike Chartak gained stamina and muscle from working in the local coal mines.

After graduating high school, he was signed by the Yankees after they saw him play with a semi-pro team in 1935. He toiled in the minors from 1935 to 1939. Called up by the Yanks on September 8, 1940, to replace an injured Tommy Henrich, he made his debut on September 13 in an 8–0 loss to the Detroit Tigers.

Pinch hitting for pitcher Steve Sundra in the eighth inning, he weakly grounded to Dick Bartell at shortstop. Chartak batted .133 in 11 games in his first stint.

Sent to Kansas City of the American Association in 1941, he appeared in five more games for New York in 1942 before Yanks management gave up on him. Fearing that he would never again be the same player he was before an ankle injury suffered in the minor leagues, he was sold to the Washington Senators on May 10. His stay in D.C. was short; he was shipped to the St. Louis Browns on June 7 along with another former Yankee, Steve Sundra, in exchange for a slumping Roy Cullenbine and pitcher Bill Trotter.

Chartak remained with St. Louis, where he was used in the outfield and at first base, for the rest of his career. He was 0 for 2 in pinch-hitting appearances during the 1944 World Series.

In the off-season of 1944, Chartak began to feel weak. Although he was scheduled to make the Browns out of spring training, he was in no shape to play ball. In April, just before his birthday, he checked himself in to the Oakdale Sanitarium in Cedar Rapids, Iowa, for an examination. Tests revealed that he had contracted pulmonary tuberculosis in his left lung.

His career was effectively over at the age of 27.

Although retired, Chartak did have hopes of making a comeback. He remained property of the Browns for the next two seasons until he was finally released on May 5, 1947.

In between hospital treatments, Chartak would work on and off as a bartender over the next 20 years. He died on July 25, 1967, at the Oakdale Sanitarium in Cedar Rapids from the effects of pulmonary TB at the age of 51.

A widower, he was buried at the Mount Calvary Cemetery in Cedar Rapids on July 28.

Jim Devlin

Jim Devlin pitched nearly all of the Louisville team's games in the National League's first two seasons of existence. He strung together 1,181 innings and seemed to be on the road to stardom when disaster struck.

In 1877 word leaked out to National League president William Hulbert that games were being thrown by members of the Louisville club. An investigation was launched, and eventually Devlin and three of his teammates were implicated.

The games in question had cost the Colonels what seemed to be a locked-up pennant. It was discovered that several players had been walking around with expensive diamond stick pins and were throwing around money. At first Devlin denied the charges, then he finally broke down and admitted to giving in to gamblers. He blamed the cheap Louisville owners as well as the gamblers for his plight. The Louisville owners were not willing to pay an honest wage, according to Devlin, and so he was driven into the arms of the gamblers by "cheapskate" owners.

Though National League president William Hulbert liked Devlin, he had no recourse but to ban him and his fellow teammates from baseball for life. Devlin did try to get reinstated, even writing legendary manager Harry Wright, begging him for help.

No help came. Driven from baseball, Devlin finally found work as a Philadelphia policeman.

He died from consumption on October 10, 1883, and was buried in an unmarked grave at the New Cathedral Cemetery (Section M, Range 5, Lot 41, 2nd East) in Philadelphia.

Fred Kommers

The son of Frank and Lora Kommers, Chicago native Fred Kommers started off in the Chicago City League in 1907 with teams such as the Elgin Nats and Anson's Colts.

Kommers made his major league debut with Pittsburgh on June 25, 1913, in a 9–1 victory over St. Louis. He played center field and went 2 for 5 in the contest. He batted .232 in 40 games total that season for the "Bucs," who released him to Columbus of the American Association on August 11.

Just before the 1914 season, Kommers jumped to the St. Louis Terriers of the Federal League. On May 27, in a game at Baltimore, Kommers was involved in an incident when he kicked an umpire in the side. The game was called for Baltimore by the score of 4–3 during the bottom of the sixth inning.

Kommers batted .306 in 76 games and played a decent outfield. He surprisingly was "loaned" by St. Louis to the Baltimore Terrapins on August 26 and remained under contract by the Federal League for the following season even though he played in the minors.

He was finally given release from his contract in January 1916.

Kommers continued to play minor league and semi-pro ball into the 1920s, eventually retiring to work as a superintendent of construction for the Cullinan Manufacturing Company.

He died from pulmonary tuberculosis at a sanitarium in Chicago on June 14, 1943, at the age of 57. He was survived by his wife, the former Lela Palmer, with whom he lived at 33 West 112th Place, a son, Fred Jr., and a daughter-in-law, Elizabeth. He was buried at the Cedar Park Cemetery in Blue Island, Illinois, on June 17, 1943.

Pat Newnam

Pat Newnam had a long and productive career as a player, manager, umpire, and executive. Mostly a career minor leaguer in the Texas League, he also played 123 games over two seasons for the St. Louis Browns (1910–1911).

Newnam started his career in the Texas League with San Antonio in 1903. The next season, at the age of 24, he got his first chance at managing with Victoria, Texas. After stints in the South Atlantic and Pacific Coast Leagues, he returned to the Texas League with San Antonio and Houston. It was while with Houston that he was drafted by the Browns in the fall of 1909. After his stint with the Browns, he was sent back to Houston, where he became manager, remaining in that capacity until 1919 when he briefly retired. He was back in the game in 1921 as manager of the Beaumont club. After managing Galveston in 1923, he turned to umpiring for a season.

Always geared for a fight, Newnam became noted for his aggressive but fair style of umpiring. But he didn't enjoy the work near enough to stay with it. He later became president of the Texas Valley League and returned to San Antonio to manage one more time in the late 1920s.

By the time he retired from the game, Newnam set 12 records in the Texas and South Texas Leagues and was considered to be one of the great baseball players in the history of the Lone Star State.

Newnam was living at 1122 West Summit Street in San Antonio when he died from pulmonary tuberculosis on June 20, 1938, at the age of 57. He suffered from the disease the last three years of his life.

He was buried at the St. Mary's Cemetery in San Antonio two days later.

Thomas "Parson" Nicholson

Thomas C. Nicholson was given the nickname "Parson" because he refused to play ball on Sundays.

Nicholson played with minor league teams in Ohio—Columbus, Barnesville, Wooster, Steubenville, and Wheeling—and Lancaster, Pennsylvania, before signing on with the Detroit Wolverines in 1888. He played 24 games that season.

After his initial stint, he moved on in 1890 to Toledo in both the International League and the American Association, after which he toiled for Sioux City, Iowa. He also managed Toledo when it was briefly in the Western League, moving to Chattanooga when the Toledo franchise folded. He soon signed with Erie of the Eastern league, with whom he remained for two seasons.

It was from there that the Washington Senators signed him in October of 1894. He played the last 10 games of his career in D.C., being released to the Southern Association where he played for two seasons.

Nicholson's last year of pro ball was 1898 with Wheeling, West Virginia. He never used baseball for his sole source of income as he was the senior owner of Nicholson and Ball, a highly prosperous shoe business. He also became the mayor of his hometown, Bellaire, Ohio.

Nicholson died on February 28, 1917, from lobar pneumonia due to pulmonary tuberculosis at the age of 53. He was buried two days later at the Rose Hill Cemetery in Bellaire, Ohio.

Willie Garoni

Of Swiss/Italian extraction, pitcher Willie Garoni had a three-game cup of coffee for the New York Giants in 1899.

The Fort Lee, New Jersey, native was signed by the Giants from the Bridgeport Warriors, where he had a 9–13 record with five shutouts for the 1899 season. He debuted on September 7, 1899, against the Baltimore Orioles. Coming on in relief for starting pitcher Charlie Gettig, he walked opposing pitcher Frank Kitson and later threw a wild pitch.

It didn't affect the outcome. New York got blown out 10–0.

Another noteworthy appearance came on September 23, when he started in the second game of a doubleheader with Pittsburgh. Trailing 4–0 in the fifth inning, umpire Al Manassau made the strange decision to call the game because of darkness.

Photograph from Frank Russo's private collection.

This would have been fine with both teams, except for the fact that the sun was still shining.

Apparently Manassau was the only person in the park who had trouble seeing, and Garoni got saddled with the loss. (Of note, 1899 was the only season that Al Manassau umpired in the National League.)

Garoni pitched with the hometown Fort Lees in 1900 and continued to throw in the minors for a few more years before getting married and starting a successful contracting business, installing sewers in Fort Lee. Working within the close confines of underground tunneling, Garoni contracted chronic pulmonary tuberculosis, which eventually ended his life on September 9, 1914.

Garoni's brief major league line: 0–1 record; 4.50 ERA; two strikeouts; two walks; and one complete game.

He is buried in the Fairview Cemetery (Section F, Block 9, Plot 5, Grave 1) in Fairview, New Jersey.

Newt Halliday

At the age of 20 he made his debut for the Pittsburgh Pirates at first base in the second game of a doubleheader on August 19, 1916. He struck out in his only at-bat. The Pirates lost the game 1–0 after winning the first 2–1.

Halliday would not have a second crack at the majors.

He joined the navy after the United States entered World War I. After being billeted at Camp Farragut, he moved on to the Great Lakes Naval Station in September 1917. Unfortunately, somewhere along the line of his training, he contracted tuberculosis. With the help of navy doctors, Halliday fought for his life gamely. Well enough to be granted leave, he visited his family one last time in late March of 1918—staying at his parents' house, which was located at 440 Keokuk Avenue in Chicago.

After a few days, he headed back to the naval station, where his condition went rapidly downhill. Confined to the base hospital, he came down with pneumonia and started suffering hemorrhages. His body wore out, and he passed away on Saturday, April 6, 1918.

Halliday's body was brought back to his family in Chicago, where he was eventually buried at the St. Joseph Cemetery in River Grove, Illinois, on April 9.

John "Egyptian" Healy

An underrated pitcher whose career started at the tender age of 19 and ended at the age of 26, pitcher John J. Healy was born in Cairo, Illinois, hence the nickname "Egyptian."

More than an eight-year major league career with seven clubs, he accrued a lifetime record of 78–136 with a 3.84 ERA in 227 games. Also known as "Long John" to his friends, his best season was 1890, when he went 22–21 for the Toledo Maumees of the American Association. He was one of the pitchers on the All-American Team that toured the world in 1888 and 1889 in what was called the "Spalding Tour."

After he left the majors, he played in the minors for several years, except for 1893, when he temporarily left the game to work for a business in St. Louis. His last season was 1896 with St. Paul, a club managed by Charlie Comiskey.

He retired from the game to become a detective with the St. Louis Police Department and continued to pitch for the department's baseball team. He was forced to leave his position in the department in 1898 because he had contracted tuberculosis.

The disease ravaged him over the final year of his life as his weight dropped down to close to 70 pounds. Healy died from pulmonary tuberculosis on March 16, 1899, and was buried in Calvary Cemetery (Section 14, Lot 424, Grave 1) in St. Louis.

Ed Hughes

The brother of pitcher "Long Tom" Hughes, Chicago native Ed Hughes was a marginally talented player who performed a heroic deed as a policeman before his passing.

Hughes made his ill-fated debut as an emergency starter at the catcher position on August 29, 1902, for the Chicago White Sox in a 10–6 loss to the Athletics. Hughes had been playing for the Elgin team in Chicago when he was signed as a back-up by Sox management. Unfortunately for Chicago, catchers Billy Sullivan and Ed McFarland went down with injuries, so manager Clark Griffith was forced to fill in with Hughes.

Hughes' debut was a disaster. The Athletics ran on him with impunity, stealing 10 bases. It was so bad that even the lumbering Socks Seybold stole a base during the contest. Eddie Plank wound up being the winner, while Nixey Callahan suffered the loss.

Hughes went back to playing semi-pro in Chicago after his stint, switching full-time to pitcher. He was with Davenport of the Three-I League when he resurfaced again after getting signed by Boston in early September 1905.

Hughes pitched a total of six games, going 3–2 in his last major league string. Lack of control confined him to the minors and semi-pros thereafter.

After joining the Chicago Police Department, Hughes gained hero status in July 1916 after a gun battle with Henry McIntyre, known to many as Chicago's "Colored Prophet." McIntyre was a religious zealot who claimed to have "divine authority." He had come to the decision that he needed to die in order to take his report to God. He and his wife went on a shooting spree.

They killed four people, including a police sergeant, and wounded five, including three officers. Police surrounded the house, eventually dynamiting it twice. Hughes, who was off duty, happened by and decided to take matters into his own hands. Against the orders of superiors, he calmly entered the house and shot the still-armed McIntyre. (McIntyre fired twice at Hughes but missed.)

Hughes continued on in the police force until he contracted pulmonary tuberculosis in 1926. A hemorrhage caused by TB ended his life on October 14, 1927, nine days after his 47th birthday.

He was buried in the Mount Carmel Cemetery in Hillside, Illinois.

Kid McLaughlin

Outfielder James Anson "Kid" McLaughlin played just three games for the 1914 Cincinnati Reds. Also known by the flowery name of "Kid Sunshine," he debuted on June 30 of that season when he pinch hit for the Reds' Murray Uhler in the ninth inning of a 5–1 loss to the Chicago Cubs.

McLaughlin retired from ball to get a teaching degree and taught for nearly 20 years at St. Bonaventure College until illness began to wear him down.

McLaughlin was living with his wife, the former Romania Griffin, at 2196 Marie Street in Allegany, New York, when he died from the effects of chronic pulmonary tuberculosis on November 17, 1934. (Most baseball records incorrectly list the day he died as November 13, 1934.)

McLaughlin was buried at the St. Bonaventure Cemetery (Section N, Lot 91) in Allegany, New York.

Tricky Nichols

From 1875 to 1882, Connecticut native Frederick C. "Tricky" Nichols alternated between the majors and minors.

He started out in his home state with the New Haven Elm Citys in 1875. His dreadful 4–29 record on the mound that season did not deter him, and he moved on to the National League for that circuit's first season in 1876. Except for a 1–0 record for the Boston Red Caps that year, Nichols was never able to have a winning season in the bigs. He occasionally filled in as an outfielder for Boston, playing 33 games there.

All told, he compiled a 28–73 lifetime record and a 3.24 ERA.

Nichols died at Grant Hospital in Bridgeport from pulmonary TB on August 22, 1897, and was buried at the Lakeview Cemetery in Bridgeport, Connecticut.

Hank O'Day

The son of James and Mary O'Day, Hank O'Day pitched seven years in the major leagues and also managed for two seasons. But his 34-year career as an umpire is what he's best known for.

As a youth, O'Day played sandlot ball with Charlie Comiskey in post–Civil War Chicago. A private and taciturn man, O'Day chose his friends carefully and never failed to keep his guard up when it came to his personal life.

He started pitching semi-pro ball in Chicago in 1882 and later that season moved on to Council Bluffs, Iowa. From there, he went to Toledo of the Northwestern League and remained with that team when it joined the American Association in 1884.

O'Day went on to pitch seven years in the majors, logging a lifetime 72–110 record. His best season was his final one, 1890, when he went 22–13 for the New York Giants of the Players League.

O'Day's career as an umpire overshadowed his playing career by far, as he went on to become one of the most famous and respected umpires in baseball history. His 35 years as an arbiter, which began in 1895, were second only to the great Bill Klem.

O'Day, who always carried a rule book on his person, was known for making firm decisions and never backing off from an argument. Once, Rabbit Maranville stole second base by sliding through O'Day's legs to reach the bag. With the crowd laughing hysterically, O'Day pulled out his rule book, thumbed through it, and, after finding no rule broken, allowed the play to stand.

Other umpires took to calling him "Groucho" due to his gruff exterior, but he was respected for his integrity and ethics.

O'Day worked the first World Series in 1903 and was second only to Klem in fall classics worked. O'Day was the umpire during the famous Fred Merkle "boner" game of 1908 and was the second-base umpire in 1920 when Bill "Wamby" Wambsganss executed the only unassisted triple play in World Series history.

Many people felt that O'Day's greatest failures in baseball were his two unsuccessful stints as a manager—in 1912 with the

Reds and 1914 with the Cubs. O'Day defended his managing record to his dying day, as it became a sore subject with him in his later years.

Despite his gruff personality, O'Day had many friends in the game, especially Comiskey and his long-time friend Connie Mack. Bob Emslie was probably his closest friend among his fellow umpires, as he often visited him at his home in Ontario, Canada.

O'Day retired from umpiring for good after the 1927 season, after which his health rapidly deteriorated. He died at 3:10 AM on July 2, 1935, at the Great Northern Hotel in Chicago, where he made his home.

The cause of death was broncho-pneumonia due to tuberculosis. O'Day, who was single, was buried at the Calvary Cemetery in Evanston, Illinois, on July 5, 1935.

John Puhl

John Puhl appeared in three games for the New York Giants—two in 1898 and one in 1899. He made his debut on October 13, 1898, against the Washington Senators at the Polo Grounds. The Giants won 5–3.

Although Puhl only batted .222, he was considered a player of promise. Signed for 1899, he appeared in his last major league game on May 31.

Puhl's life, and career, were cut short when he contracted pulmonary TB during the summer of 1900. He was living at 94 West Nineteenth Street in Bayonne, New Jersey, at the time of his death on August 24, 1900.

Puhl, just 24 years old, officially passed away due to phthisis. He was buried at Holy Name Cemetery in Jersey City, New Jersey.

Yank Robinson

Philadelphia-born Yank Robinson played 11 major league seasons between 1882 and 1892, making stops with the Detroit

Wolverines, the Baltimore Monumentals, the St. Louis Browns, the Pittsburgh Burghers, the Cincinnati Porkers, and the Washington Senators.

In all, Robinson appeared in 978 games, batting .241 with 825 hits and 399 RBIs in 3,428 at-bats. He also collected 272 stolen bases.

One of baseball's first "super subs," Robinson was acquired by Chris Von der Ahe's St. Louis AA team from the Baltimore Onions team of the Union Association. This turned out to be a wonderful opportunity for Robinson, who fell under the tutelage of manager Charlie Comiskey and blossomed as a player. Never a great hitter, in 1885 and 1886 he wound up playing every position except shortstop for the Brownies, and in 1886 stole 51 bases.

He would continue on in this capacity for the majority of his career, even doing a little pitching for the Browns in 1886.

Robinson was involved in one of the most controversial baseball episodes of the 19th century. During the 1889 season, Robinson was suspended and fined after a shouting match with owner Von der Ahe. The Browns players nearly went on a sit-down strike in support of their teammate. In fact, they became so indignant at the treatment of their teammate that many refused to go to Kansas City to play the Cowboys for their next series.

After much debating, and on pleas from Robinson, the team made a last-minute decision and boarded the train. Controversy would not stop there, though. The Browns would then proceed to drop three in a row to the Cowboys amid charges from Von der Ahe that they lost on purpose.

All this proved to be too much for Robinson, who eventually had enough of Von der Ahe. Eighteen eighty-nine would be the last full season for Robinson, who jumped to the Players League in 1890.

He would never again play more than 98 games in a season for the rest of his career.

Settling in St. Louis after his career was over, he died on August 25, 1894, as a result of phthisis pulmonalis (wasting of the pulmonary system), another term for consumption, or TB.

He is buried in the Calvary Cemetery in St. Louis, Missouri, in an unmarked grave (Section 11B).

John Skopec

A southpaw, Chicago native John Skopec learned his baseball on the streets and sandlots of the Windy City. Skopec, who went to Avondale Elementary School, chose not to go to high school, instead opting for a career in baseball.

He joined the Chicago White Sox from Wheeling of the Interstate League in 1901, picking up their first franchise victory as a major league club on April 24 versus the Cleveland Blues. Skopec pitched good ball, yielding single runs in the first, second, and sixth.

That season, Skopec went 6–3 for the Sox but was ineffectively wild, as he walked 45 and threw nine wild pitches in 68⅓ innings pitched.

When the team headed east on a road trip in early June, he was left home in Chicago. Skopec was soon released but found work pitching for the Gunthers of the Chicago City League. Later that season, he signed on with Little Rock of the Southern Association.

The Sox invited him back to spring training in 1902, and then decided to let him go back to Little Rock to get in more work. While there, he began playing the outfield, patrolling mostly left and center field. He was then sold to Shreveport on August 20, where he continued to spend time in the outfield when he was not pitching.

In 1903 he began the season with the Spalding Club of the Interstate League. It was while there that he was signed by Detroit in August, appearing in his first game with them on August 15. In a sloppy affair, Skopec saw his new team commit six errors (three by shortstop Herman Long) in a 6–3 loss to Boston.

Skopec's trial with the Tigers lasted all of six games.

Amazingly, in mid-September, Skopec decided to jump his contract because he felt that he had been unfairly treated by management. Apparently, he was put in the upper berth of a sleeper car on one of the team's trains, and that was just not acceptable to him.

He played with Newark of the Eastern League in 1905 and later with the Logan Squares and Felix Colts of the Chicago City League.

Due to his lack of education, when not playing ball, Skopec was forced to work as a laborer. Eventually his health went downhill, and he died at his home, located at 2071 North Western Avenue in Chicago on October 20, 1912. Skopec, who was 32 years old, passed away as a result of pulmonary TB and was buried at the Bohemian National Cemetery in Chicago on October 22, leaving his wife, the former Adeline Lamberti.

Fred Warner

A native of Philadelphia, Frederick John Rodney Warner played 257 games in the majors for seven different teams—three of those in the City of Brotherly Love.

Warner started out in the National Association with the Philadelphia Centennials in 1875, then he played with the Athletics of the National League in 1876. After a season in the minors, Warner was back with the Indianapolis Blues in 1878. He then moved to the Cleveland Blues, Philadelphia Quakers, and Brooklyn of the American Association, where he finished out his career.

Used almost entirely as a utility man during his career, his career high in games came in his final season (84). Never much of a hitter, the best he could do at bat was .227 in 1883. Lifetime he had one home run and a modest 47 RBIs.

Warner was working as a clerk in his hometown when illness overtook him. He died from consumption of the lungs (pulmonary TB) on February 13, 1886, at his home located at 1601 Christian Avenue. Warner, who was married, was laid to rest at the Woodlands Cemetery (Section G, Lot 267) in Philadelphia on February 16, 1886.

Marsh Williams

Marsh Williams was a student at both the Presbyterian College of Clinton, South Carolina, and the University of North Carolina. With the ink on his term papers barely dry, he was signed by Connie Mack, who always had great faith in college players.

Williams appeared in 10 games for the A's, accruing a 0–6 record with a lofty 7.89 ERA. He joined the United States Army during World War I and served in France. Gassed by the Germans, he was sent back stateside to recover. Unfortunately for Williams, his lungs would never fully regain their function.

With a career in baseball out of the question, he remained in the army, retiring with the rank of major. It is believed he contracted pulmonary tuberculosis in 1927, and the disease eventually prompted him to move to Arizona. Williams' doctors thought the dry desert air would provide a better climate for his condition.

Settling in Tucson with his wife, Lucy, he lived at 1542 Spring Street. It was there that he passed away on the afternoon of February 22, 1935, from the effects of pulmonary tuberculosis. He also had suffered from myocarditis in the last year of his life—a condition that was only compounded by his tubercular condition.

Williams, who was only 42, was brought back to his hometown of Faison, North Carolina, for burial.

Rube Waddell

Rube Waddell was as eccentric as he was talented.

With his great fastball, effective curve, and excellent control, he was one of the greatest left-handers in major league history.

He was also one the game's all-time kooks. Case in point: Waddell's three passions in his life were baseball, fishing, and following fire engines.

Even if he wasn't the most cerebral ballplayer of all time, he was an easygoing, slow-witted sort who loved to have a good time. Oh, and yes, he also liked to tend bar and chase the ladies around.

Photograph courtesy of Dave Lotz.

Growing up near Bradford, Pennsylvania, Waddell signed with Louisville of the National League in 1897 and transferred to Pittsburgh when the two franchises merged. Unhappy with the stern discipline of manager Fred Clarke, he jumped the club. Clarke, preferring not to have to deal with the flaky hurler, let him go.

Connie Mack "borrowed" Waddell from the Pirates' Barney Dreyfuss for his Milwaukee team in the AL for the 1900 season. Waddell followed Mack to Philadelphia to join the Athletics in 1902 and went 24–7, leading the AL in strikeouts for the first of what would be six straight seasons.

In 1904 he struck out 349 batters. In 1905 he led the league with 26 wins, leading the A's into the World Series against the Giants. As the series approached, rumors abounded that gamblers paid Waddell off to fake an arm injury and sit it out. The truth was that Waddell had fallen on his left arm while horsing around with teammate Andy Coakley at a train station. It stiffened up overnight, and he didn't pitch again that season.

Waddell never made more than $2,800 a year, and he spent money as fast as he got it. For a time the A's paid him in dollar bills, hoping to make his money last longer. He was forever borrowing or conning extra money out of Mack. Waddell enjoyed waving his teammates off the field and then striking out the side.

He enjoyed wrestling alligators in Florida, hung around in firehouses, married two women who then left him, and tended bar when he wasn't the saloon's best customer. He held up the start of games he was scheduled to pitch while he played marbles with children outside the park.

One legend about Waddell is that there was a provision in his contract barring him from eating animal crackers in bed. In those days, two players had to share a double bed on the road, and Ossie Schreckengost was Waddell's catcher and roommate. "Schreck wouldn't sign unless he saw that clause in Waddell's contract," said Mack, "so I wrote it in there, and the Rube stuck to it."

Despite being a fan favorite, Waddell's erratic behavior and declining effectiveness strained the tolerance of his teammates. In the spring of 1908 Mack traded him to the Browns after some of his teammates threatened not to report. By 1910 Waddell was back in the minors. He won 20 games for Joe Cantillon's Minneapolis AA club in 1911. In the spring of 1912 he was staying at Cantillon's house in Hickman, Kentucky, when a nearby river flooded. Standing in icy water, Waddell helped pile sandbags on the embankments. The incident affected his health. He still managed to pitch one more year in the minors, but after being badly weakened by the river incident, he became an easy target for tuberculosis.

In early 1914 he went down to San Antonio, Texas, to rehabilitate in a sanatorium. He died there, fittingly, on April Fools Day, 1914.

For several years there was no headstone on Waddell's grave. The president of the San Antonio ballclub told Connie Mack and John McGraw that Waddell had no headstone, and they raised enough money to put up a six-foot granite marker.

Waddell, who was elected to the Hall of Fame by the Committee on Baseball Veterans in 1946, is buried in San Antonio Mission Burial Park, the same final resting place as fellow Hall of Famer Ross Youngs.

Lew Richie

Nicknamed the "Giant Killer" by his Philadelphia teammates for his propensity for beating John McGraw's New York squad, Lew Richie pitched several years for the Phillies with lukewarm results.

The Pennsylvania native was traded to Boston on July 16, 1909, and then to the Chicago Cubs on April 13, 1910, in a deal that occurred right before the game when Boston was in the Windy City's West Side Park. In fact, when he was swapped for Doc Miller right before the opening pitch, the two players simply switched uniforms and took the field in time for batting practice.

Under Chicago manager Frank Chance, Richie excelled, going 11–4 in 1910 and making a brief appearance in that season's fall classic against the Athletics.

Richie won 15 and 16 games in 1911 and 1912, respectively, before getting sent to Kansas City of the American Association on August 9, 1913, for Hippo Vaughn. The trade proved to be a solid one for Chicago, as Vaughn established himself as the Cubs' ace during the World War I era, becoming a five-time 20-game winner.

Richie ended up with a 74–65 lifetime record with a solid 2.54 ERA. He took up the occupation of plumber after his career and made his home in Philadelphia. Illness forced him to cut back on his activities—he contracted tuberculosis in the mid 1920s. He eventually was forced to move to the Mt. Alto Sanatorium in South Mountain, Pennsylvania, where he succumbed to the effects of pulmonary TB on August 15, 1936—eight days before his 53rd birthday.

He was buried at the Rose Hill Cemetery in Ambler, Pennsylvania, three days later.

Virgil "Ned" Garvin

Ned Garvin possibly could go down in history as the meanest man in baseball. A devout racist, alcoholic, and rabble rouser, Garvin, to put in mildly, was one mean hombre.

Hailing from Navasota, Texas, he was aptly nicknamed, "the Navasota Tarantula."

Trouble always seemed to follow Garvin, who had a personality only an axe murderer could love. He once was reported to have emptied his gun into a young black man because he didn't shine Garvin's shoes to his liking.

When asked about the incident, Garvin replied, "Texans don't like niggers anyhow."

On October 20, 1904, Garvin smashed in the face of R. N. Sheffey, a New York insurance man, in the lobby of the Hotel

Kensington in Plainfield, New Jersey. The reason? Sheffey preferred to read a newspaper rather than have a conversation with the loquacious Garvin.

They settled out of court for a whopping $50.

Garvin was in Plainfield at the time because he was in the midst of a lawsuit with the Plainfield Athletic Club, which he had pitched for but was not paid by because of his poor performance on the field.

Garvin had a wide range of interests and hobbies. At one point in his life he studied to be a dentist. He was also an avid hunter and wrote and recited poetry. He worked as a scout at times, and not the Boy Scout kind either.

He was as handy with a gun and bow as he was with a baseball.

Garvin made his Major League debut with the Philadelphia Phillies on July 13, 1896, starting and losing a 9–8 decision to the Chicago Colts. The game featured four home runs by Phils outfielder Ed Delahanty. After two games, Garvin was sent back to the minors.

Garvin resurfaced in the majors in 1899 with the Chicago Orphans. He spent two years with them before a one-season stint with the Milwaukee Brewers in 1901. He was then signed by Charlie Comiskey to play for the White Sox in 1902. Garvin managed to keep his nose clean until late August, when he was involved in a wild brawl on Chicago's West Side. The incident occurred at a place called Flanagan's Bar. Garvin had been to about a dozen saloons before he strolled into the place at about 8:00 that evening. After a few minutes, he got into an argument with his friend, Lawrence Flanagan—the saloon's owner, who was bartending that evening.

It might be safe to surmise that Garvin was half in the bag when he asked to borrow money from Flanagan, who refused him. Garvin then shot him in the shoulder. When a police officer eventually entered through the establishment's swinging front doors, he was immediately bashed in the head by Garvin, who used his pistol like brass knuckles. Garvin took off down the street pursued by several dozen people. He doubled backed and eluded the angry mob by jumping on a streetcar that whisked him away to safety.

After hearing of the incident, Comiskey sent Garvin packing via waivers.

Amazingly, Garvin didn't have to wait long to find work. The Brooklyn Superbas management decided to take a chance on him, signing him in mid-September of 1902. It was ironic that Garvin, a sub .500 pitcher for his career, amassed his best record that tumultuous year, going 11–11 overall with Chicago and Brooklyn.

Garvin stayed with the Superbas for the better part of the next two seasons, but never pitched winning ball because his temper usually got the best of him. After going 5–15 in 1904, he was selected off waivers by the New York Highlanders for their late-season stretch drive on September 9, 1904. Garvin went 0–1 in two games for New York, which lost the pennant by a game and a half to the Boston Pilgrims.

Garvin played with Portland in the Pacific Coast League in 1905 and with Seattle in 1906 before closing out his career with Butte of the Northwest League in 1907.

He was living in Fresno, California, when he died of consumption at age 34 at the county hospital on June 16, 1908. Garvin was eventually laid to rest at the Mountain View Cemetery in Fresno several days later. Upon his death newspapers lauded his life, speaking in flowery terms of his fine disposition and wonderful demeanor.

You could say that when they buried Ned Garvin, the newspapers buried the lead.

Hump Days: Tales of Hunchbacked Mascots

Where to spit and where not to step. Pregame rituals and game-day meals. Routines before pitches and routines before at-bats. Curse of the Bambino. Curse of the billy goat. Uniform numbers. Don't lend your bat to a fellow player. Sleep with your bat to stay in a groove or break out of a slump. Never talk to a pitcher when he has a no-hitter or a perfect game in progress.

And by the way, stick a wad of gum on your hat for good measure.

Baseball is replete with superstitions, but none has ever been stranger than the one which held that the presence of a hunchbacked mascot bestowed good luck.

Always a welcome sight to players on a ball club, even those on opposing teams, hunchbacked mascots often served as batboys. More than anything, they were a combination of lucky charm and dugout jester—and players even took their mimics and jibes in good-nature. Players also took to rubbing their humps for good luck as they headed to the plate.

175

Often, management went to great lengths to keep them with their teams.

The three most famous hunchbacked mascot/batboys—Louis Van Zelst, Hugh McLoon, and Eddie Bennett—had a few things in common. They all made their appearances in the first two decades of the 20th century. They each exuded an irrepressible, flamboyant style that grew to be considered a vital part of their teams' chemistry.

And, unfortunately, all three met untimely demises.

Louis Van Zelst

Louis Van Zelst was the mascot/batboy for the powerhouse Philadelphia Athletics teams of 1910 through 1914. Born in 1895 in Philadelphia, he was a normal, happy-go-lucky boy until the age of eight, when he fell off of a wagon, sustaining a spinal injury. Paralyzed for one month after the fall, his growth became stunted, and he never exceeded dwarf-like proportions. He also developed a hunched back, which had painful side effects.

Spasms were a part of his everyday life.

Van Zelst grew into an avid sports fan and became a well-liked regular at the University of Pennsylvania's football, baseball, and track and field games. The Quakers facilities were just down the road from his house, so the trek to the fields was an easy one. One day in 1909 he wandered over to Shibe Park and, on seeing Connie Mack, manager of the A's, asked if he could manage the bats. Being superstitious, Mack let him become a batboy for the day.

The A's won, and Mack decided to keep Louis on as a permanent mascot.

A's players rubbed Van Zelst's hump, and he encouraged the practice. An immediate hit with the team, he fell under the benevolent watch of Jack Coombs and Jack Barry. Van Zelst did his job only at home games in the beginning, and did not take his first road trip with the team through the American League circuit

Photograph courtesy of Russ Dodge.

until 1911—although he did go with the team when they appeared in the World Series of 1910.

Once on the road, Barry saw to it that "Little Louie" always got to bed on time and that he went to church on Sundays. He became a particular favorite of Nap Lajoie, Ty Cobb, and Big Ed Walsh. He went to his first spring training camp down in San Antonio, Texas, in 1912, and was a huge hit with the fans. He had a mischievous, devil-may-care attitude and even took to doing imitations—mimicking opposing managers like Hugie Jennings and John McGraw.

His kidding was always taken with good cheer.

Van Zelst never complained about his physical struggles, even though there is evidence that he also likely suffered from sciatic nerve damage as well as spinal degeneration from the effects of his boyhood injuries.

In this regard, he was an inspiration to the players.

Once, Frank "Home Run" Baker slid into second base at Shibe Park, cutting open his leg on the hard surface. When asked afterward why he did not take himself out to get treatment, Baker replied, "Every day I see that little guy [Louie] doing his job, without fanfare. He never complains, yet he is in the most pain of anyone I have ever seen. I think I might be able to brave a few bruises and bumps after witnessing that."

A written account at the time said Van Zelst was considered to be an "exceptionally bright chap, winsome and clever." He never drew a salary for his job with the A's; instead, the players anted up and gave Louie a gift of about $250 dollars at the end of each season. Eventually, the strain of his physical condition caused other problems for him. He was diagnosed with Bright's disease and died after a two-day illness in March 1915.

On his death, a somber Ty Cobb said, "I shall miss that little rascal dearly. He never failed to greet me when I saw him on the field and was as full of vim and vigor as one could hope to expect from a person in his condition. All the boys throughout the league will miss his smile and good cheer. I know I will."

Van Zelst was laid to rest at the Holy Cross Cemetery (Section M, Range 4, Lot 39, Center Grave) in Yeadon, Pennsylvania. He is buried between his father, John, and mother, Mary.

Hugh McLoon

Heir apparent to Van Zelst as mascot/batboy for the Philadelphia A's, Hugh McLoon found a place in society outside the baseball diamond and went on to modest fame until brought down by a hail of gunfire in the late 1920s. His gangland-style murder was a catalyst that got the wheels of justice rolling in what became known as the "Philadelphia Bootleg Wars."

Being an Irish hunchback from Philly, McLoon was a natural to replace Van Zelst. But the McLoon era was highlighted by some of the most dreadful teams in baseball history, as Connie Mack had begun dismantling his team after the 1914 series.

It was after his career as a mascot that life became interesting for McLoon, who used the contacts he had made during his days at Shibe Park to situate himself as a manager of prize fighters in the city. The change from mascot to boxing manager proved to be more lucrative, since his share of the take from a bout was much greater than the paltry few dollars he received from the miserly Mack, who had the reputation of a banker with the heart of an undertaker.

One of the fighters McLoon managed was lightweight Eddie "Kid" Wagner. Managing to accumulate his resources, and with the help of many famous friends, he was able to open a "cabaret establishment," as he liked to call it. In truth, McLoon ran a fully functioning saloon supplied with beer and alcohol by his friends—members of one of the two prominent bootlegging rings operating within the city confines.

On the evening of Wednesday, August 9, 1928, McLoon was walking with two companions, William Meister and Joseph Fries, in the downtown section of Philadelphia. They had just left McLoon's saloon on Cuthbert Street when a car with three men in it approached. Shots rang out, and the car sped away. Lying on the ground was McLoon, dead from a shotgun blast. Meister, 21, was seriously wounded while Fries, 22, was shot in the leg. A pistol found at the scene showed that someone had attempted to return fire on the speeding sedan. Police began an investigation as burial arrangements were made for McLoon.

More than 3,000 people attended the funeral on August 13, as celebrities from the political, sports, and theatrical worlds gathered together to pay homage to a former friend. His body was taken from St. Monica's Church to Holy Cross Cemetery (Section 34, Range 9, Lot 14) in Yeadon, where he was laid to rest.

The authorities, however, weren't about to bury the episode.

For openers, police weren't even sure if McLoon was the intended target of the gunmen. Was he just in the wrong place at the wrong time? Were Meister and Fries, who had bootlegging connections, the intended targets? The plot thickened when cops received a tip and sought the whereabouts of a man named Daniel J. "Joseph" O'Leary in connection with the killing. O'Leary was the head of the so-called "O'Leary Gang" and apparently was hired to kill Meister and Fries. Unfortunately for O'Leary, cops found him too late—he was found dead in bed, shot five times, in his North Park Avenue apartment. The gunmen, who had used silencers, had found him to be easy pickings, and an 18-year-old girl who went by the name of Jennie Brooks had apparently drugged O'Leary. When police found two shotguns of the same type that killed McLoon in O'Leary's apartment, they realized that the two murders were connected.

O'Leary's murder was in retaliation for McLoon's.

Brooks was nicknamed "Little Miss Iceberg" by police, undoubtedly for her warm demeanor. After a week of grilling by the cops, she broke down and provided information on bootleggers ranging from Atlantic City to New York. Her real name was Mrs. Anna Marcello. Married at 14 but separated from her husband for some time, she found herself in the company of "wise guys" and her knowledge helped widen the investigation.

Theories were floated on McLoon's slaying. One idea had it that McLoon might have been murdered because of a dispute over a woman. (Though a hunchback, McLoon had no problem putting himself in the company of attractive women.) In any case, the bloodshed did not stop with the McLoon/O'Leary murders. On August 19, 24-year-old James Daly was shot to death in a bar while defending McLoon's reputation. A bartender named H. J. McAtee, who was connected with the rival bootleg-ger ring, was arrested as the shooter.

The city was in desperate need of a strong-willed personality to get to the bottom of what was happening. It found its man in Quarter Sessions Court Judge Edwin O. Lewis. Known for his integrity and honesty, he ordered a sweeping grand jury investi-gation to look into alleged racketeering. Widespread corruption was suspected on a grand scale between bootleggers, outside mob forces, and police. Lewis tabbed District Attorney John Monoghan as his point man. His job was to conduct raids and gather evidence in an attempt to discover the sources of illegal booze flowing to the more than 13,000 cabaret/saloons in Philadelphia.

Meanwhile, the grand jury went after several police officials, including Captain of Detectives Charles C. Beckman and four of his subordinates.

The case was blown completely open when the district attor-ney's office obtained what they called a "Bootleg Blue Book." All hell broke loose as numerous city officials were brought to their knees. Many notable underworld names were mentioned in the book, including Max "Boo Boo" Hoff, the so-called "King of Philadelphia Bootleggers" and a friend of his from Chicago by the name of Al Capone. The book was evidence that the tentacles of the underworld had reached out beyond Philadelphia to places as far away as California. The grand jury uncovered evi-dence that graft was widespread. Hundreds of thousands of dollars had been paid out to police officials of all rank to turn a blind eye to the illegal distilleries situated throughout the city.

It was a mess of the first magnitude. In early September, the grand jury made the following statement: "The information that we have derived thus far is amazing in character and almost unbelievable in significance. It clearly shows that there has existed in the County of Philadelphia during the last several years and up to the present time, a group of lawless men who have violated the law upon a wholesale scale...which has systematically flaunted the law with the connivance of police officials high and low."

Eventually Francis Peterson and Samuel A. "Shorty" Feldman were both arrested in connection with the McLoon slaying. All told, four men and two women were held in police custody. Although it took the strength and resolve of the Virginia–born and bred Judge Lewis to get to the bottom of the Philadelphia Bootleg Wars, it was the untimely demise of a former Philadelphia A's mascot that sparked an eventual blaze of justice.

Eddie Bennett

The Chicago White Sox. The Brooklyn Robins. The New York Yankees. Wherever he hung his cap, Eddie Bennett brought his own brand of baseball magic as well as pennants to the teams he served.

Born an orphan circa 1903, not much is known about him until he became a batboy for the Chicago White Sox in 1919 when the Sox were in the midst of listless play. There, he became the personal tender of Happy Felsch's bats. In a world where baseball players looked at hunchbacks as good luck, Bennett became a highly prized commodity. Bennett made $18 a week for Chicago and was promised $200 from the World Series pool money. The first of five straight October Classics was in 1919 for Little Eddie, who refused to report in 1920, instead opting for Brooklyn.

The Robins went on to win the pennant, but Brooklyn president Charlie Ebbets, who did not believe in mascots, elected not to bring Bennett with the team on the road against the Indians for financial reasons. Many fans felt that the Robins needed Bennett's good luck and blamed the loss directly on Ebbets and his cheap ways.

"Too expensive" was the response from the tightwad Ebbets.

Bennett's response to him: "It'll cost you more to ditch me. You will lose for sure."

His words were prescient; the Indians won the Series 5–2.

Ebbets' antics so embittered Bennett that he signed with the Yankees on January 28, 1921. In his contract, the Yankees brain trust, Ed Barrow and Jake Ruppert, stipulated that Bennett would appear as a batboy/mascot in every World Series game should the New Yorkers win the pennant. Bennett became a fixture with the team over the next 14 years, and the Yanks won the pennant seven times, making it to the October Classic on four of those occasions.

Bennett always received shares of World Series money, win or lose, starting in 1920 when he received $500 of the $74,192 losers' share. Known for taking losses as badly as the players and management, Bennett was always cheerful yet serious in his work. He counted on himself to bring good luck to the Yankees players. They rubbed his hump for luck as they went to bat. Bennett liked to make it a habit to greet Babe Ruth at home plate after his numerous home runs, sticking out a glad hand to the Bambino in celebration.

When the Yanks finally won the Series in 1923, it was said that Eddie Bennett was the happiest young man in the United States. Bennett was close to the Babe on the team, and later Lou Gehrig, whose mother felt sorry for the physically challenged mascot. Opposing players as well had soft spots for Little Eddie, including Ty Cobb and Harry Heilmann of Detroit. Wilcy Moore of the Yanks always threw his first warm-up ball to Bennett for luck whenever he came into a game, and Urban Shocker, after he rejoined the Yankees, had Bennett room with him on the road.

Bennett continued on as the Yanks' good luck charm until May 21, 1932, when the car he was driving in was involved in a crash. He severely broke his leg, and other more minor injuries compounded his hunchbacked condition. He was unable to continue his job with the Yanks, although he did appear on crutches in the World Series to urge the boys on.

Even though Ruppert took over and paid for his medical and living expenses and said that he would never have to want for anything, Bennett nonetheless took to drinking to ease the pain. His self-medication got worse and worse as the thought of never again gracing the field at Yankee Stadium grew stronger.

He was living at 115 West 84th Street in New York when he passed away on Wednesday, January 16, 1935. His landlady, Mrs. Scholtz, had gone down to his apartment to check on his him when she found his body amidst a treasure trove of trophies and memorabilia that he had collected during his tenure in the majors.

He was buried a few days later with the entire funeral being paid for by the Yankees organization. He was laid to rest in St. John's Cemetery (Section 20, Row H, Grave 99) in Middle Village Queens.

Officially, Eddie Bennett died as a result of complications from alcoholism. Those who knew him best said he died from a broken heart.

Last Call

Oh, that demon rum! Some say it's the devil's brew, not to mention beer, wine, liquor, and any and all alcoholic beverages resulting from the fermentation process.

Strange how there's never been a product so romanticized that has wrecked so many lives. Alcohol is the ultimate double-edged sword of pain and pleasure, and woe to the wretched souls who make the fateful leap from sips at the bar to daily binges and weekend benders.

For those of age, there are few simple pleasures better than taking in a great ballgame on a warm day with a cold beer. There are also few things sadder than watching a promising career, let alone a life, cut short due to alcohol addiction.

Hall of Famers Mickey Mantle, Grover Cleveland Alexander, Dennis Eckersley, and Mike "King" Kelly are but a handful of players whose bout with the bottle has been well-chronicled. Mantle's alcoholism contributed to his death from liver cancer.

The players profiled in this chapter are some who have died as a direct result of alcoholism, like accomplished pitchers Allen

Sothoron and Larry Corcoran and prolific catcher Earl Smith. The majority succumbed to some form of cirrhosis of the liver.

That fact is printed on their death certificates.

Perhaps the saddest fact of all is that alcoholism remains a disease without a cure.

Allen Sothoron

A spitballer, Allen Sothoron was one of a handful of pitchers still allowed to throw that trick pitch when it was abolished after the 1919 season.

He spent the bulk of his career for St. Louis teams in the National and American Leagues and flashed signs of brilliance with regularity. After seeing him pitch once, the famous sportswriter Bugs Baer wrote of his performance, "Allen S. Sothoron pitched his initials off yesterday."

Sothoron made his debut on September 17, 1914, with the St. Louis Browns and got his breakthrough season in 1916 when he won 15 straight games for Portland of the PCL. His best year in the majors, by far, was 1919, when he won 20 and finished with a 3.31 ERA.

Sothoron left the Brownies just as they were starting to become one of the American League's top teams. From 1921 through 1926, he bounced from Boston to Cleveland and then back to St. Louis where, on December 29, 1926, he was released by the Cardinals as a player and named as a coach, replacing Otto Williams.

His career record stood at 91–100 with a respectable 3.31 ERA.

Sothoron remained as a coach with the Cards until May 31, 1928, when he signed with the Boston Braves in the same capacity. He managed in the minors with Louisville from 1929 to 1931 and with the Milwaukee Brewers from 1934 to 1938. In between, he coached for and was interim manager for the Cardinals. While in the minors, he began to gain a reputation as a keen judge of talent.

By 1939, however, his health began to take a serious turn for the worse. A full-blown alcoholic, Sothoron came down with hepatitis as a direct result from his years of drinking. In late May he entered a St. Louis hospital for treatment, and it was here that he would spend the last four weeks of his life. He died at 10:30 PM on June 17, 1939, at the St. John's Hospital, leaving his wife of two years, wealthy New York socialite Dorothy Clemens.

Sothoron's body was brought back to New York for burial, with services conducted on June 20. For 65 years, it was not known exactly where he made his final resting place. It was not until the fall of 2004 that it was discovered he was resting in anonymity in the Woodlawn Cemetery in the Bronx, New York.

Alan Sothoron's body rests in the Clemens Family Mausoleum (Section 137/138, Lot 12482) located in Parkview.

Barney Olsen

Massachusetts native and outfielder Barney Olsen appeared in a total of 24 games for the 1941 Chicago Cubs, batting a strong .288 in 73 at-bats.

He was sent to the Los Angeles Angels of the Pacific Coast League after spring training the next season and never made it back to the bigs.

The Cubs eventually sent Olsen to the Philadelphia Athletics, but the deal became moot when he enlisted in the Navy. After his service time was up, he tried to make a comeback, joining the Angels just in time for spring training in 1946. But his time in the service appeared to have hurt him—his timing was off both in the field and at bat.

Olsen wound down his days in baseball with the Columbus Red Birds, the Houston Buffs, and the Rochester club. He eventually became a truck driver for the Standard Electrical Supply Company in Everettt, Massachusetts.

He died from esophageal bleeding and arterial bleeding due to cirrhosis of the liver from excessive drinking on March 30, 1977. He was living with his wife, Alice, at 11 Dunster Road at the time and was buried at the Holy Cross Cemetery in Malden, Massachusetts, on April 2.

Bill Hart

Bill Hart was also known as "Two Gun" after silent-screen cowboy hero William S. "Two Gun" Hart. The Pennsylvania native played in 95 games over parts of three seasons for the Brooklyn Dodgers from 1943 to 1945.

Hart started out with his hometown Harrisburg team of the New York-Penn League in 1935. His tour of minor league stops continued over the next few years with Portsmouth of the Mid-Atlantic League, New Orleans of the Southern Association, and Cairo of the Kitty League.

He was brought up from New Orleans on September 18, 1943, for his debut with the Brooklyn Dodgers in a twin bill against the Giants. The Dodgers lost both games, 3–1 and 7–4, with Hart starting at third base. Hart and Dodgers manager Leo Durocher were often at odds with each other. Leo "the Lip" often laid into the rookie infielder during his tenure with the Dodgers, and Hart was optioned several times to New Orleans.

In 1945, after batting .230 in 58 games, the Dodgers optioned Hart to St. Paul of the American Association on August 11, ending his major league career.

The move to the cooler air of Minnesota invigorated him—he smashed 17 homers and drove in 48 RBIs in only 38 games. On September 4 of that season, he cracked four homers and drove in nine RBIs while tying two AA records. Hart later managed Santa Barbara of the California League and Asheville of the Tri-State League before calling it a career in 1952.

After he quit playing, he settled in Wiconisco, Pennsylvania, where he worked as a machine operator. Hart, who had a fondness for liquor, died as a result of portal cirrhosis of the liver on July 29, 1968, at the Holy Spirit Hospital in East Pennsboro, Pennsylvania.

He was 55 and left a wife, Anna. He was buried at the Calvary United Methodist Cemetery in Wiconisco, Pennsylvania, on August 1.

Bill Whaley

An Indianapolis native, outfielder Bill Whaley appeared in 13 games for the 1923 St. Louis Browns.

After his stint with the Browns, he was eventually sold to New Orleans in 1926, after which he became a journeyman minor leaguer. He made 11 stops with 11 other minor league organizations before his retirement from the game in 1932.

Whaley got a job with the US Postal Service, eventually working as a special delivery postman. His health deteriorated the last year of his life, and he checked into the Methodist Hospital in Indianapolis in late February 1943. He passed away there on the afternoon of March 3 from cirrhosis of the liver due to alcoholism at the age of 47.

Whaley, who was survived by his wife, Ann, was buried at the Crown Hill Cemetery in Indianapolis a few days later.

John "Brewery Jack" Taylor

He didn't work in a brewery, but he often smelled like one.

Staten Island native John Budd Taylor was nicknamed "Brewery Jack" because of his fondness for beer.

Pitching for one of the hardest-hitting teams ever in baseball history, the 1894 to 1897 Philadelphia Phillies, he won 85 games. His career-high victories in a single season was 26 in 1895.

That was also the last year in which he would amass a winning record.

In 1896 he managed to lose 21 games, although he did also win 20. His final year in Philly saw him slump to a 16–20 record,

Photograph from Frank Russo's private collection.

after which he was traded off to the St. Louis Maroons in 1898. Over the course of nine seasons, he accrued a 120–117 record with a 4.23 ERA with seven shutouts and nine saves in 270 league games.

His final year in the majors was 1899, when he went 9–10 for Cincinnati. During that campaign, Taylor's health slowly began to fall apart. He was diagnosed with Bright's disease and died at his home in the New Brighton section of Staten Island on February 7, 1900. He was only 26 years old.

Jack's mother, Phoebe Ann Taylor, predeceased him by only 17 days.

Taylor is buried at the Fairview Cemetery (Section M, Plot 47) in Staten Island next to his beloved mother.

Buzz Murphy

Buzz Murphy had a bit of a quirk about him—he hated to ride on trains. This posed a bit of a problem, especially for someone who played in the days before teams traveled by air or by bus.

He managed to persevere—barely.

Murphy broke in with Waco, Texas, in 1914, eventually making stops with Marshalltown, Iowa, and San Francisco of the PCL, and Houston and Des Moines of the Western League, from whom the Braves recruited his services in 1918.

In his major league debut on July 14, he drove in four runs and scored twice to lead Boston to an 8–4 win over the Cardinals in the first game of a doubleheader. The Braves also won the second contest 4–3.

Murphy had a pretty good outing, collecting five base hits. Newspaper accounts that day erroneously reported Murphy's first name as Richard.

Murphy batted a hefty .375 during his nine-game stay with the Braves. He was back playing with Des Moines in 1919 when he was picked up by the Washington Senators. Murphy batted a respectable .262 in 70 games that season.

The following January, Minneapolis of the American Association purchased his contract. He stayed with the Millers until 1924, when he was released to Denver. By this time Murphy had grown tired of train travel and decided to quit.

He was put on the suspended list by the National Commission and remained so until 1928, when he was reinstated, at which time officially retired.

Murphy was working as a truck driver in his hometown of Denver at the time of his death. He passed away on May 11, 1938, at his residence, 3826 Franklin Street, where he lived with his wife, Mae.

Murphy died as a result of chronic alcoholism and was laid to rest at the Mt. Olivet Cemetery in Wheat Ridge, Colorado, on May 14.

Chris Rickley

Christian Rickley appeared in just six games at shortstop for the 1884 Philadelphia Keystones of the Union Association, making his debut in a 6–4 win over the Washington Nationals on June 9. Overall, he batted .200 in his brief stay in the majors, going 5–25.

Rickley, a Philadelphia native, had a listed occupation as a laborer and was living with his wife in his hometown at 1203 W. Leithgow Street at the time of his death.

After his bout with the bottle, he died at St. Mary's Hospital as a result of alcoholic croupous pneumonia just 18 days after his 52nd birthday on October 29, 1911. He was buried that same day in Philadelphia's Greenmount Cemetery.

Cy Blanton

Darryl "Cy" Blanton was known for his breaking pitches, one of which he named "Dewdrop" due to its precipitous drop when crossing the plate. Many close to him felt that he could have been a great pitcher if not for his fondness for alcohol.

Blanton broke in with the Shawnee club in 1930, subsequently pitching for six more minor league teams before the Pittsburgh Pirates purchased his contract in 1933. He made his debut the following season on September 23, starting and pitching eight innings in a 3–2 win over the Cubs.

Back with the Pirates in 1935, Blanton became the outstanding rookie pitcher in the majors, going 18–13 with a 2.58 ERA. He never was able to duplicate the success of his rookie season, although he still remained effective. On May 21, 1940, after six seasons in "Steel City," he was granted free agency by Commissioner Landis. The Phillies almost immediately signed him to a contract in the hopes that a change of scenery would help him. Unfortunately, it was not to be. Blanton was a mere shadow of himself at this point in his career. Arm injuries and excessive drinking were taking their toll.

The best he could do with Philly was a 4–3 mark in his first season in 1940, followed by a miserable 6–13 in 1941. His 0–4 record in 1942 earned him a pink slip on June 12.

Blanton tried to regain his old form with the Hollywood Stars of the Pacific Coast League. But on March 27, 1945, he was suspended by Hollywood management for breaking training rules, having failed to get into shape since arriving at spring training.

By this time in his life, the bottle had begun taking a toll on him. Amazingly, Blanton got a letter from Uncle Sam, asking for him to report for pre-induction tests. Of course, Blanton did not pass, and in fact was recommended by doctors to get more tests and treatment. Blanton returned home to Oklahoma, where he eventually was admitted to the Central Oklahoma State Hospital in Norman on August 31.

While there, friends and relatives who visited could hardly recognize him. He was emaciated and at times acting erratic due to toxic psychosis. He was also suffering from cirrhosis of the liver, hepatic failure, and hemorrhages.

The painful end came on September 13, 1945, 13 days after entering the hospital. Blanton, who was just 37 years old, left a wife and four children.

He was buried in the Tecumseh Cemetery (Second Addition, Block 8, Lot 6, East Half, Grave 5) in Tecumseh, Oklahoma.

Dan Marion

Dan Marion had all the tools to star at the professional level, but alcohol addiction hammered him into an early grave.

He made his debut with the Brooklyn Tip Tops of the Federal League on April 24, 1914, in a 5–4 loss to the Pittsburgh Rebels. Marion started and got a no-decision in the contest and went on to appear in 17 games that season, going 3–2 with a 3.93 ERA.

The next year he accrued a 12–9 mark with a 3.20 ERA. After the Federals folded, his contract was awarded to Bloomington for 1916. He later played with Vernon in the PCL and Wichita.

After he hung up his spikes, he went back to Milwaukee, where he bartended, eventually operating a roadhouse called The Maple Leaf. Though noted as a first-rate bartender, he was never able to save any money, with his pay usually going to his rent and booze.

By 1933, even though his alcoholism had progressed to a dangerous point, he was still able to work at the roadhouse, and did so until a short time before his death. Marion lived at a rooming house located at 816 North 5th Street in Milwaukee at the time of his sad demise on January 18, 1933. He was found in his room, hemorrhaging from the mouth, and rushed to the Milwaukee County Emergency Hospital, where he died at 7:30 that night.

The cause of death was a ruptured esophageal varix caused by cirrhosis of the liver. When authorities informed his wife, Mae, of his passing, she informed them that they had been separated since about 1919 and that she was unable to provide funds for burial. If not for the good graces of some of his old baseball friends, Marion would have been buried in a potter's field. Officials from the Milwaukee Brewers of the American Association opened up their hearts and wallets and paid for all of his funeral and burial expenses.

Dan Marion was laid to read at the Mount Olivet Cemetery in Milwaukee on January 22, 1933. Besides officials from the Brewers, most of the people who showed up at his wake and funeral were either old teammates or patrons from the roadhouse.

His only known relatives, two sisters who lived in Cleveland, Ohio, never made it to the funeral.

Earl Smith

A catcher for five pennant winners, Arkansas native Earl Sutton "Oil" Smith was one of four Earl Smith's to play in the majors.

Simply put, he was the best of the bunch.

A lifetime .303 hitter, Smith usually won wherever he went. He was on two pennant-winners with the New York Giants, two with the Pirates, and one with the Cardinals.

Hard-drinking, tough as nails, and always ready for a brawl, Smith liked to call his own game as catcher, which usually put him at odds with managers, particularly the Giants' John McGraw.

Smith started his pro career in 1916 with Dallas of the Texas League and followed that up with stays in Waxahachie, Fort Smith–Tulsa, and Rochester before service in World War I. Smith signed with the Giants in 1919, playing solid baseball until an argument with McGraw forced his trade from New York on June 7, 1923, along with Jesse Barnes, to the Braves for Hank Gowdy and Mule Watson.

His stay with the Braves only lasted a year before the Pirates purchased his contract the following July. With Pittsburgh, he found life to be more pleasant due to manager Bill McKechnie's easier-going style. Under McKechnie's leadership, Smith enjoyed his best season as a pro in 1926, when he batted .346.

Released by the Pirates on July 9, 1928, he was signed the next day by the pennant-bound Cardinals, with whom he made his last World Series appearances. He stayed with the Cardinals until 1930, after which he played five years in the minors before switching over to managing in 1935.

Smith's last stop as manager was with Allentown of the Interstate League in 1940.

Smith retired to Hot Springs, Arkansas, in 1940, living in happy retirement until the early 1960s, when his health began to deteriorate. He spent the last 24 days of his life at the Little Rock Veterans Hospital, passing away at 9:00 PM on June 8, 1963, at the age of 66.

The cause of death was laennec cirrhosis due to alcoholism. Smith was buried at the Little Rock National Cemetery (Section 14, Grave 1238).

Fritz Henrich

A baseball, basketball, and football star at St. Joseph's College in Philadelphia, Fritz Henrich was reported to have played professional football for a while before the Phillies signed him off his semi-pro baseball team in the spring of 1924.

Henrich played 32 games for Philadelphia, making his debut on April 21, 1924, in a 7–4 loss to the Brooklyn Robins, pinch-hitting for pitcher Hal Carlson in the tenth inning. Later in the season, he was optioned to Williamsport, Pennsylvania, of the NY-Penn League but was recalled late in the season to finish out the year. The Phils optioned him to Beaumont of the Texas League for 1925, after which he retired from the game and moved back to his boyhood home of Philadelphia, where he lived at 358 West Mt. Airy Avenue.

He worked for the Sweda Cash Register Machine Company in Philadelphia as a sales rep, retiring in the mid-1950s. A heavy drinker, Henrich passed away due to esophageal bleeding and cirrhosis of the liver on May 1, 1959, eight days before his 60th birthday.

A widower at the time of his passing, he was buried at the Holy Sepulchre Cemetery on May 6, 1959.

George Watkins

The always-hustling and fiery George Watkins spent much of his career with St. Louis and once hit three homers in a game against the Phillies. His biggest home run, though, was a two-run shot in the third inning of Game 7 of the 1931 World Series off A's pitcher George Earnshaw.

Watkins, who also played for the Giants, Phillies, and Dodgers, wound up with a career .288 average with 73 homers and 420 RBIs.

Originally, Watkins was a semi-pro player playing in the Houston area when he was signed to a contract to play with Houston of the Texas League managed by Marv Goodwin. Watkins made additional stops with Marshall, Austin, and Beaumont before his breakthrough season came with Rochester of the International League, in 1929, in which he batted .346.

Signed by the Cardinals as outfield insurance, Watkins debuted with St. Louis on April 15, 1930, as a 28-year-old rookie. Watkins saw more action than he bargained for when Chick Hafey went down with an eye ailment. Forced into full-time service, Watkins batted .373 with 17 homers and 87 RBIs.

After a final season with Houston in 1936, Watkins retired. He went on to work as a laborer—working mostly in construction— and he served in the Navy during World War II. He died three days before his 70th birthday on June 1, 1970, at the Austin State Hospital. His death resulted from cirrhosis of the liver due to his lifelong consumption of alcohol. Watkins was buried at the Broyles Chapel Cemetery in Palestine, Texas.

Guy Lacy

Tennessee native Guy Lacy had a fierce temper and few temperate habits. In a shockingly violent and explosive incident in September of 1934, Lacy, while manager of the Jackson, Mississippi, club of the East Dixie League, shot and killed his 65 year old father–in–law, Lee Payne. The incident happened in front of the Payne home where Lacy's estranged wife Lela was staying. Lacy, who posted $5,000 bail, proclaimed his innocence in the matter and managed to escape the clutches of the legal system.

In another explosive, but far less violent incident, Lacy assaulted an umpire as manager of the Lynchburg club in the Virginia State League in 1940. He was fined $75.00 and suspended 10 days. To get around the suspension, Lacy watched the games from atop a tombstone that was located in a cemetery across from the ballpark.

On his request, he was given his release in February 1942 to pursue other opportunities.

The high-point of Lacy's pro career was a brief stint with the Cleveland Indians in 1926. He batted .167 in 13 games. The Indians released him to Newark, and he later played with Georgia and Bridgeport and managed Charlotte for three years.

His long, controversial career behind him, Lacy retired from the game and operated a fruit and dairy farm in his native Cleveland, Tennessee. Lacy died on November 19, 1953, as a result of myocardial decompensation due to cirrhosis of the liver caused by his long-standing drinking habit. To top that off, at the time of his passing, he also suffered from bronchiectasis—a rare lung infection.

He was survived by his ex-wife, a son, and two daughters. He was buried on November 20, 1953, at the Triplett Cemetery in Cleveland.

Harry Lochhead

A shortstop by trade, Harry Lochhead made his debut for the Cleveland Spiders on April 16, 1899, in a 6–5 loss to his former team, the St. Louis Perfectos. (Lochhead's name was spelled "Lockhead" in most of the box scores of the time.) Lochhead batted .238 that season for the Spiders—the worst team in major league history with a 20–134 record.

One could argue that playing for a team like the Spiders could drive any man to drink, but Lochhead had made a good friend of John Barleycorn well before joining Cleveland.

After appearing in one game for Detroit in 1901, Lochhead was sold in late April to Connie Mack's Athletics. Lochhead was sent out after nine games in which he batted .088. He later turned to umpiring in the Pacific Coast League and performed admirably until his health took a turn for the worse.

Lochhead, who was single, died at his mother Ellen's residence, located at 929 N. San Joaquin Street in Stockton, California, on August 22, 1909.

His passing was the result of cirrhosis of the liver due to his long-standing drinking problem. He was laid to rest in the Stockton Rural Cemetery on August 24.

John Jackson

Pitcher John Jackson, a resident of the Keystone State, played briefly for the Philadelphia Phillies in 1933. Coming out of the

University of Pennsylvania, Jackson signed with the National League club, making his pitching debut in the first game of a doubleheader against the Cincinnati Reds.

Jackson started and scattered eight hits in a 7–4 win. Jackson went 2–2 with a 6.00 ERA in 10 games during his short stint. He later pitched in the minors for the Albany Senators and the Charlotte Hornets of the Piedmont League, among others.

A veteran of World War II, he owned his own clothing retail business in Ocean City, New Jersey, where he also lived at the time of his death.

Jackson died at the Shore Memorial Hospital in Somers Point, New Jersey, on October 22, 1957, from cirrhosis of the liver due to chronic alcoholism. His body was brought to Philadelphia, where he was cremated at the West Laurel Hill Cemetery on October 25. He was just 48 years old.

Larry Corcoran

Larry Corcoran's name remains largely forgotten among the all-time greats in the history of baseball, even though, for a brief few years, he was probably the sport's best pitcher.

Corcoran teamed up with catcher Frank "Silver" Flint and became the acknowledged star hurler for Cap Anson's Chicago White Stockings. His pitches included a fastball and a breaking pitch that seemed to have an "up shoot" movement to it.

His won an amazing total of 170 games over a five-year period, from 1880 to 1884. He turned even more heads with three no-hitters.

Corcoran was one of the first pitchers to work out a set of signals with his catcher. He would chew tobacco, and at the suggestion of Flint, he would move his chew from one side of his mouth to the other, indicating when he would throw a curve ball.

By the 1885 season, the overworked right-hander was found to have an injured arm. After stints with New York, Washington, and Indianapolis, he was out of the league for good at the age of 27.

He worked as an umpire for a time in the Atlantic League. A heavy drinker, Corcoran died from Bright's disease in 1891 at the age of 32.

His .663 winning percentage is eighth best all-time. His brother, Mike, pitched one game for Chicago in 1884.

Larry Corcoran was buried in an unmarked grave in the Holy Sepulchre Cemetery (Section J, Lot 148, Grave 3) in East Orange, New Jersey.

Logan Drake

Sammy Strang, President of the Chattanooga Lookouts and a former major leaguer himself, said he once saw Logan Drake down 20 shots of whiskey on a bet from one of his teammates.

It is not known how much money Drake won, but one can only assume he was not fit to spend it right away—or even stand.

Drake began drinking at about the age of 15 and would continue to do so for the rest of his life. L.G., as he was known to his

Photograph courtesy of the Elmwood Cemetery, Columbia, South Carolina.

friends, spent the majority of his pro career playing for minor league teams in the South.

His major-league career lasted all of 10 games over parts of three seasons (1922–1924). He debuted for the Cleveland Indians on September 21, 1922, in a 15–5 blowout at the hands of the Boston Red Sox. Drake was one of five pitchers used in the contest.

His career mark was a 0–1 record with a hefty 7.71 ERA.

On June 17, 1924, Drake was optioned by the Indians to Wichita Falls, Texas, ending his major league career. Logan became a self-employed caterer/sandwich maker upon his retirement from the game.

He lived the last two years of his life at 1002 Elmwood Avenue in Columbia, South Carolina, with his wife, Iva. Drake's excessive alcohol abuse finally came to a head in 1940, when he was admitted to the Columbia Hospital on May 26. Drake began suffering from delirium and tremors after a minor operation to relieve hemorrhaging. He died on June 1, 1940, as a result of alcohol poisoning at the age of 40.

Drake's attending physician stated that the onset of his demise started 25 years earlier, just about the time when he discovered the bottle. Drake was buried at the Elmwood Cemetery (Square 61, West Half of Lot 18, Grave 3) in Columbia, South Carolina.

Mike Roach

Mike Roach had a less-than-memorable career as a major league baseball player, briefly serving with the National League's Washington Senators in 1899. But it was from his career in the minors and in private business that he became successful and wealthy.

Roach made his debut as a 29-year-old rookie on August 10, 1899, in a 5–4 loss to the Chicago Orphans. He batted .218 during his 24-game stint in the majors. Sold by Washington to Toronto of the Eastern League the following March, he later played with Los Angeles of the PCL, Ilion of the New York State League, and Wilkes-Barre, among others.

The Los Angeles team he played on was chock-full of former major leaguers, including Charley Atherton, Nick Altrock, Harry Spies, Patsy Dougherty, and Frank McPartlin.

Later, Roach purchased the Binghamton, New York, club with his friend, Mike Mooney. Roach eventually sold his baseball holdings and went into the hotel business full-time, owning the McDonald Hotel and later the Cadillac Hotel until his health forced him to slow down.

For the last two years of his life, he was forced to seek medical treatment in New York City from his brother, Dr. Charles P. Roach.

Mike Roach, who was an alcoholic, died as a result of cirrhosis of the liver complicated by chronic nephritis on November 12, 1916. Roach was survived by his wife and two small children. Roach's body was taken back to Renova, Pennsylvania, for burial.

Mike Slattery

Born and raised in South Boston, Mike Slattery played parts of five seasons in the majors, starting with the 1884 Boston Reds of the Union Association. That first season would be the busiest of his career as he appeared in 106 games.

His best season was for the 1890 New York Giants of the Players League when he batted .306.

In between his playing time at the big league level, Slattery played in the minors, most notably in the New England League and later, after his major league career, with Binghamton, Wilkes-Barre, and Worcester.

Injuries forced his retirement in the mid-1890s, but he and his wife were not wanting for money after she inherited $30,000 from a relative in 1892. Slattery did quite well after his retirement. His notoriety preceded him with customers in his job as chief salesman of a Boston haberdashery.

Upon his death in 1904, obituaries stated that he died as a result of stomach trouble, but the truth was a bit more insidious. Slattery died at the Carney Hospital in Boston, Massachusetts, on October 16, 1904.

His demise at the age of 37 was the result of hypertrophic cirrhosis of the liver due to alcoholism, complicated by chronic gastroenteritis. Hypertrophic cirrhosis of the liver was also known as "gin drinker's liver."

He was buried at the Holyhood Cemetery in Brookline, Massachusetts.

Monk Dubial

Monk Dubial was a pitcher for seven seasons from 1944 to 1952 with the New York Yankees, the Philadelphia Phillies, and the Chicago Cubs.

In 1944 he joined the wartime Yankees for two years, winning a combined 23 games and losing 22 before being sent to the minors when players started to return from military service. (He himself was excused from serving because of an eye ailment.)

Dubial returned to the bigs in 1948 with Philly, where he

spent only one year as a starter and reliever before being traded to Chicago. The Cubs used him primarily as a relief pitcher over three seasons, but Dubial was seriously hampered by back and hip injuries and would pitch in only one game in 1952 before being released.

His career totals were a record of 45–53 in 187 games pitched with 289 strikeouts, 11 saves, and a 3.87 ERA.

Dubial, who worked for the post office after baseball, died from cirrhosis of the liver on October 23, 1969. He was buried in the Center Cemetery in Rocky Hill, Connecticut.

Pete Childs

An infielder by trade who could also play the outfield when called upon, Pete Childs appeared in 205 games in the majors over two seasons.

He logged time between 1901 and 1902 with the St. Louis Cardinals, Chicago Orphans, and Philadelphia Phillies.

Nicknamed "Petie" by his teammates, Childs made his debut with the Cardinals on April 24, 1901. After batting .266 in 29 games, mostly in a utility role, he was released in early August. The Chicago Orphans picked him up for a song and, although he did not hit much, he played heady ball for Tom Loftus' troops. The following March, Childs signed a contract with the hometown Phillies. He played 123 games that year, all at second base, and batted just .194.

Childs played in the American Association for several years before turning to managing. He managed Portsmouth of the Ohio State League to a pennant in 1910 before retiring from baseball after the 1916 season.

He lived with his wife, Ella, at 2528 West York Street in Philadelphia at the time of his death. Only a few months before his demise, during the holiday season of 1921, some of his old teammates ran in to him while he was selling Christmas trees on a lot near the Phillies Stadium, the Baker Bowl.

One of them, Roy Thomas, said that Childs "had the face of a beaten man about him."

Little did they know that Childs was not long for this earth. An alcoholic, he died from cirrhosis of the liver on February 15, 1922. He was laid to rest on February 20 in the West Laurel Hill Cemetery (Rockland Section, Lot 509). Childs was just 50 years old.

Rudy Schwenck

Rudy Schwenck was a lifetime minor leaguer except for the three games he pitched for the Chicago Cubs in 1909.

He made his debut as the starting pitcher, and loser, in the first game of a doubleheader against Brooklyn on September 23. Schwenck got off to a bad start in that game when he failed to cover fist base on a bunt by leadoff hitter Al Burch. After allowing three runs in the first inning, he settled down and pitched well, letting up only a single run in the third.

The final score was 4–1 in favor of the Superbas.

Schwenck posted his lone major-league victory, 5–1, on October 6 in the second game of a doubleheader against the Cardinals. Schwenck went with the Cubs to spring training in 1910 but was "sent out" by manager Frank Chance after he failed to make the midnight curfew. Kicked off the team, Schwenk was then sold to his hometown Louisville Colonels on April 8, from which he was eventually sold to the New Orleans Pelicans that August. He later hurled with Spokane of the Northwest League and the Sacramento Senators of the PCL.

After his baseball career, Schwenck became a real estate salesman in his hometown of Louisville, where he lived with his wife, Mabel, at 57 Fairlawn Road.

Schwenck died at 11:30 PM on November 27, 1941, at a sanitarium near Anchorage, Kentucky, from the effects of hyperstatic pneumonia due to alcoholism. Schwenck, who was 57 years old, was buried at the Cave Hill Cemetery (South Half, Section P, Lot 806) in Louisville, on December 1.

Jimmy Hudgens

Already considered by major league scouts to be a fine young hitter, Jimmy Hudgens was only 20 years old in 1923 when he led the Nebraska State League in home runs (13) while playing for the Fairbury Jeffersons.

The Newburg, Missouri, native's contract was purchased that September by the St. Louis Cardinals, with whom he made his major league debut on September 14.

A lefty-swinging first baseman who could also play the outfield, he appeared in six games for St. Louis, batting .250. Even though he was invited to spring training the next year, the intent was to eventually send him to the minors for seasoning.

In April 1924 the Cards sent him to the Fort Smith, Arkansas, team. After a year in the minors, he reappeared with the Reds in 1925, appearing in three games for them. In the spring of 1926, Cincinnati looked to find a place for him on their roster, but with first base already occupied by Wally Pipp and back-up Rube Bressler, it was decided to send him to the minors.

He spent time that season with both Seattle of the PCL and the Minneapolis Millers of the American Association. In between minor league duty, Hudgens came up for a total of 17 games at the big league level and batted .250. With his final game in the majors on September 25, 1926, Hudgens' lifetime average stood at .282.

He played with Seattle in the PCL for several seasons, but eventually moved back east, where he played for the Charlotte Hornets, Asheville Tourists, and the Huntington, West Virginia, club.

After his career, he moved back to Missouri, where he eventually became employed by the Magic Chef Corporation as a laborer.

Hudgens died two days after his 53rd birthday, August 26, 1955, at the St. Louis City Hospital from laennec cirrhosis and hepatic insufficiency due to alcoholism.

The next day, with little fanfare, he was buried at the St. Matthew Cemetery in St. Louis.

Suicide Squeeze

The annals of human history are teeming with suicides, and scores of famous and well-liked personas are among them. All walks of life are represented—artists, musicians, politicians, authors, poets, comedians, and even psychoanalysts, with their granddaddy, Sigmund Freud, heading the list.

Still, suicide remains taboo in many religions. No question, it's a big-time moral stigma in some orthodoxies. But as religions and institutions have evolved over time, one thing has remained constant: the human condition and the pain it can bring.

For some unfortunate souls, there will always be pain that is profound and persistent. The pain can be physical, emotional, or psychological. For some, suicide is what finally puts the pain to rest.

Baseball players are no different, and the ones in this chapter took the "suicide solution" for a variety of reasons. Mostly, it was to end depression or physical suffering.

There was the case of love-sick Bob Langsford who poisoned himself at the turn of the century while gazing at the picture of a young actress.

There was "baseball acrobat" Jackie Price, who made millions in ballparks laugh at his antics but was unable to bring any lasting joy to himself.

There was Fraley Rogers, who killed himself when his malaria became unbearable, and Eddie Hohnhurst, who ended it all after being racked with guilt for killing a man in the line of duty as a police officer.

And how about back-up-catcher-turned-starter Willard Hershberger, who slashed his throat after a couple of losses in the middle of a pennant race because he didn't think he played well enough?

Coroners are obligated to put suicide on the death certificate if that's what they think happened. Sometimes, it's a judgment call.

For the rest of us, what's needed most is compassion, not judgment.

It doesn't help getting too philosophical about the matter. Remember, Socrates himself put a cup of hemlock to his lips.

Willard Hershberger

Willard Hershberger has the dubious distinction of being the only baseball player to commit suicide during the season. It appears he simply cracked under the pressure of being a major league catcher in a pennant race.

Traded by the Yankees to the Cincinnati Reds for Eddie Miller and $40,000 cash on December 3, 1937, Hershberger became the backup to future Hall of Famer Ernie Lombardi. In late July 1940, Hershberger was forced into the starting role when Lombardi sprained an ankle in a game at Philadelphia.

Mentally, Hershberger was just not prepared to deal with the situation. "Little Slug," as he was affectionately called by his teammates, obsessed about his game, particularly in the way he called pitches. A 5–4 loss to the Giants the Wednesday before his death seemed to affect him greatly. The Reds were in the heat of

a pennant race, and there were rumblings in the clubhouse that the team might have fared better if Lombardi were behind the plate.

Then a doubleheader loss to the Boston Braves really sank his spirits.

Cincy manager Bill McKechnie took to talking to him to ease his mind, since he knew that his player worried about literally every facet of the game. But it was to no avail. When Hershberger failed to show up at Braves Field for the game on August 3, 1940,

Reds traveling secretary Gabe Paul called the hotel where he was staying.

Hershberger's reply to Paul was, "I'm sick and can't play, but I will come out right away anyway."

Later, when Hershberger still failed to report, Paul sent Cincinnati businessman Sam Cohen, who was also a close friend of Hershberger, to check in on him. When Cohen got to the hotel, he found the door to Hershberger's room locked. With the aid of a maid, he entered the room and found a grizzly discovery.

Lying there, slumped over the bathtub, face first, was Hershberger. He had slit his own throat with a razor.

Evidently, the pressure had just been too much. With the Reds, Hershberger found himself playing behind an All-Star catcher for the second time in his career. (He backed up Bill Dickey with the Yankees.)

Still, friends and teammates could only surmise. There was no note given. The only thing police found were a few uncashed checks. His death was a devastating shock to his teammates. Even though Hershberger was known as a bit of a hypochondriac, he never once spoke of ending his life. There was, however, a recent history of suicide in his family. His father had taken his own life in 1928.

When news of his death reached the Reds, Bill McKechnie was said to have cried like a baby. The Reds, as expected, went into a deep mourning.

The grand irony is that the Reds went on to win the World Series that fall over the Tigers. Most of the players dedicated the rest of the season to their friend.

Hershberger, who had just bought his mother a new house, was laid to rest in the Visalia Cemetery in Visalia, California.

Jackie Price

John Thomas Reid Price literally made millions laugh as he entertained crowds, both large and small, from coast to coast as a base-

ball entertainer and stuntman in the 1930s and 1940s.

Ironically, his life ended in the saddest of fashions when he hanged himself from a light fixture on October 2, 1967.

Price only appeared in seven games in the majors—four of them at the shortstop position. Yet he was remembered by countless fans who saw his on-field act, which was like no other.

Unlike Al Schacht and Nick Altrock, who performed a vaudevillian style of comedy for fans, Price was more of a "baseball stuntman" who would perform wild physical stunts that would make most entertainers performing on *The Ed Sullivan Show* jealous. His brand of baseball comedy was often called "screwball baseball."

Some of his stunts included him shooting a baseball out of an air gun, then jumping into a jeep and speeding out to the outfield to catch the plummeting sphere. Price was limber enough to bat a baseball upside down from a trapeze or a backstop. He also would perform a trick that reminded one of the old tale of David and Goliath, hurling a baseball out of the park using a sling.

Price would amaze fans by pitching two balls at the same time, one a curve and the other a fastball, and batting two balls with a fungo bat at the same time, sending them in opposite directions.

He perfected his act in the minors, where he started as a semi-pro player in 1934, then moved on to minor league stops in Union City, Asheville, and Daytona Beach before entering the U.S. Army. Discharged with the rank of Tech 5, he restarted his career in 1944 with Columbus, Ohio.

Splitting the 1945 season between Columbus and Milwaukee, he moved to the Pacific Coast League's Oakland Oaks, managed by Casey Stengel in 1946. It was while at Oakland that Price, by now well known for his baseball antics, was purchased by Bill Veeck for the Cleveland Indians.

The Yankees under Larry MacPhail tried to grab him first, but Veeck beat them to it, stating, "He won't hit much, but he is the greatest baseball entertainer in the country."

At the height of his popularity, Price was making between $250 and $500 per appearance and usually averaged about 40,000 miles a year in travel, mostly by car. He packed the majority if his work in a three-month time frame during the baseball season, often traveling to such places as Canada and Cuba.

For the last seven years of his life, Price supplemented his income by working as a bartender, and he was working at the J&J Bar in his adopted hometown of San Francisco. For reasons known only to himself, Price attached a leather belt to a light fixture while in an intoxicated state (his blood-alcohol level was .028), then wrapped the belt around his neck and hung himself at approximately 10:25 PM.

His body was taken to Olivet Memorial Park, where it was cremated. His remains were then buried at the Golden Gate National Cemetery in San Bruno, California (Section Z, Grave 1929-A).

Price, who was only 54 years old, had lived with his wife, Martha, at 1563 Treat Street in San Francisco.

Fraley Rogers

There's nothing more annoying than that last mosquito of summer—especially if it bites you and gives you a case of malaria so severe that you're prompted to take your own life.

Pity poor Fraley Rogers. He played 45 games with the National Association's Boston Red Stockings in 1872, batting .278 with 1 homer and 28 RBIs. After one game the next season, he left baseball to work for L. Schepp & Co.—eventually rising to head clerk status.

Unfortunately for him, by 1881 the level of parasites coursing through his bloodstream was also rising. Chills, fever, sweats, and general weakness are the telltale symptoms of malaria, and Rogers' physician suggested he take a trip to Bermuda to try and regain his health.

The warm tropical breezes and climate did him little good, and his condition worsened. When he arrived back in the States, his actions became alarming. He would mutter at times and showed signs of delirium.

Rogers went to bed on Monday night, May 10, and according to his wife, had a restful night's sleep. He arose the next morning at about 8:00 AM, got partially dressed, walked out of his bedroom into a sitting room, pulled out a pistol, and shot himself in the left temple.

A longtime New Yorker, Rogers was residing at 100 West 129th Street and was thought by physicians to be temporarily insane at the time of his death.

His body was brought to Westborough, Massachusetts, for burial. When Fraley's brother, Mort, received the news of his brother's death, he was overcome with grief and wound up dying three days later on May 13.

Fraley and Mort played their first organized baseball together with an amateur club, the Brooklyn Resolutes. Mort eventually moved on to work as part of the National Association's rules committee.

Even though it was reported that Mort died from shock, more romantic thinking by friends and acquaintances suggested that he died from a broken heart.

Bob Langsford

Love-sick, star-struck Bob Langsford poisoned himself to death with the picture of a young actress before him.

A one-game wonder in the majors, he made his debut at the age of 34 at shortstop for the Louisville Eclipse on June 18, 1899, in a 7–2 loss to the Baltimore Orioles before 3,500 fans at Eclipse Park.

Newspaper accounts used his real name in wire stories and box scores of the time. (He was born Robert Hugo Lankswert in Louisville, Kentucky, on August 5, 1865.)

Langsford became well-known in local baseball circles as first an amateur then a semi-pro—he made his mark as a professional in the minors. Some of his minor league stops included Evansville in the Northwestern League, Mobile, New Orleans, Memphis, and Atlanta of the Southern League and the Southern Association.

That New Orleans team was filled with former major leaguers, including Abner Powell, Count Campau, King Bailey, Pat Luby, and Kid Baldwin. Langsford was severely beaned while playing with Mobile in the early 1890s and had fits of strange behavior for the rest of his life, though it did not affect his play in the field.

On January 10, 1907, Langsford decided to take his own life in a curious manner. He sat before a mirror while gazing at a picture of a young actress named Elsie Cresey. Apparently, Langsford had been smitten by the young girl, who appeared in a play at the Avenue Theatre in Louisville two years earlier.

No one was quite sure as to Langford's relationship with the woman, but it was believed the two had a brief and torrid affair. Langsford fixed the picture so that Cresey's face would be the last thing he ever saw as he downed one ounce of carbolic acid. He died before reaching the hospital and was buried at the Cave Hill Cemetery in Louisville, Kentucky (Section 8, Range 216, Grave 24).

Oh, and the name of the play? *To Die at Dawn.*

Art Irwin

Art Irwin was a player and manager whose first claim to fame was "discovering" Lou Gehrig as a scout for the New York Giants in 1921.

His other claim is that he is credited for inventing the football scoreboard.

Irwin played with Worcester, Providence, Washington, and Philadelphia of the National League, along with Boston Clubs in both the Players League and American Association. He had a lifetime .241 average over 13 seasons.

He was also a manager with the Washington, Philadelphia, and New York Clubs of the National League and the Boston club of the Players League. He went 416–427 overall as a skipper.

In ill health and suffering from depression, he committed suicide by jumping off the Metropolitan Line steamer *Calvin Austin* into the Atlantic Ocean. He had been on his way to Boston to see his "legal" wife and family. After his death it was learned that he had, in fact, two families—one in New York and one in Boston and that he had lived a double life for more than 30 years.

Some have suggested that the possibility of a scandal was the direct cause of his suicide.

Bob Gandy

Bob Gandy got one shot to play in the majors with Philadelphia in 1916. The Phillies signed him to a contract on August 22 of that season, and Gandy appeared in his only major league game on October 4 in a 7–5 win by the Phillies over the Boston Braves.

The win clinched second place for Philadelphia.

Gandy started off his professional career with Waycross, Georgia, of the Florida State League, part of the F.L.A.G. (Florida-Alabama-Georgia) League in 1913. He eventually moved on to Portsmouth, Virginia, in 1916.

Gandy continued to pitch in the minors for several more seasons in cities such as New London, Hartford, and Charleston, South Carolina.

After his career, Gandy, a Jacksonville, Florida, native, worked as chief paymaster for the McGiffin Coal Company.

On June 19, 1945, in ill health, Gandy took his own life with a gun sitting in his driveway at 2103 Gilmore Avenue in Jacksonville, Florida. He left a widow, Ethel, and was buried at the Oaklawn Cemetery in Jacksonville, Florida, on June 21. He was 52 years old.

Bob Rothel

Robert Burton Rothel chose to end his own life with a self-inflicted gunshot on Wednesday, March 21, 1984.

He made his major league debut with the Cleveland Indians on April 22, 1945, in a 6–3 loss to the Tigers at Detroit. Starting at third base, he was one of four Indians players to commit errors in the game. Allie Reynolds was the starter and loser in the game that was seen by 23,063 fans at Briggs Stadium.

Heading to spring training that season, Indians manager Lou Boudreau was looking for a replacement for veteran star third baseman Ken Keltner. Rothel was one of three third basemen in the mix, along with Eddie Wheeler and Roy Cullenbine. Cullenbine was said to have the big advantage due to his experience and good bat. Rothel would only appear in four games that April for Cleveland, batting .200 on two hits in 10 at-bats.

The Indians soon solved their third base problem with a trade on April 27.

Cullenbine was sent to the Tigers for Dutch Meyer and third baseman Don Ross. Rothel would undergo a pre-induction examination in early May, but fail. He soon was optioned to Wilkes-Barre. He was recalled by the Indians in September but failed to appear in a single game. Rothel was kept on the 40-man roster by Cleveland for the 1945 season and then optioned to Baltimore in February 1946.

After his retirement from the game, Rothel, whose favorite hobby was trout fishing, became president of State Sales Inc. of Elyria, Ohio. He moved to Huron, Ohio, three years before his death at age 60.

He left a wife, daughter, and stepson, and was buried at the York Chapel Cemetery in Bellevue, Ohio.

Ed "Cannonball" Crane

A standout athlete, Crane could play outfield, catch, and pitch. His strong throwing arm, which once hurled a ball 405 feet, earned him the nickname "Cannonball."

Crane also enjoyed getting blasted. Alcohol was his drug of choice, and his eventual addiction, coupled with a bout of emotional trauma, would lead him to take his own life by ingesting poison.

Crane honed his skills as a youth on the sandlots of South Boston and joined the hometown Boston Reds of the Union Association in 1884 where he was used primarily as an outfielder and catcher. He showed superior power by smacking 12 home runs, good enough for second place behind league leader Fred Dunlap's 13.

Spending the 1887 season in the minors with Toronto, he joined the New York Giants the next season where he became a full-time pitcher. Although future Hall of Famers Mickey Welch and Timmy Keefe were considered to be the heart and soul of the pitching staff, Crane nonetheless did quite well, especially in the postseason where he accrued a 5–2 lifetime record in the World Series (before 1903 the World Series contests were considered exhibition games). In the 1888 World Series, he went 1–1, and in 1889 he pitched to a sizzling 4–1 record.

Crane was invited to join the famous Spalding World Baseball Tour, which was to be a vehicle to introduce the game of baseball to foreign countries. It was while Crane was on tour that he took up the practice of drinking. Crane did not start his imbibing until the Spalding Conglomerate reached Paris, but he found liquor to his liking.

Crane jumped to the New York Giants of the Players League in 1890, hurling to a 16–19 record. In 1891 he split time between Cincinnati teams in the American Association and the National League. (He led the AA in its final season with a 2.45 ERA.) He returned to the Giants in 1892, going 16–24.

By 1893 the drinking had pretty much taken its toll as Crane appeared in only 12 games total for the Giants before being released. Brooklyn signed him in early July, but he was just as ineffective. After Brooklyn released him, he negotiated with Providence for a contract but never came to terms.

Because Crane had some experience as an umpire at the big-league level in 1892 and 1893, Eastern League president Pat Powers gave him a job as an umpire in 1896, but he soon lost his job due to unsatisfactory work caused by his drinking. That, coupled with two failed attempts at playing with Providence and Springfield, put him over the edge.

When Crane was informed that he was about to be evicted from his hotel room in Rochester, he decided that enough was enough. He went to his room and swallowed a bottle of Chloral. He died almost instantly. Friends and family were taken aback, but not surprised by his death, thinking that he had slowly been committing suicide with alcohol for several years.

Crane, who was 34 years old, left a wife and young child. He was buried at Holyhood Cemetery in Brookline, Massachusetts.

Charlie Hollocher

When healthy, Charlie Hollocher was a top-flight shortstop who even took part in two triple plays and twice led the

National League in field-ing average. But he was snake-bitten when it came to injuries—so much so that people thought he was a hypochondriac.

He wasn't faking any-thing on August 14, 1940, when he shot himself in the neck with a shotgun he had just purchased from a mail-order store. His body was found on the side of the road, lying near his car on a highway in Frontenac, Missouri.

Early in his playing career, Hollocher had joined the crack Wabada Amateur Team under the tutelage of John B. Sheridan. He then moved on to Muscatine and Keokuk of the Central Association and was drafted by Portland of the Pacific Coast League, which sent him to their affiliate at Rock Island of the Three-I League for seasoning.

From there he was drafted by the Chicago Cubs.

A right-handed thrower and left-handed batter, Hollocher was a good hitter who rarely struck out. As a rookie in 1918, he smacked out 161 hits to lead the National League, helping the Cubs reach the World Series where they lost to the Boston Red Sox. His .340 average in 1922 was the highest mark for a short-stop since Honus Wagner batted .354 in 1908.

Over the course of his major league career he accrued a life-time batting average of .304 in 2,936 career at bats with 14 home runs and 241 RBIs.

Because of injuries, real and imagined, he never fulfilled his promise. The Cubs team captain, he actually quit the team several times—one time seeking advice from a doctor over a stomach ailment that had been giving him problems for several years.

After he retired from baseball, he took time off, spending it mostly golfing. He eventually opened up a tavern in St. Louis, became an investigator for the St. Louis County Attorney, and worked as a watchman for a drive-in theater.

Hollocher even returned to baseball in 1931 as a scout for the Cubs.

He was only 44 years old at the time of his death. There were some who surmised that Hollocher was suffering from syphilis, and many of his former teammates said they suspected that it was that insidious disease that caused the stomach ailment years earlier.

Syphilis may well have been in its third and final stage by the time of his suicide. No one can say for sure. Hollocher's death certificate listed his death as suicide by gunshot, and the coroner never looked to see if he was suffering any form of infection.

Hollocher is buried on the Oak Hill Cemetery in Kirkwood, Missouri.

Chet Chadbourne

Chet "Pop" Chadbourne paid plenty of dues in the minors to earn his time in the majors. He was even an umpire before punching out in his retirement years by a self-inflicted gunshot in Los Angeles.

In the majors, he logged time over five seasons with the Boston Pilgrims/Red Sox in the American League (1906–1907), the Kansas City Packers of the Federal League (1914–1915), and the Boston Braves of the National League (1918).

More significantly, Chadbourne was a minor league star, collecting 3,216 hits over 21 seasons in the Pacific Coast League.

In the mid 1920s he became an umpire in the PCL and then retired to become a bartender in L.A. He was living with his wife, Gladys, at 5028 South Harvard Street when he took his own life.

He was cremated at the Rosedale Crematory three days later, and his ashes were given to his wife.

Drummond Brown

During the Great Depression, after a modest career in baseball, Drummond Brown pulled the plug, or rather trigger, on himself in January 1927.

Brown was a catcher/first baseman who played for the Brooklyn Robins (Dodgers) of the National League and the Kansas City Packers of the Federal League. Over parts of three major league seasons, he appeared in 123 games, batting .241 on 77 hits, with two home runs and 33 RBIs in 319 at-bats.

Starting off with the minor league Kansas City Blues, he made his major league debut with a 15-game stint in 1913 for the Boston Braves, in which he batted .324.

He jumped to the newly formed Federal League for the 1914 season.

Over the course of the next two seasons, he appeared mostly as a part-time player. After the Federal League collapsed, he went on to manage several small town teams in the South Western League.

He later became a Kansas City detective and then an appliance salesman before becoming unemployed. He suffered for weeks from depression, unable to find a job, before finally committing suicide with a revolver four days before his 42nd birthday.

He left a wife, an 18-year-old daughter, and six-year-old son. He is buried in the Line Creek Cemetery in Platte Woods, Missouri.

Eddie Hohnhorst

While working as a policeman in Kentucky after his baseball career, Eddie Hohnhorst shot and killed a black man in the process of arresting him. Guilt-ridden and emotionally tormented by the incident, he became beset by alcoholism, lack of sleep, stomach pains, and depression that turned into temporary insanity.

Hohnhorst then turned his service revolver on himself on March 28, 1916.

Edward Hicks Hohnhorst was a native of Covington, Kentucky. He developed into a first baseman with a good glove, who could hit for average with occasional power. He played with teams such as the New Orleans Pelicans, Augusta Tourists, Atlanta Crackers, and San Antonio of the Texas League.

Purchased by the Cleveland Naps from Boston in 1910, he made his major league debut on September 10, 1910, in a 15–3 loss to the Tigers. Hohnhorst replaced George Stovall at first base.

In 18 games, Hohnhorst batted .318 with six RBIs.

After stops with Toledo in 1911 he ended up with Montgomery of the Southern Association in 1913 and soon retired to become a member of the Covington, Kentucky, police department.

It was 1915 when he accidentally killed the man in the line of duty. Although he was found faultless for the shooting, the incident haunted him to the end. He was married and living at 1910 Jefferson Avenue when he decided to end his suffering.

The death certificate cited temporary insanity.

Buried at the Highland Cemetery in Fort Mitchell, Kentucky, on March 30, he was just 31 years old.

Elmer Leifer

Elmer Leifer appeared in only nine major league games for the Chicago White Sox in 1921. He then suffered a career-ending injury after being sent down to Arkansas Travelers of the Southern Association.

During a game against the Atlanta Crackers, in Atlanta, on Wednesday, May 10, 1922, Leifer and shortstop Jarvis Jackson were involved in a frightful collision in short left field when they attempted to catch a pop-up. They smashed headfirst into each other and crumpled to the ground.

Leifer was the more seriously injured of the two, sustaining severe damage to the optic nerve of his left eye. At the hospital, there was talk of an enucleation (removal of the eye) if complications set in, but he was eventually released after several weeks.

Several benefit games were played throughout the Southern Association to help defray medical expenses for Leifer, who was forced to find an occupation outside of baseball. Eventually, he settled back in his home state of Washington where he became a foreman at a lumber mill. Through the years he was sometimes bothered by the complications from his injuries, including severe headaches.

On September 26, 1948, Leifer committed suicide by ingesting an overdose of Nembutal, a barbiturate that is often used for the treatment of insomnia. Leifer, who lived at the Avon Hotel in Everett, Washington, with his wife, Leola, was also survived by four brothers and two sisters.

He was buried in the Leifer Family Plot (Row-18 in the Pine City Cemetery) in Pine City, Washington.

George Jeffcoat

After hanging up the spikes and picking up the Bible, George Jeffcoat was a Baptist minister when he inexplicably and unexpectedly shot himself to death at his home in Leesville, North Carolina, on October 17, 1978.

The motive for taking his own life was not made public, but there was some suspicion that he may have been in ill health.

The older brother of major league outfielder/pitcher Hal Jeffcoat, George was a football and basketball player at the University of South Carolina. Jeffcoat pitched in 70 games in the majors with the Brooklyn Dodgers and Boston Braves.

Appearing mostly in relief, he accrued a 7–11 lifetime record.

Jeffcoat pitched with Allentown before joining the Dodgers, with whom he was noted for having an outstanding curveball. He made his debut on April 20, 1936, in an 8–4 loss to the Boston Bees. Jeffcoat relieved Dodgers starter George Ernshaw in the first inning.

In the minors Jeffcoat played for the Nashville Vols, managed by Larry Gilbert, from 1939 to 1942. On September 5, 1942, Nashville sold his contract to Boston, where he finished out his major league career with a 1–2 record in eight games. He later played with Indianapolis, Shreveport, and Nashville again.

In 1948, after his career was over, Jeffcoat, who was deeply religious, enrolled in the Baptist Theological Seminary in New Orleans. For the last 17 years of his life, he led the Old Lexington Baptist Church in Leesville, South Carolina.

Jeffcoat was buried at Old Lexington Baptist Church Cemetery, Leesville, South Carolina.

Guy Morrison

West Virginia native Walter "Guy" Morrison broke into pro ball in 1920 with Evansville after leaving Virginia Wesleyan College. He played for Bloomington in 1922 and St. Paul in 1923 before the New York Giants purchased his contract, sending him outright to San Antonio.

In 1924 he returned to Bloomington and then toiled for several minor league teams, including Decatur, Quincy, and Idaho Falls. In 1927 the Pirates obtained him, sending him to Waterbury. It was from that franchise that he was purchased by the Braves in 1927. He played 12 games for Boston over parts of the 1927 and 1928 seasons. After a one-game appearance in 1928, he was back in the minors for good with Bloomington.

Morrison retired in 1930 to become the director of physical education for the city of Grand Rapids. It was while in this position that he committed suicide by shooting himself in the head on August 14, 1934.

He was buried in the Sunset Memorial Park in South Charleston, West Virginia.

Jim McElroy

A graduate of St. Mary's College of California, James D. McElroy appeared in 15 games in the majors in 1884 for the Philadelphia Phillies and Wilmington Quicksteps of the Union Association.

It is unclear whether his death by morphine overdose was a suicide or an accident caused by a fellow addict administering a larger, stronger dose than intended.

Released by Wilmington, he later pitched for Norfolk, Memphis, and then Topeka of the Western League in 1886. McElroy and his battery mate from Topeka, Harry Smith, were signed by Abilene, and in late December they took a Santa Fe Railroad train to Albuquerque, New Mexico, where they hooked up with the Hutchinson semi-pro club.

McElroy's stay in the "Land of Enchantment" was a rough one. He never really got into playing shape and lost his day job. Some legal trouble followed in which he had to pay a fine. After only a year's stay, he moved back to his home state and settled in Needles, California, where he got a job tending bar.

By this time in his life, his arm had pretty much given out, although he still had hopes of pitching with some success again. Much worse, he had apparently gotten into some bad habits that included drugs. His demise, which occurred just six months after his arrival, was due to a morphine overdose.

Many newspaper accounts stated that his overdose was self-inflicted, while dispatches from *The Needles* reported that he was administered a fatal dose by a fellow opium fiend.

McElroy died at approximately 1:30 PM on July 24, 1889, at the age of 26.

Suicide or accidental overdose? The only thing that's for sure is that McElroy's life ended before he had a chance to really live.

Jim Oglesby

Jim Oglesby's big-league career consisted of three games with the 1930 Philadelphia Athletics. A spiking from a sliding opponent curtailed his stay with the A's, and he soon found himself back in the minors.

After several more years in the minors, he retired to become manager of the Chicago Cubs farm teams in Sioux Falls, South Dakota, and Springfield, Illinois.

He left baseball and became a security guard for the Douglas Aircraft Corporation in Tulsa, Oklahoma. Suffering from ill health and depression, he killed himself with a shotgun blast to the head in 1955. He was 55 years old.

Limb McKenry

Frank Gordon "Limb" McKenry was also known as "Big Pete" due to his 6'4", 205-pound frame. He logged plenty of minor league time from 1912 to 1915 in the Washington State, California, and Northwest Leagues before he was brought up to the Reds in June. In 13 games he accrued a 5–5 record.

The next year, after going 1–1 in six games, he left Cincinnati, retiring to a fruit farm in Selma, California.

By the mid 1950s, McKenry, who was divorced, was beginning to get depressed due to chronic rheumatoid arthritis that was taking a persistent and painful toll on him.

On Thursday night, November 1, 1956, at about 8:20 PM, McKenry put a shotgun to the roof of his mouth and fired while inside his apartment located at 1426 Delmar Avenue in Fresno.

He left no note. He was survived by a brother, two sisters, two daughters, and two grandchildren, and was laid to rest on November 5 at the Mountain View Cemetery in Oakland, California. McKenry was 68 years old.

Lyle Bigbee

Lyle Bigbee was one of a host of young pitchers Manager Connie Mack was counting on to give his Philadelphia Athletics a lift when spring training rolled around in Lake Charles, Louisiana, in 1920.

Bigbee made his debut for the A's on April 15 in a 4–1 loss to the Yankees. He was used as both a pitcher and outfielder/utility man in 38 games that season—going 0–3 on the mound while batting .187 with one homer and eight RBIs.

It wasn't quite the lift Mack was hoping for.

Bigbee was released to the Newark Bears in 1921 and wound up bouncing around with several teams, with stops in Pittsburgh, Milwaukee, Louisville, and finally Los Angeles of the Pacific Coast League, which released him in June 1924, effectively ending his career.

Bigbee did some farming for a while until he got a job as a shipfitter for the Kaiser Ship Yard in Vancouver, Washington. For the last 10 years of his life, he lived at 927 SW 11th Avenue in Portland with his wife, Ellen.

On August 5, 1942, at the age of 48, he committed suicide at the Portland Motel by shooting himself in the right temple with a pistol.

Bigbee, brother of major league outfielder Carson Bigbee, was buried at the Liberty Cemetery in Sweet Home, Oregon.

Morrie Rath

Morrie Rath played his first major league game in 1909 and his last, 11 years later, in 1920. He spent more time struggling in the minors than he did playing in the majors due mainly to his inability to consistently hit big-league pitching until late in his career.

In the majors, he was a second and third baseman for six seasons with the Philadelphia Athletics, Cleveland Indians, Chicago White Sox, and Cincinnati Reds.

Rath had a five-year stint in the minors and also spent a year in the navy during World War I before he was brought up by the Reds in 1919 as their starting second baseman. He responded with a great year in the field (leading National League second basemen in double plays, chances, assists, and putouts) while hitting .264 with 29 RBIs and 77 runs.

His efforts helped propel the Reds to their first National League pennant and an appearance in the World Series against his former White Sox team.

As the Reds leadoff batter in Game 1, he was hit by pitcher Eddie Cicotte, which turned out to be the sign to gamblers that members of the White Sox team had agreed to throw the Series.

Rath played in all eight games of the best-of-nine Series, batting .226 with seven hits as the Reds won the Series 5–3. The team's triumph was forever tainted with the revelation of the "Black Sox" scandal.

The next year he hit .267 and led all National League second baseman in fielding percentage, but his on-base average dropped greatly. The Reds released him at season's end, ending his career.

His career totals were 565 games played, 521 hits, 291 runs, four home runs, 92 RBIs, and a career .254 batting average.

Rath settled in Philadelphia, and ran a sporting goods store. However, he was given to bouts of depression, and he committed suicide in 1945 in his residence by shooting himself. He was 58.

Pea Ridge Day

An eccentric free spirit, Clyde Henry "Pea Ridge" Day was known as the "Hog-Calling Pitcher" due to his tendency to let loose his rebel yell.

It is believed that unsuccessful elbow surgery coupled with family tragedies prompted him to take his life on March 21, 1934, when he slashed his own throat with a hunting knife.

Day broke into professional baseball with Joplin, Missouri, in 1922. After stops with Fort Smith, Little Rock, and Muskogee, his contract was purchased by the Cardinals, with whom he made his debut on September 19, 1924. He pitched a six-hitter and went the distance in a 4–1 win. All told, Day pitched in three games that season, going 1–1. In 1925 he hurled to 2–4 in 17 games. Sent back to the minors, Day was with Syracuse when he was drafted by the Cincinnati Reds, with whom he pitched in four games in 1926.

Day bounced around the minors over the next few years, appearing with clubs such as Omaha, Wichita, Los Angeles of the Pacific Coast League, and Kansas City. The Brooklyn Robins purchased his contract in 1930, and he joined them the next year. In 1931 Day enjoyed the busiest season of his major league career, appearing in 22 games, going 2–2, mostly in relief.

Brooklyn sent him to Minneapolis the next season, by which time he had started having arm problems.

There is reason to suspect that Day was experiencing an injury that, these days, would have required Tommy John surgery. Of course, in the early 1930s, the procedure was unknown. Still, Day committed to undergo surgery on his pitching arm after the 1933 season. He went to Rochester, Minnesota, and reportedly spent almost $10,000 on the surgery. It was never made known what kind of operation was performed on his arm.

Whatever the case, it proved to be a complete failure.

Day became increasingly depressed over the matter and returned home and began drinking heavily. He got into a squabble with his wife on Sunday, March 18, 1934, after which he left his home to visit a former teammate, Max Thomas, in Kansas City.

On March 21, 1934, Day killed himself.

Day had his own share of tragedy even before his arm went bad on him. His brother, also a ballplayer, had a leg amputated and later died from blood poisoning. His mother committed suicide by drinking poison in 1929, and his father had dropped dead of a massive coronary in 1932. No doubt these family tragedies could have contributed to his depressed state.

Day, who had been married 11 years at the time of his death, left his wife and infant son, John Charles. On March 22, his funeral was held at the Pea Ridge Baptist Church and was attended by more than 300 people, many of whom brought gifts for Day's infant son. He was then laid to rest at the Pea Ridge Cemetery in Pea Ridge, Arkansas.

Andrew "Skeeter" Shelton

Some suicides are a little more grisly or a touch more violent than others. In some instances, like that of Andrew Kemper "Skeeter" Shelton, the method is common but much more thorough.

For good measure, Shelton managed to shoot himself not once, but twice, in the head with a .38 caliber revolver on the morning of January 9, 1954, in the bedroom of his home located at 1207 5th Avenue in Huntington, West Virginia. He was rushed to a hospital where he died two hours later.

Sixty-five years old at the time, he had suffered for years from artherosclerotic heart disease; as the ailment became worse, Shelton became more despondent.

Severe depression set in as the heart condition made him a shell of the man that he once was.

A native of Huntington, Shelton played both football and baseball at Huntington High School, continuing his dual sports career at both Marshall College and West Virginia University.

In 1907 he signed with Huntington of the Mountain State League. In 1909 he was signed by the Pirates, playing in their organization for two years until purchased by Columbus.

Shelton, who was known for his speed, was usually ranked highly in runs scored and stolen bases. He was purchased by the Yanks from Augusta of the Southern Association in 1915, making his debut on August 25 in center field in a 3–2 win over Cleveland. After 10 games with New York, he was sent back the next season to Columbus, which then sent him to Huntington for his final pro stop.

He retired after the 1917 season and landed a job with the West Virginia State Liquor Commission. He later managed the Elks Lodge in Huntington.

Shelton was laid to rest at the Spring Hill Cemetery in Huntington, West Virginia.

Stan Pitula

In the early morning hours of August 16, 1965, Bergen County police found Stan Pitula in the front seat of his car at his northern New Jersey home. The engine was running and a hose was connected from the exhaust pipe to the inside of his auto. Attempts to revive him were futile.

Separated from his wife and haunted by a baseball career that was cut short by an arm injury, Pitula was overcome by growing despair.

After five years in the minor leagues, he finally got his shot with the 1957 Indians, pitching in a total of 22 games that season, going 2–2. Unfortunately, he tore a muscle in his elbow that June and sat out the rest of the season.

Although he would continue to pitch for the next few years in the minors, he was basically washed up at the age of 26. He did attempt a comeback a few years later, but his arm just never regained the form that originally made him a star athlete at Hackensack High School, where he went 18–3 in three seasons.

Signed by the Cleveland Indians as an amateur free agent before the 1950 season, he pitched well for several minor league teams and did military service from 1952 to 1953 before his brief stint with the Indians.

After his retirement in 1958, he took up the profession of sheet metal worker. By 1965 his life had gotten to the point where he had had enough.

Pitula was buried at Hackensack Cemetery, Hackensack, New Jersey.

Tom Miller

It's a recurring motive in the realm of suicides: failing health leads to depression leads to self-inflicted gunshot wound to the head.

Native Virginian Thomas Royall Miller added another chapter with this familiar ending on August 13, 1980. He had just recently celebrated his 83rd birthday on July 5.

In his prime, Miller appeared in nine games for the Boston Braves over parts of two seasons, briefly in 1918, and after service with the Navy during World War I, in 1919. He made his debut on July 29, 1918, pinch-hitting for Boston pitcher Pat Ragan in the seventh inning of a 3–2 Braves' victory over the Cubs.

In the minors, Miller played for Richmond and Worcester among others, being sent to Worcester for Hugh McQuillan on May 14, 1919, the day after his final major league appearance.

Miller credited Art Nehf, one of his teammates with the Braves, as the person who helped make his brief stay in the majors a most pleasant one. Nehf spent a lot of time helping the rookie when he came up.

After his career, Miller worked as a clerk in the Husting Court House in Richmond, Virginia. He was residing at 612 West Franklin Street in Richmond at the time of his death.

Wally Roettger

The younger brother of Oscar Roettger, Walter Henry Roettger played eight seasons in the majors with the Cardinals, Giants, Pirates, and Reds from 1927 to 1934.

By 1951, however, Roettger's health had been deteriorating at an alarming rate due to out-of-control high blood pressure. The medical technology that we now take for granted was just not available in the early 1950s, and Roettger was left with only about 15 percent of his vision.

On September 15, 1951, Roettger, driven by depression and despair and the thought of going blind, committed suicide by slitting his wrists and throat with a razor at his home.

Roettger honed his baseball skills on the sandlots of his native St. Louis and attended the University of Illinois. He made his big-league debut on May 1, 1927, in a 12–4 pasting of the Reds at St. Louis. Roettger was a late-inning replacement for Chick Hafey in left field. He appeared in five games that season and got off to a fine start with the Cardinals in 1928 until a July 4 game when he broke his ankle sliding into third base.

Batting a head-turning .341 at the time, he was out for the rest of the season, although he was able to put on a uniform and stand in the Cardinals dugout with the aid of crutches during the World Series.

The ankle continued to be an issue the next season as his average dropped to .253 in 79 games. Never the speediest player, the injured ankle made him even more "base-path challenged." He was traded to the Giants on April 10, 1930, for Showboat Fisher and Doc Farrell and found new life under the tutelage of Manager John McGraw. He posted his best overall season—batting .285 in 114 games and helping "McGraw's Minions" to a third-place finish.

After his last season in the bigs, Roettger moved on to coaching college athletics full time. He had gotten his feet wet some years earlier coaching the Illinois Wesleyan University basketball team during the off-season and he was hired by the University of Illinois, where he spent the next 17 years as the baseball and assistant basketball coach. Noted for sound fundamental training techniques, Roettger developed several major leaguers during his tenure, including Lou Boudreau, Hoot Evers, Jack Brittin, and Howie Judson. His teams finished in the first division 11 times during his tenure, winning four championships.

In a strange coincidence, Roettger was once a teammate with three other ballplayers who took their own lives—Wattie Holm, Benny Frey, and Harvey Hendrick.

Roettger is buried at the Riverview Cemetery in Streator, Illinois.

Walt Goldsby

Here's another familiar final box score: cause of death—gunshot wound, self-inflicted.

A lifetime minor leaguer except for 73 games over parts of three seasons, Walton Hugh Goldsby worked as a railroad clerk after leaving baseball. He shot himself at the Campbell House Hotel in Dallas, Texas, on January 11, 1914.

The son of a minister, Goldsby broke into the majors by playing for three teams in his first season after his debut on May 28, 1884. That year he played for the St. Louis Browns, the Washington Nationals, and the Richmond Virginians.

Purchased by the Baltimore Orioles in 1888, he logged the best numbers of his major league career, batting .288 as the team captain. The Baltimore correspondent for *The Sporting News* said of him, "His good and earnest work has won him a host of friends, and he is one of those players who work to win, not for the record."

In 1903 Goldsby briefly became an umpire in the Southern League and found himself at the center of controversy when Shreveport hosted Montgomery on June 14. The game had to be called after eight innings when a near riot ensued over calls made by Goldsby. He needed a police escort off of the field and submitted his resignation to league president Kavanaugh the next day.

He was buried on January 13 at the Oakland Cemetery in Dallas, Texas. A widower, Goldsby was 53 years old.

Tom Warren

Tom Warren left a suicide note saying that he was ending his life due to ill health. He shot himself in the chest with a .16-gauge shotgun in a motel on the south side of Tulsa on Tuesday January 2, 1968.

It was a sad ending for a former big-leaguer who did so much for young kids by devoting his time and talent to a baseball school in Oklahoma.

A native of Tulsa, Warren was always a fine all-around athlete, capable of not only pitching but also playing second base and outfield. He had a year of minor league ball under his belt, playing for Midland, Texas, before enlisting in the navy the day the United States entered World War II. He was wounded during landing operations at Casablanca, spending the next 11 months in the hospital recovering from a severe concussion.

After his release from the service, he signed with the Brooklyn Dodgers organization. He made his major league debut on April 18, 1944, in a 4–1 loss to the Phillies at Shibe Park before 10,128 fans. The Dodgers sent him to their farm team at Montreal in 1945, and he helped the Royals to the International League championship, batting an amazing (for a pitcher) .330 in 58 games.

In 1946 he logged his best season in the minors, going 20–6 for the Tulsa Oilers. He later managed in the minors briefly with Corpus Christi and Borger, Texas, and Seminole and Miami, Oklahoma.

In 1947, after visiting the Tulsa Children's Home, he began getting involved with children. Working with young, disabled, and disadvantaged children became one of his main focuses in life. He helped conduct Oklahoma's first baseball school for kids with then–*Tulsa Tribune* sports editor Jack Charvat.

The school became a huge success and a real joy for Warren, who once remarked, "Young boys seem to retain correct instructions in baseball fundamentals better than older ones, and that's why I like to work with them."

During offseasons, Warren was a deputy sheriff in Tulsa County and ran a place called the Woodland Lounge. In 1949 Warren ran into trouble while sheriff when he was charged with larceny by fraud for taking money from friends and acquaintances and, in return, promising them automobiles from the factory at a reduced price.

Warren supposedly took the money and used it to pay off gambling debts that he had accrued. He also supposedly used some of the money to make new bets. He was convicted and sentenced to three years in jail, but an appellate court reversed the decision.

The legal trouble continued in 1951. While a minor league manager in Oklahoma, he was again convicted for bilking a used car dealer of $6,600. Warren was to purchase new cars in Detroit but failed to deliver the goods.

He later admitted to racking up over $68,000 in gambling losses while sheriff.

Warren was buried at the Memorial Park Cemetery in Tulsa. At his funeral, there were flower arrangements from many of his friends in and out of baseball and, in particular, from former members of the baseball school for children that he ran with such passion and commitment.

Too Young to Die

By any standards and in any area, dying before the age of 30 can be considered too young to die. About half of the unlucky 13 players in this chapter did just that.

There were budding lawyers Alan Storke and Bill Vinton, who went in their twenties, and exceptionally promising left fielder Austin McHenry, who was cut down at age 27 by a brain tumor.

A few players here passed away in their forties—also leaving a lingering feeling that their lives, and careers, were cut short. Take Sherry Magee for example, the fiery competitor during the "dead-ball era" who put up numbers worthy of the National Baseball Hall of Fame before succumbing to pneumonia at age 44.

More recently, there was the passing of former Blue Jays pitcher and TV color analyst John Cerutti from a massive heart attack at age 44.

Modern-day medical technology and procedures could probably have saved "cup-of-coffee" players Pat Kilhullen and Pembroke Finalyson, who died young after very brief major

241

league stints. Kilhullen was taken by small pox in 1922 at age 32. Finlayson died from complications due to heart surgery in 1912 at age 22.

Influenza, hemorrhages, Bright's disease—it was all out there and still is.

It's always sad when folks suffer ailments and diseases that kill them. It's tragic when it happens to those who are young.

Alan Storke

Born in Auburn, New York, and a graduate of Amherst College, Al Storke played four years in the majors, gaining a reputation as a jack of all trades in the infield. Never a great hitter, his career high was .282 with St. Louis in 1909, but he stuck in the majors due to his heads-up play and versatility in the field.

After graduation from Amherst, he joined Auburn of the Empire State League in 1906 before moving to Providence and then the Pittsburgh Pirates in late September. Storke played parts of four seasons with the Pirates before being traded to the St. Louis Cardinals on August 19, 1909, along with Jap Barbeau for Bobby Byrne. The Cardinals traded him the following February 3, along with Fred Beebe, to the Reds for Miller Huggins, Rebel Oakes, and Frank Corridon.

Storke studied law at Harvard during his playing career (his father was also a lawyer) and was in the third year of his degree as the spring of 1910 rolled around. Unfortunately, sickness would end both his career and his life at the age of 25. While visiting a friend in Newton, Massachusetts, Storke was taken ill, and entered the Newton Hospital on March 7. His stay there lasted five days.

Storke suffered from empyema, a disease caused by an infection that spreads from the lungs and creates an accumulation of fluid in the pleural space. An operation was performed to remove the fluid and relieve the pressure, but the resulting complications were too severe.

On March 12, Storke died as a result of a general streptococcus infection due to empyema. He was buried at the Fort Hill Cemetery in Auburn, New York, on March 21, 1910.

Austin McHenry

After three so-so seasons with the St. Louis Cardinals, Austin McHenry burst into stardom in 1921 when he batted .350—third-best in the National League. He was also fourth in home runs (17), tied for third in RBIs (102), and second in slugging average (.531).

Cardinals' manager Branch Rickey said he considered the versatile McHenry to be one of the best left fielders he ever saw.

McHenry was diagnosed with a brain tumor, and his average tailed off to .303 in 64 games in 1922—his last season. He died at age 27 that November 27, and was buried at Moore's Chapel Cemetery in Jefferson Township, Ohio.

Upon his death, Rickey, a notorious cheapskate, was asked if he was going to send flowers to McHenry's funeral. Supposedly, Rickey replied, "Flowers won't help to bring the poor boy back."

McHenry accrued a lifetime average of .302 with 34 home runs and 286 RBIs in 543 career games.

Bill Vinton

The son of a clergyman, Bill Vinton attended the prestigious Phillips Academy in Andover, Massachusetts, where he pitched brilliantly for the baseball team. After his graduation in 1884, he signed a contract to pitch for the Philadelphia Quakers managed by the legendary Harry Wright. Vinton's father, the Reverend Porter Vinton, was not pleased with his son's decision to put down the books and pick up the bat.

Nonetheless, on July 3, 1884, the 19-year-old Rhode Islander won his major league debut—a 15–13 win over the Chicago White Stockings at Lake Front Park II in Chicago. Vinton showed good form the rest of the season, accruing a 10–10 record and a stingy 2.23 ERA.

The next season he was less effective, showing signs of arm problems. He went 3–6 before he was released in August. He found work almost immediately, signing with the Athletics of the American Association. For the A's, he made his debut in rather grand fashion—shutting out the Metropolitans 7–0 on August 21. Despite an overall 4–3 record with the Athletics, he was released in mid-September.

Soon after he gave up the game due to his arm problems, he entered Yale University, where he managed the school newspaper and coached and managed the baseball team. (He was ineligible to play on it due to his previous pro career.) At Yale, he became friends with Amos Alonzo Stagg, a pitcher on the team at the time who would go on to gain legendary status as a college football coach.

After graduation, Vinton entered law school and interned at a number of law firms. His promising future came to an abrupt end on September 3, 1893, when he passed away at the age of 28 at his parents' home in Pawtucket.

Vinton died from what his physician termed *Cholera morbus*, the definition of which is acute gastroenteritis occurring in summer and autumn and marked by severe cramps, diarrhea, and vomiting. The term is no longer in scientific use today.

Blaine Thomas

A product of California semi-pro baseball, Thomas played with the St. Vincent's club before heading to the Northwest League in 1911.

Also known as "Baldy" (reason self-explanatory), he was called up by the Red Sox that season and made his debut on August 25 against the St. Louis Browns. Thomas pitched four innings, allowed two runs, and was relieved in the fifth by Charley "Sea Lion" Hall.

Thomas' second, and last, game in the majors was an interesting affair against the New York Highlanders, who knocked him out of the box in the first inning. In the brief appearance, Thomas hit Bert Daniels and walked two others before getting the hook.

Thomas later played with Centralia of the Washington State League and Sacramento of the Pacific Coast League. He was staying at the Herron Hotel in Payson, Arizona, when he passed away from a pulmonary hemorrhage at the age of 27 on August 21, 1915.

His body was sent back to Compton, California, for burial.

Frankie Hayes

The pride of Jamesburg, New Jersey, Frankie Hayes went on to become a five-time major league All-Star after a rough start as a rookie.

He was recommended to A's manager Connie Mack by a local umpire in 1933 when Hayes was just 18. Hayes played with the Montreal Royals of the International League in 1934 and was called up at the end of that season for a three-game stint. After batting just .226 in 92 games the next season, he was sent back to the minors for seasoning.

And seasoned he was.

Hayes returned to the major leagues utterly transformed and blossomed into a dynamic fielding catcher and hitter.

Defensively, he went on to lead the AL three times in total chances per game. He twice led the league in fielding percentage, put-outs, and double plays. His 29 double plays in 1935 was the second-highest total ever for a catcher. When he caught 155 games in 1934, he set an AL record that has still not been broken.

Offensively, his best season was 1939, when he hit .283 and had career highs in home runs (20) and RBIs (83). The following season, he hit a career-high .308 with 61 walks in 465 at-bats. On July 25, 1936, he tied the major league record with four doubles in a game.

In April 1946 he caught Bob Feller's no-hitter against the Yankees with his home run accounting for the lone run in the

Cleveland Indians' 1–0 victory. Ironically, after getting traded to the Chicago White Sox later that season, Hayes broke up Feller's bid for a second no-hitter by hitting a single.

Hayes' major league career ended with his unconditional release by the Red Sox on May 21, 1947.

Hayes went into business the next year, becoming co-owner of a sporting goods store located in Point Pleasant, New Jersey. Hayes died at the Point Pleasant Hospital on June 22, 1955, at the age of 40. His death was due to a retroperitoneal hemorrhage complicated by a ruptured pancreas and fatty cirrhosis of the liver.

Hayes, who lived at 92 East Main street in Freehold, New Jersey, was laid to rest in his boyhood home of Jamesburg at the Fernwood Cemetery (Plot 424, also known as the Hayes Family Plot).

John Cerutti

A first-round draft pick in 1981 by Toronto Blue Jays, left-hander John Cerutti made his big-league debut for the Blue Jays in 1985.

For his first few seasons, the native of Albany, New York, alternated between a starter and a reliever. He overcame his tendency to give up the long ball and settled into a rather effective, if not very good, starting pitcher.

Not blessed with an overpowering fastball, he relied on good off-speed stuff to get the job done. His control was also good, except for his one outing on July 2, 1986, when he set a record by throwing four wild pitches against Boston.

Cerutti's best seasons were 1987, when he went 11–4, and 1989, when he went 11–11 in 31 starts while posting a 3.07 ERA. He helped the Jays to an AL East title in 1989, but the next season his ERA rose to 4.76, prompting the Jays to grant him free-agent status.

Signed by the Detroit Tigers on January 14, 1991, he played one last season in the majors—going 3–6.

Over the course of his career, he accrued a lifetime record of 49–43 with a 3.94 ERA and 861 innings pitched in 229 league games.

After his playing days were over, he turned to broadcasting, eventually becoming lead analyst for Jays' broadcasts on Rogers Sportsnet. As a broadcaster, he was noted for a great work ethic and attention to detail. His likeability on and off the air, where he also showed a great sense of humor, were traits carried over from his playing days.

On October 3, 2004, after failing to show up for a pregame production meeting, he was found dead in his hotel room from a massive heart attack.

Cerutti, who was only 44, left a wife and three children. His body was cremated and his ashes given to his family.

Marty Honan

Marty Honan's numbers in the majors didn't add up to success. And his numbers while keeping the books as a tax collector in Chicago were equally suspect.

Honan played a total of six games in the majors and had a lifetime average of .167. He finished out the 1891 season with his old club, the Whitings, helping them to the Chicago City League pennant.

In 1894 he won the election for the office of tax collector for the city's Sixth Ward as a Democrat. It was later found out that he had been quite a "juggler of the books." Although only 65 men were sworn in to work with him as "deputies" to help with the collection of funds, Honan drew salaries for as many as 132 men, often using "dummy names."

In the process, he pocketed the money for himself.

After two years of these shenanigans, Honan took a public scolding from the press and managed get away free and clear. He ran for alderman in the Fifth Ward in 1899 but lost. In 1900 he appeared at a rally to help get future Hall of Fame first baseman

Cap Anson elected as Circuit Court Clerk and again in 1905 to help Anson with a run for Chicago City Clerk.

Honan, who later worked as a salesman, lived at 2573 Emerald Avenue at the time of his death, which occurred on August 20, 1890, at the age of 39. His official cause of death was from Bright's disease and albuminuria (albuminuria is usually seen in conjunction with kidney failure and is recognized by a high presence of a protein called "albumin" in urine).

Honan left a his wife, Jennie, a brother, and three sisters, and was buried at Calvary Catholic Cemetery, Evanston, Illinois.

Pat Kilhullen

One appearance and one at-bat with the 1914 Pittsburgh Pirates.

That's the major league career of Joseph Isadore "Pat" Kilhullen in a nutshell. His debut on July 10 came on the short end of an 11–3 annihilation to the Boston Doves.

After attending Villanova University, Kilhullen played for New Bedford in 1913 and Fitchburg in 1914, both of the New England League. While with Fitchburg, he was signed to a contract by the Pirates. A catcher by trade, he also logged time as a first baseman. After his lone appearance in the majors, he was back with Fitchburg, and later made stops with Manchester and Portland of the Eastern League.

In October 1922, Kilhullen was still playing baseball and living in Southern California when he came down with a case of small pox. He was admitted to the Alameda County Hospital on October 9 with the hopes that he might somehow recover. In the hospital he was isolated from other patients as doctors tried to stabilize his condition. His battle with the dread disease lasted for 16 days, before he finally succumbed on the 25th of October.

Due to the infectious nature of his disease, Kilhullen's body was specially prepared by an undertaker and was eventually buried at the St. Mary's Cemetery in Oakland, California, on October 26. He was 32 years old.

Pembroke Finlayson

Pembroke Finlayson pitched two games in the major leagues for the Brooklyn Superbas—one in 1908 and one in 1909, hurling a total of 7⅓ innings with a 2.58 ERA.

A career minor leaguer, his family actually moved to Brooklyn from Cheraw, South Carolina, when he was 12 years old. He was signed by Brooklyn after making his mark with the minor league Marquettes and George Gould's Missouri-Pacific team.

Finlayson's final bush-league stop was with Memphis of the Southern League in 1911. While there, he underwent an operation for his heart, and before he fully recovered, began to practice pitching in early 1912. The wound from the operation reopened, and he was recommended by specialists to return home to Brooklyn to recover. He never did, passing away at age 22 due to general peritonitis and myocardial adenitis.

He left a wife and two children, a boy and a girl, and was buried in the Green-Wood Cemetery in Brooklyn, New York.

Sherry Magee

Although his name lacks the recognition of his contemporaries like Ty Cobb and Honus Wagner, Sherry Magee was one of the greatest players of the so-called dead-ball era—a formative period in the game from 1901 to 1919.

A fierce competitor, Magee was the Phillies' only bona fide star before the arrival of Grover Cleveland Alexander. Magee could hit for power, had an excellent glove, and was a heady base runner.

He also criticized himself and teammates for poor play.

By 1905 Magee was entrenched as the Phils' left fielder, a position he would hold for a decade. In 1907 he hit .328 (second only to Wagner's .350) and led the National League in RBIs with 85.

He would go on to bat over .300 four times.

In 1910 he achieved his finest season, leading the National League in runs scored (110), RBIs (123), and batting average (.331). His numbers dipped the next year (although he socked 15 homers), but he showed his defensive prowess by leading all outfielders in fielding percentage.

On July 10, 1911, he also showed his volatile side when, after being ejected by umpire Bill Finneran for arguing a called third strike, he knocked out Finneran with one punch. He was slapped with a one-year suspension that was reduced to five weeks after an appeal.

On July 20, 1912, he set a National League record by stealing home twice in a game against the Chicago Cubs. In 1914 he would put together another great season, batting .314 and leading the NL in hits (171), doubles (39), and RBIs (103).

When the Phillies managerial position became vacant after the 1914 season, Magee was assured he would become the team's player/manager. However, the position went to Pat Moran. Feeling slighted by the Phillies, he asked for a trade, which he got on Christmas Eve, 1914, when he was shipped to the World Champion Boston Braves for outfielder Possum Whitted and infielder Oscar Dugey.

This move caused him to miss the Phillies' appearance in the 1915 World Series. After two and one-half mediocre seasons in Boston, he was sold to the Cincinnati Reds. In 1918 he regained some of his old form for the Reds and led the NL in RBIs with 76. In 1919 he played only 56 games, but was part of the Reds' National League pennant–winning team.

After 16 seasons he would finally get to a World Series, but it would be one that was forever marred due to the Black Sox scandal. In the Reds' tainted 5–3 series victory over Chicago, Magee had only two pinch-hitting appearances, managing a single. It was his last hurrah in the majors.

In his 16 seasons as an outfielder from 1904 to 1919, his totals were 2,087 games played, 2,169 hits, 1,112 runs scored, 83 home runs, 1,176 RBIs, and a career .291 batting average. He still holds Phillies team records for most career triples (127) and most career stolen bases (387).

Magee became a major league umpire in 1928. That second baseball career was tragically cut short after only a year when, on March 13, 1929, he died at age 44 at his home in Philadelphia from pneumonia.

He is buried in the Arlington Cemetery in Drexel Hill, Pennsylvania (Sunnyside Section, Lot 688).

Gene Krapp and Tony Suck

Other than a feeble attempt at fifth-grade humor, there is really no reason to package Gene Krapp and Tony Suck here together.

They never even played on the same team at the same time.

Krapp, a pitcher, appeared in 118 games in the majors over four seasons (1911–1912, 1914–1915) with Cleveland and Buffalo. Suck, a catcher, appeared in 56 games for three teams in two leagues from 1883 to 1884 (Buffalo, Chicago/Pittsburgh, and Baltimore).

Still, they're unanimous selections for the All-Time Name Team. It's rife with endless possibilities for newspaper headlines, creative leads for sportswriters, and colorful statements for heckling fans.

Besides their terrible last names, both players actually had a lot in common. Both had relatively brief major league careers. Both lived in the Midwest—Krapp in Detroit, and Suck in Chicago. And both died in their mid-thirties—Krapp at 35, Suck at 36.

Krapp pitched in the Southern Michigan League with Tecumseh and Flint, and with Portland of the PCL, before his purchase by the Cleveland Naps. He appeared in 44 games total in 1911 and 1912 with an overall 15–14 record.

He eventually moved to Buffalo of the Federal League, where he gained his greatest success as a pitcher, going 16–14 in 1914. He went 9–19 the following season.

251

Krapp left the game to join the army during World War I but came back to manage Battle Creek of the Michigan-Ontario League in 1920. He retired after that season to go into the automobile business with his brothers.

For the last two years of his life, Krapp suffered from cancer. He entered the Evangelical Deaconess Hospital in Detroit in late March of 1923 with the hopes that an operation might save his life. He died from carcinoma of the colon on April 13, 1923, and was buried at the Woodmere Cemetery in Detroit on April 16.

Tony Suck was actually born Charles Anthony Zuck on June 11, 1858, but inexplicably changed his playing name to Tony Suck. (Obviously, the idiom was different back then.)

Suck made his debut for the National League Buffalo Bisons in a 14–5 loss to Cleveland on August 9, 1883. Suck, a semi-pro player of note in Chicago, ran into problems over his two years in the majors. Besides the fact that he had a horrendous .151 lifetime batting average with only two extra-base hits (doubles), he was also dreadful in the field, making 53 errors in 61 games. But to be fair, he did play in the days when every fielder except the catcher and first baseman wore no gloves and errors were as common as rain.

Suck played amateur and semi-pro ball almost to the end of his life, which occurred on January 29, 1895, at the age of 36 after a bout with pneumonia.

He left a wife and two small children. He was buried on January 31 at the Oakwoods Cemetery (Section B1, Lot 44). His flat headstone is engraved with his real last name, Zuck, but lists only his wife, Cora, who outlived him by more than 50 years. The marker makes no mention of him being buried there.

Matty McIntyre

Matty McIntyre played 10 seasons and more than 1,000 games in the American League as an outfielder for the Philadelphia A's, Detroit Tigers, and Chicago White Sox.

JUNE 12 1880-APRIL 2 1920
MATTY McINTYRE
WORLD FAMOUS
BALL PLAYER

Photograph from Frank Russo's private collection.

While with the Tigers, McIntyre became one of the acknowl-edged leaders of an anti-Cobb faction who had open disdain toward the "Georgia Peach." McIntyre's dislike of Cobb likely stemmed purely from jealousy. With the lack of job security that permeated baseball at the turn of the century, it was not surprising for an average player such as McIntyre to be protective of his own job. In the days before guaranteed contracts, players held onto their jobs for dear life and usually never took kindly to rookies, especially ones with the level of talent that Cobb possessed.

Able to play all three outfield positions, McIntyre usually patrolled center and left. He appeared in 120 games or more on five different occasions, with a career high 152 in 1904—his first season with Detroit. His services were always in demand due to his versatility in the field, and on more than one occasion trade rumors regarding him surfaced.

McIntyre, who appeared in two World Series for Detroit, had an injury-plagued 1910 season. The Tigers eventually sold him to the Chicago White Sox on January 12, 1911. The purchase price was between $2,000 and $3,000. In his first year on the South Side, he batted a career-high .323. The next season he dropped to .167 in just 49 games and was sent to the San Francisco Seals of the PCL on September 9, ending his major league career.

He later managed both Lincoln of the Western League and Mobile of the Southern Association, with whom he managed until the end of the 1917 campaign.

McIntyre settled back in Detroit, where he was content to play semi-pro ball. He came down with influenza in March of 1920 and entered St. Mary's Hospital on the 29th. He passed away at 9:30 in the evening of April 2 from the effects of the influenza, complicated by acute nephritis.

McIntyre was just 39 years old. His wife, the former Grace Kennedy, brought his body back to Staten Island, New York, for burial.

It was not until 2004 that his grave site, long forgotten and lost to anonymity, was found. McIntyre rests in Staten Island's St. Peter's Cemetery (Section 32, Range 6, Grave 2).

His headstone is marked with the inscription: Matty McIntyre, World Famous Ball Player.

Afterword: Grave-Hunting for Dummies

He was no ordinary caretaker. But then again, this was no ordinary cemetery—mercilessly split down the middle like a ripe watermelon by the sharp lanes of the Garden State Parkway.

Surrounded by housing projects on the hardscrabble side of East Orange, New Jersey, Frank Russo lit out into the Holy Sepulcher Cemetery in search of Larry Corcoran, one of the great pitchers of the late 1800s.

"I knew I was in trouble when I got there and the caretaker was driving around with a sawed-off shotgun and a 9mm handgun in a red Mazda pickup truck," said Russo. "He was missing his right hand and spoke broken English with an Italian accent. He said they closed the cemetery at 2:30 PM because that's when school gets out. Then he told me a couple of weeks before, a college woman had been raped in the cemetery. I was just glad to have him there. And we found Corcoran's grave—it had been unmarked for 110 years."

So maybe the first lesson in grave-hunting is the most obvious one: safety first. Graveyards can be the most desolate of places. Frequently, the terrain is unkempt and treacherous, increasing the likelihood of a fall.

Best to bring a friend, a dog if you have one, and a cell phone.

To Russo, it's well worth the effort of actually finding the graves. The thrill of the chase, so to speak, means a lot to him. It validates all the homework. It brings scholarly closure out in the elements after hours of sitting behind a desk with microfilms and a computer.

Over the years, he's gone to and catalogued the final resting places of thousands of deceased major leaguers. For him, the key to success is preparation—meticulous research time spent looking up obituaries in the local library or National Baseball Hall of Fame, contacting funeral homes for death certificates, locating cemeteries and calling up their offices for the exact burial location (plot and section).

Then the fun begins—the part where it often seems that all his best-laid plans go to waste in long, frustrating stretches where he can't find the headstone. With great persistence, the site eventually turns up and the payoff is more than you'd expect.

"To me, it's like looking at history," said Russo. "Crazy as it sounds, what better way to do research than to physically go out and get your butt in the grass? And sometimes, you'll be the only person to have visited that grave in a long time.

"Like Larry Corcoran. He'd been dead 110 years, and maybe I was the first person in who-knows-how-long to visit it."

Needles and Haystacks

The most difficult grave hunt Russo ever made was trying to locate "Turkey" Mike Donlan, teammate of Giants legend Christy Mathewson. Donlan was managed by John McGraw and was an accomplished actor with 30 movie appearances to his credit, including *Casey at the Bat*.

His grave was somewhere in Greenwood Cemetery in West Long Branch, New Jersey, and Russo needed more than eight trips, some lasting four to six hours, to eventually find a plot he said was "right under my nose."

Managed by a construction company, the cemetery was without an on-site office, and Russo, with the help of the local police department, got the phone number of the company that provided Donlan's exact location. He's buried in a family plot with the marker prominently placed at a fork in the road near the cemetery's entrance. For quite a while it was a blind spot for Russo, who eventually spotted it during a light snowfall in the dead of winter.

"Sometimes you miss the obvious," said Russo who also had a rough time locating the grave of "Wee" Davie Forc upstate in the Riverview Cemetery in Englewood. Even with the exact section and plot, he needed five trips to eventually uncover what was a flat marker covered with ivy, leaves, and debris.

"I literally tripped over it when I found it," Russo said. "There were no attendants at the cemetery. It was deserted, right next to a hospital. I found it in the rain—a 1' x 2' granite headstone."

There's one deceased major leaguer whose grave continues to elude Russo—"Broadway" Alex Smith, buried somewhere in Woodlawn Cemetery in the Bronx. Russo's been there once, spending an hour and a half with a girlfriend and two security guards pacing off a small area they suspect has a slanted marble head-stone bearing the name of one of the first Jewish ballplayers—a catcher for the New York Giants.

The search was eventually called off due to darkness, and the only thing Russo had to show for his efforts was a bad case of bronchitis from the damp chill in the air. So here's another tip: bring a sweater. And while you're at it, bring a pen, water to drink if it's a warm day, and a camera to document a successful mission.

Hot on the Trail of Billy Gilbert

Section 35. Plot 8. Grave 8.

The directions sounded specific enough, and finding the tombstone of former big leaguer William O. "Billy" Gilbert should have been a piece of cake.

But graveyards are tricky terrain—with hills and steps and slopes, bushes, and bends. And on a sweltering August day at the Gate of Heaven Cemetery in Hawthorne, New York, the heat grew more oppressive the longer the search wore on.

We had just come from the deep-cooled, air-conditioned comfort of the main office, where the caretaker opted to continue running copies of something on a Xerox machine as we asked him if he wanted to come out and help find the grave.

You couldn't blame him for saying he was busy.

Twenty minutes later, dripping with sweat in the far corner of the gothic-style grounds, weaving in and out of lines of marble and granite, we found what we had been looking for, right there in front of us.

Photograph from Frank Russo's private collection.

Somehow it always is, or seems that way, in this life-size version of "Where's Waldo?"

In terms of where's William O. Gilbert, there was nothing hidden about the headstone, though it had to be the plainest one in the joint. Nondescript, rectangular, and chalk white, its inscription read nothing more than: Gilbert, William O., Aug. 8, 1927. It was visible from the roadside, under the speckled shade of a sycamore tree. No way on earth to tell that the man buried there once played for the New York Giants and was a teammate of the legendary Christy Mathewson—the man who once pitched three shutout victories in the 1905 World Series to help the Giants win.

It would be nice to change that.

Final Thoughts

"Is this a morbid hobby?" Russo wonders aloud. "I think grave-hunting is becoming kind of a chic obsession in the world. It's a genealogy kind of thing. For me, as a researcher, I like to physically go there and know they're there. And it's always nice to know whether the graves are marked or unmarked."

And what of the final resting place awaiting Russo: born June 16, 1959, in New Brunswick, New Jersey? (His best games are still ahead of him.)

"Some people want a big deal, they do," Russo said. "All you've got to do is go to Arlington National Cemetery. Just go there.

"Me, I want to be donated or stuffed or propped up in a chair holding a beer in one hand and a cigar in the other. I could care less what happens to me. Scatter my ashes in my cat's litter box. They can throw me in the water as chum."

He talks a big game and laughs at the thought. But at the end of the day, Russo also carries no organ donor card and has a plot reserved for himself and his mother—next to where his father rests in a quiet corner of St. Peter's Cemetery in New Brunswick, New Jersey.

—Gene Racz

How to Be a Grave-Hunter: Some Helpful Tips

1. If you're interested in locating a deceased player or famous person, look into the various grave-finding resources on the Internet. The largest website for getting grave site information on famous celebrities is findagrave.com. Additionally the website thedeadballera.com can be helpful when looking for players. Retrosheet.org provides statistics for baseball players and is linked with SABR (Society for American Baseball Research). Baseball-reference.com is another useful site for data. There are also websites such as Internment.net and the Nation Wide Gravesite Locator, which can be helpful in finding the graves and locations of veterans. Sometimes a cemetery is not mentioned in obituaries, so look for any mention of church services or funeral homes.

2. After you find out in what cemetery the person you are looking for is buried, get the exact internment location. At the saying goes, it's all about location, location, location. You don't want to run around a cemetery without knowing exactly where you are going, especially if the grave is unmarked—you could be outside for hours with no luck and nothing to show for your time but two sore feet. So call the cemetery and get the internment location, lot, section, grave, etc., if is not yet known.

3. Call ahead to the cemetery to make sure someone will be there when you arrive. There are several reasons for this. Most people who work in cemeteries are usually very helpful in pointing you in the right direction. Many cemeteries have maps with marked routes to the graves. Some cemeteries have rules against roaming around unescorted and mandate that you be accompanied in your grave hunt.

4. Bring grave-hunting tools with you. No, not a shovel. Besides a camera, a spray bottle with water and a magic marker are helpful.

Many grave stones and monuments are weathered, and the engravings do not always show up well on a photo. Usually wetting the engraving area brings words out enough so that they will show up on camera. If that does not work, a magic marker will help. Just follow the outline of the engraving. A pair of gloves is good in case you have to move any weeds or brush. A flashlight is also a good idea.

5. Dress appropriately. Treat your grave hunt like any other outdoor activity. If it's hot, wear light clothing. If it's cold, bundle up. It sounds so simple that people often overlook it. Also, in the summer, don't wear sandals or light footwear. The grounds of cemeteries, particularly the older ones, can have uneven surfaces because of ground settlement.

6. Safety first! Research ahead of time to see if the cemetery is located in a dangerous side of town. Cemeteries are not always located in the safest of places. If you feel confident enough, that's fine, but don't take chances. Bringing a dog with you is not always allowed. Bringing a friend is always best. Some cemeteries provide security, such as Woodlawn Cemetery in the Bronx, and they will often help you find your way.

7. Know the cemetery regulations and, of course, the hours of operation. Some places allow you to take photos as long as you fill out a form. Others totally prohibit it. Some of the famous cemeteries in California, such as Forest Lawn in Hollywood Hills, are basically run like Fort Knox.

8. Always act in a professional and courteous manner. Grave-hunting is a hobby that can be fun and rewarding. When you are looking for that famous person and finally find the grave, it can be a most satisfying experience. But remember to always have the utmost respect when you go. It is the least you can do.